THE T

Ralph Hammond B
at Hounslow Colle
journalism and t
writing and severa
the Windmill Theatre before the wa
joined the RAF as a wireless-operator /air-gunner and completed 2,000 flying hours before demobilization. He worked as a radio officer in a civil aviation company until 1948, when he rejoined the RAF and was posted to Germany as a public relations officer on the Berlin Airlift: subsequently he worked on the official airlift history. In 1961 he left the RAF to become a full-time author.

His first book, *Down in the Drink*, a collection of true stories about members of the Goldfish Club, was published in 1955 and followed two years later by *The Ship-busters*, the story of the RAF torpedo bombers. He has since written seven more books with an aviation background including *The Thousand Plan* and *Great Mysteries of the Air*.

He describes himself as an 'obsolescent but compulsive cricketer' and has written three books on the subject. He lives with his wife in Surrey and they have one daughter.

By the same author in Pan Books

STRIKE HARD, STRIKE SURE

GREAT MYSTERIES OF THE AIR

THE THOUSAND PLAN

RALPH BARKER

UNABRIDGED

PAN BOOKS LTD : LONDON

First published 1965 by Chatto & Windus Ltd.
This edition published 1967 by Pan Books Ltd,
33 Tothill Street, London, SW1.

ISBN 0 330 20205 7

2nd Printing 1972
3rd Printing 1973

Printed in Great Britain by
Cox & Wyman Ltd, London, Reading and Fakenham

CONTENTS

MAPS AND DIAGRAMS

ILLUSTRATIONS IN PHOTOGRAVURE

ACKNOWLEDGEMENTS

In gathering material for this book I have been greatly helped by various departments of the Ministry of Defence (Air), and particularly by the Historical, Public Relations, Records and Casualty Branches and the Library.

In reconstructing the planning stages of the raid I have had much valuable assistance from Air Marshal Sir Robert Saundby, formerly Deputy Commander-in-Chief, Bomber Command. I am also indebted to Dr B. G. Dickins, formerly Head of the Operational Research Section at High Wycombe; to Group Captain Dudley Saward, formerly Command Radar Officer; and to Marshal of the Royal Air Force Sir Arthur Harris.

The stories from the various stations, squadrons and training units, covering preparations for the raid and experiences on the raid, have come from the surviving aircrews, the men of Bomber Command. There would have been no book without their resolution at the time and their generosity twenty years later.

The evaluation of the raid is based on the relevant Bomber Command Night Raid Report, prepared by the Operational Research Section at High Wycombe; photographic cover of raid damage obtained by the Photographic Reconnaissance Unit, RAF; and the files of the Police President, Cologne.

I have made considerable use of BBC and Imperial War Museum material, which I gratefully acknowledge.

I have been greatly helped in tracing survivors by the RAF Record Office; the Department of Veterans' Affairs, RCAF; the Department of Air, Commonwealth of Australia; the Director of Public Relations, RNZAF; the Admiralty Historical Section; the Royal Air Forces Association; and the Pathfinder Association.

ACKNOWLEDGEMENTS

Several writers and students of air history have very kindly lent me material from their private collections, and among these I must specially mention David Irving, Philip Moyes and Leslie Hunt. Above all I must acknowledge my very great indebtedness to G. J. Zwanenburg, of Amsterdam, for his researches into the fate of crashed aircraft.

A valuable account of the raid as seen through German eyes was provided for me by Claus-Dieter Maass, of the Bundespresse und Informationsamt, Bonn.

I acknowledge the copyright of the photographs of Air Marshal A. T. Harris with Air Vice-Marshal R. H. M. S. Saundby, Wing Commander Dudley Saward, Group Captain S. C. Elworthy, 'Bave' Baveystock, George Gilpin, Cologne after the raid, and the railway workshops at Cologne-Nippes, to the Imperial War Museum.

The loan of the remaining photographs, from private sources, is gratefully acknowledged.

I have appended a list of books, documents and papers from which factual information and background, and in some case quotations, have been extracted. Acknowledgement is made in all cases to the authors and publishers of these works.

The arrangement of material, treatment, opinions expressed and final assessment are of course entirely my own.

R.B.

SOURCES

THE STRATEGIC AIR OFFENSIVE AGAINST GERMANY (History of the Second World War, United Kingdom Military Series): Sir Charles Webster and Noble Frankland (HMSO)

NO. 5 BOMBER GROUP RAF (1939–1945): W. J. Lawrence (Faber and Faber)

BOMBER OFFENSIVE: Marshal of the Royal Air Force Sir Arthur Harris (Collins)

BOMBER PILOT: Group Captain Leonard Cheshire (Hutchinson)

THE BOMBER'S EYE: Group Captain Dudley Saward (Cassell)

AIR BOMBARDMENT, THE STORY OF ITS DEVELOPMENT: Air Marshal Sir Robert Saundby (Chatto and Windus)

THE DESTRUCTION OF DRESDEN: David Irving (Kimber)

ROYAL AIR FORCE 1939–1945: Denis Richards and Hilary St G. Saunders (HMSO)

THE SECOND WORLD WAR: Winston S. Churchill (Cassell)

THE BUSINESS OF WAR: Major-General Sir John Kennedy (Hutchinson)

NO MOON TONIGHT: D. E. Charlwood (Collins)

THE GOEBBELS DIARIES: Translated and Edited by Louis P. Lochner (Hamish Hamilton)

THE RCAF OVERSEAS: THE FIRST FOUR YEARS (OUP)

RAAF OVER EUROPE: Edited by Frank Johnson (Eyre and Spottiswoode)

OPERATIONAL RESEARCH IN THE RAF: Air Ministry (HMSO)

'*The United States Strategic Bombing Survey*', Overall Report, European War (United States Information Service)

'*The Battle of Britain*', General Adolf Galland (Forces Aériennes Françaises, Nos 61–65, October 1951 to February 1952)

Bomber Command Review (HQ Bomber Command)

Articles by Air Marshal Sir Robert Saundby in *Royal Air Force Review* and *Royal Air Force Association Annual*

Paper read by Air Marshal Sir Robert Saundby to the Royal United Services Institution, 8th December 1943

THE FIRST THOUSAND: A Radio Documentary, script by Cecil McGivern (BBC Recording)

BBC Monitoring Reports (Imperial War Museum)

BBC News Broadcasts (Sound Publicity Officer, BBC)

The Times

Files of the Police President, Cologne

Dokumente Deutscher Kriegsschaeden (Bunderministerium fuer Vertriebene, Fluechtlinge und Kriegsgeschaedigte, Bonn, 1958)

Prologue

THE BOMBING COMPETITION

The twin-engined Vickers Vernon, development of the old Vickers Vimy bomber in which Alcock and Brown had flown the Atlantic four years earlier – in 1919 – banked ponderously above the confluence of the Tigris and Diyala rivers before settling down on its bombing run.

Ahead lay the great circular *bund*, or bank, the sloping embankment which enclosed the Royal Air Force station of Hinaidi, eight miles south-west of Baghdad, protecting it from flooding when the Tigris and Diyala burst their banks. And perched on the top of the *bund*, facing east, sheltered from the fierce sun by a huge multi-coloured umbrella, in the manner of an Eastern potentate, sat Air Vice-Marshal Sir John Salmond, Air Officer Commanding Iraq.

Like most of his officers in Iraq, Salmond was aware of the extravagant claims of bombing accuracy attributed to one of his squadrons, and to end all argument he had ordered a bombing competition, in which two aircraft and crews of the boastful squadron were pitted against two representatives of each of the other bombing squadrons in Iraq, of which there were seven.

Fifteen hundred yards east of the *bund* had been erected a white post, round which was drawn a circle fifteen yards in radius. Fifteen yards! That was the kind of error – if such it could be called – which the squadron commander of No 45 Squadron had repeatedly put forward in his assessments of squadron practices, drawing on his squadron a wave of ridicule which gradually hardened into irritation. Other squadrons had previously been well content to keep their average error down to between one and two hundred yards. Now, under the impartial eye of the AOC, the exaggerated claims of 45 Squadron were about to be exposed.

The truth was that the commander of 45 Squadron had devised an entirely new method of aiming bombs. The crews of the other squadrons – Vernons, DH 9a's and Bristol Fighters, from Kirkuk, Mosul, Shaibah and Hinaidi itself – aimed their bombs by peering over the side of their cockpits. It was a job entrusted to the second pilot or observer. The crews of 45 Squadron aimed their bombs in the prone position, flat on their bellies under the high cockpit of the Vickers Vernon, with the aid of a standard drift sight, gazing down through the rectangular hole they had cut in the ply-wood nose. And the task was given to the most experienced men. Flying straight and level was an essential, but it was something that any competent pilot ought to be able to achieve. The men stretched out in their khaki shirts and shorts on the hard unyielding floor of the two Vernons were the commanding officer and his senior flight commander.

The competition started soon after dawn. That had been mandatory if all the squadrons were to drop their bombs before the convection air currents of mid-morning jolted the ground about in their drift sights. Soon the 13 lb practice bombs, filled with stannic chloride to give off a tell-tale white puff as they hit the ground, were tumbling down from an azure sky. Sweating airmen out on the bombing range were busy measuring distances. The two Vernons of 45 Squadron, several miles apart, commenced their bombing run.

The secret was to fly dead into wind. This reduced speed and cut down error. To line up on the target, the angle of approach which gave no drift was carefully sought, as revealed in the parallel wires of the drift sight. Supporting themselves on their elbows, around which they had affixed leather pads, and with legs splayed out behind as though they were firing a rifle, the two bomb-aimers peered ahead and downwards at the target, 3,000 feet below them, adjusting their aim.

'Left left. Right right. Steady.'

The bomb-aimer's instructions reached the pilot in the cockpit directly above him by means of a speaking tube. Both men worked up to a smooth crescendo of concentration as the drop drew near. Having cut down the drift to nil, and made allowance for speed and height, they waited for the target to centralize in their drift sights. Then they pressed the release button.

'Bombs gone.'

And so to make another circuit, dropping a brace of bombs each time, until the competition was over.

The results showed that there was no doubt about it. The men of 45 Squadron had pointed the way to the future. Their average error had been under twenty yards, less than a quarter the average of the best of their competitors. With no new equipment, but simply by applying a little ingenuity and thought, a revolution had been brought about in the method of aiming bombs.

The name of the squadron commander of No 45 Squadron was 'Bert' Harris.[1]

His senior flight commander was Bob Saundby.

1. Harris acquired his nickname in an Officers' Mess in Baghdad that was full of ex-Royal Naval Air Service men. In the Navy, just as all Wilsons are 'Tug' and all Millers are 'Dusty', so all Harrises are 'Bert'.

PART I

MOTIVATION

1. WHO STARTED IT?

THE ORIGINS OF unrestricted bombing are not obscure. The bombing of civilian populations to disrupt production and undermine morale had been begun by the Germans with the Zeppelin raids of 1915 onwards and supplemented later by the day and night raids of the Gothas. The shock of these raids lingered in Britain in both the public and the official mind. Indeed it was these raids, provoking as they did a demand for reprisals on German cities, which did much to stimulate the formation in 1918 of the Royal Air Force, to carry the war to the enemy. And it was this argument – the ability to hit direct at the means and will of an aggressor nation to wage war – to which RAF leaders continually returned when under pressure between the wars. Strategic bombing was fundamentally the RAF's reason for existence. Yet it was a method of warfare which, in its fully unrestricted sense, Britain could never start. Public and world opinion would never stand for it. Public opinion, perhaps, might somehow be moulded or silenced, but world opprobrium was something we couldn't afford. We could never enter into conflict with a major European power without the moral and material support of the English-speaking world.

Hitler was under no such inhibitions. He controlled public opinion, or could mould it by propaganda, and for world opinion he cared little. Yet even Hitler, surprised and perhaps dismayed by the emotional rallying to Britain's cause in America after the first bombing attacks by the Luftwaffe, tried to find an excuse.

For the first few months of the war, Britain had taken the greatest care to avoid air action which might result in the loss of enemy civilian life. This was a political decision, as much expedient as humanitarian when one bears in mind the much greater strength of the German bomber force. But even in this period we recognized two basic truths – first, that when the shooting started we should be forced, for reasons of self-defence, to make a determined attempt to destroy vital German military and industrial targets by bombing, and not be squeamish about the inevitable civilian casualties that would result; and second, that our restraint in the meantime was unlikely to influence Hitler one jot. This was the lesson of Warsaw, and later of Rotterdam. When the Commander of Warsaw refused to surrender, Hitler ordered continuous large-scale air attacks on the city; the same thing happened at Rotterdam, where nearly a thousand people were killed by bombing. We knew well enough what to expect.

It has since been suggested that the bombing of Rotterdam, which was regarded as one of the major German atrocities, for which the German people must one day expect to pay, was all a hideous mistake; and it is clear that General Schmidt, the local German army commander, did his best to call it off, and did in fact succeed, by the use of warning flares, in stopping about half the bombers. The evidence strongly suggests that Goering himself intervened, because he was determined not only to hasten the Dutch surrender but to issue a timely warning to the Allies in the shape of the destruction of an Allied town: but this is speculation. What is certain is that the mistake could not have occurred had the intention not been there all along. Schmidt's orders from the headquarters of the German Eighteenth Army, issued on the evening of 13th May 1940, were ruthless and clear: 'Resistance in Rotterdam will be broken with every means; if necessary destruction of the town will be threatened and carried out.'[1] At 10.30 next morning the 'complete destruction' of the city was duly threatened; at 13.30, while negotiations for the surrender were in progress, the bombers went in.

1. *History of the Second World War*, Vol. II – 'Grand Strategy' (HMSO).

Our own expectations of aerial bombardment rose steeply with the fall of France. 'As our enemies still reject peace,' said Hitler on 6th June 1940, after Belgium and Holland had surrendered and with French resistance ceasing, 'they shall have war of total annihilation.' He could only be referring to Britain. It was clear now to even the most optimistic politician that unrestricted bombing was and would be an integral part of Nazi war policy when it suited them, and from this point on, while Fighter Command prepared for the onslaught to come, Bomber Command was allowed to attack selected military and industrial targets in Germany.

The first bombs to be dropped on central London since 1918 fell on the night of 24th August 1940, at the height of the Battle of Britain. The British Government, reacting immediately, ordered a heavy raid on Berlin the following night as a reprisal. Eighty-one aircraft set out, and although the specified targets were military and industrial, most of the bombs, inevitably for that period, fell wide of their targets, and there were civilian casualties. The effect of this reprisal raid is uncertain. The Nazis were super-sensitive about the raining of bombs on German soil, and it has been suggested that the raid on Berlin was an important factor in the decision, taken in the next few days, to switch the main weight of the Luftwaffe attack from airfields to London. If so, it had a decisive effect on the battle, which up to that point had been in the balance. But it seems more likely that the Germans were forced to change their tactics through their own prohibitive losses, and that this switch demanded the less precise objectives offered by London and other large cities.

Before the war the Nazis had firmly believed that Britain, through fear of the air war that would result, would never enter into major conflict with Germany. When it became evident that this was wishful thinking, it was thought that England could be intimidated by mass air attacks.[1] Operation 'Sealion', the plan for the invasion of Britain, depended for

1. General Adolf Galland, *The Battle of Britain* (Forces Aériennes Françaises).

success on the prior destruction of the Royal Air Force, and when it was clear, at the end of the second phase of the Battle of Britain, that RAF resistance had still not been swept away and that the invasion would therefore have to be postponed, the Nazi leaders were not unduly depressed. While the threat of invasion was maintained, Britain was to be brought to the point of surrender by the bombardment of her capital city. This was in line with the successful pattern of previous campaigns, in which the Polish and Dutch armies had capitulated after the bombing of main centres of population and the Danish Government had capitulated at the threat of it.

On 2nd September, in an order to the Luftwaffe, Hitler directed that attacks should now be made on the populations and defences of the larger cities, particularly London, by day and night. The RAF raid on Berlin of a week earlier provided him with a useful pretext, and he decided to announce the impending assault on Britain's civil population in a speech at the Berlin Sports Palace two days later, placing the blame for the resort to all-out air warfare firmly on Britain. However, a single RAF raid on Berlin seemed a flimsy excuse for a punitive war on an entire population, so Hitler decided to fabricate a picture of British atrocity bombing in the war so far, claiming that it had gone on for many months, and investing one particular incident with as much infamy and notoriety as possible – the alleged bombing of the town of Freiburg in south-western Germany on 10th May 1940.

In the course of this speech Hitler developed his theme. 'For three months I did not reply,' he said, 'because I believed they would stop, but in this Mr Churchill saw a sign of our weakness. The British will know that we are now giving our answer night after night.' Secure in the belief that he had overwhelming air superiority, he promised that British towns and cities would be 'wiped off the map'. His speech was followed three days later by the first of a series of the biggest air attacks of the war on London. Even the German News Agency admitted that much of the bombing was indiscriminate. 'Bombs,' it said, 'fell all over the place.' The German newspapers, too, acknowledged that the bombing of London was not of a purely military character. And the German propaganda services let themselves go. The bombardment of London was compared with the catastrophe of Sodom and Gomorrah. The day of judgement had broken over the British Empire, the German sword in the sky had struck at the heart of the island, the hour of military vengeance had come. Sneering at the reported singing of 'There'll always be an England' in a London night club after a raid, one broadcast offered a flat contradiction. 'We can tell them that the German air arm will see to it that there won't be an England, because this is only the beginning, and other cities will get their turn.'[1]

Amidst all these threats there were solemn assurances on wave-lengths beamed at neutral audiences that the raids were confined to legitimate military objectives and were anyway of a retaliatory nature. Hitler returned to the subject many times. 'We did not want the war in the air either,' he said on 11th December 1940, 'but having accepted it we shall continue it to the end ... this great strategist Churchill had the idea of starting unlimited warfare at night. He started it with Freiburg and then he went on.' Again on 1st January he repeated his story, hoping perhaps to square himself with neutral audiences. 'In May,' he said, 'England began her attacks on Freiburg ... for months I watched this inhuman cruelty ... now, however, this war will be waged to the end. ... We are not talking useless phrases but are in deadly earnest when we affirm that for every bomb ten or, if necessary, a hundred will be dropped in its place.' All this was justified, so the story went, first and foremost by the infamous Freiburg raid, the so-called start of unrestricted air warfare.

The truth was that the bombs which fell on Freiburg on 10th May 1940 had been dropped in error – by German planes. They were Heinkel 111's, briefed to bomb the airfield at Dijon, but they lost their way in cloud and attacked what they thought was an alternative target.[2] It turned out to be Freiburg. Fifty-

1. BBC Monitoring Service.

2. *The Destruction of Dresden*, by David Irving (Kimber).

seven people were killed. The Germans checked the bomb fragments and thus discovered the culprits for themselves. All Hitler's accusations against us for firing the first shot in the war on civilians stemmed from this trumped-up piece of propaganda based on evidence which he and all the other Nazi leaders knew from the start to be false. It was for the bombing of Freiburg by German planes that Britain was to have her cities wiped off the map in so-called reprisal raids.

Why did Hitler and his propagandist teams bother to dream up the chimera of Freiburg? Although RAF bombing was still directed in theory against precise military and industrial objectives and could not be seriously challenged, in practice it had caused civilian casualties, and since a pretext was needed it was the obvious target for a specious and scurrilous attack by Hitler. Why wasn't this enough? The most compelling answer may be that Britain had to be blamed for indulging in this kind of warfare from the very beginning: Hitler was still smarting under the opprobrium of Rotterdam and something had to be found to ante-date it.

To prove that Britain started unrestricted bombing remained a Nazi obsession to the end of the war, and they clung with pathetic faith to their mendacious Freiburg story. As late as June 1943 Goebbels was still plugging it when, in an address at a mass funeral of air raid victims at Wuppertal, he brought out the old accusation. 'A long chain of human suffering in all German cities blitzed by the Allies', he said, 'has borne witness against them and their cruel and cowardly leaders – from the murder of German women and children in Freiburg on 10th May 1940, right up to the present day.'

This repeated insistence on the myth of Freiburg underlines the weakness of the Nazi case even in their own eyes. But the full hypocrisy of their position is best illustrated by an instruction Hitler gave to Brauchitsch, Raeder, Goering and Keitel on 9th October 1939, when stressing the importance of capturing bases in the Low Countries from which to mount a strategic air offensive against Britain. 'The ruthless employment of the Luftwaffe', he wrote, 'against the heart of the British will-to-resist can and will follow at the given moment.' The switch to an attack on the morale of the British people was a part of the plan, clearly foreshadowed eleven months before it was begun.

2. *'GIVE IT 'EM BACK!'*

BEFORE THE WAR the official Air Staff attitude had been that the bombing of targets in enemy territory would be carried out by day. This did not mean that training for night bombing was ignored – simply that no reason was apparent why our bombers should not fly to their targets and identify and bomb them in daylight. So while the policy was ostensibly a flexible one, allowing for both day and night bombing, in practice the crews were insufficiently trained in flying long distances in all weathers to find and bomb pinpoint targets at night.

Our early war experience, and that of the Germans, showed that plans for defending the bomber in daylight were inadequate, and perhaps impracticable. A decision to confine the bombing of targets in Germany to darkness became inevitable. But the requirement for aids to navigation and blind bombing that was inherent in this decision was swamped by the natural preoccupation of air leaders and scientific establishments and committees with the problems of air defence, and obscured by the absence of any scientific evaluation of the results of our night bombing. There were people who had their doubts, but the general impression given was one of highly trained crews fighting their way unerringly through stubborn enemy defences and dropping their bombs with pinpoint precision. It was taken for granted that targets were wrecked.

This was a legacy from the pre-war over-emphasis on the immediate bomber threat and over-estimate of its destructive power as then constituted. When the German air raids began, people in the big towns, and indeed outside them, confidently expected to be obliterated. It was only with experience that they learned that although a raid might cover a wide area, the wounds were generally scattered and the casualties supportable, bad as they often were. Citizens developed a resistance to the bomber threat and hoped to survive it. It was only in comparatively few instances that an effective and terrifying concentration was achieved.

There were several lessons to be learnt from the German raids. One was that morale might be toughened rather than weakened when bombing was on a relatively minor scale. In total war, civilians welcomed the chance to share dangers and divert enemy effort from their relatives and friends in uniform. 'The sublime but also terrible experiences and emotions of the battlefield,' said Churchill in a broadcast on 27th April 1941, 'are now shared for good or ill by the entire population. All are proud to be under the fire of the enemy.' Another important lesson was that damage to the war effort was not confined to the destruction of industrial plant. If the heartbeats of a city, its transport, water, power, housing and administrative services, could be interrupted, the effect on output was immediate and widespread.

In his broadcast Churchill had averred that the British nation, stirred and moved by their experiences as never before in their history, were determined to conquer or die. They knew well enough by this time that they could certainly die: in air raids alone, over 40,000 of them had already done so. But, how, in the spring of 1941, were they to conquer? The only possible answer seemed to be by the proper application of air power. Just as the U-Boat was the natural weapon of the vastly inferior naval power, so the destruction of industrial capacity by bombing was the natural weapon of a power outclassed on land.

There were two principal factors which dominated the public subconscious mind. First was a revulsion against the trench warfare of 1914–18; even the horrors of bombing seemed preferable to that. Second was the realization that Britain could never win a Continental war unless her adversary were first fatally weakened by some indirect means; by blockade, by the intervention of a powerful Continental ally – or by bombing

Between the wars the British were continually assured that the next war would be a war in the air, and that the bomber would always get through; to that extent they were conditioned to the idea of aerial bombardment. Since then they had accustomed themselves to the realities of day and night bombing by the full weight of the Luftwaffe and were ready to back themselves to stand up to it. The Germans, on the other hand, had been promised by Goering that not a single bomb would fall on the Ruhr. The British were anxious to see how they would react to similar treatment.

There can be no bilking the fact that the people of Britain, sick of defeats and humiliations at the hands of aggressor nations, desired nothing more than to see the people of Germany hurt. They had been caught up involuntarily in a war of survival against an evil tyranny, a war that had quickly become an intensely personal matter. (The fate awaiting them if they lost it is too easily forgotten.) They had been the victims of an unprovoked assault, as a nation, in their homes, on their persons, on their lives, and it was natural that they should come to identify themselves with a bomber offensive. 'On every side,' said Churchill in the House of Commons on 8th October 1940, 'is the cry "We can take it!", but with it there is also the cry "Give it them back".' This analysis of the feelings of bombed-out Londoners, with its hint of retribution for the future, was greeted with prolonged cheers. For two months, from September to November 1940, London was bombed by an average of 200 bombers a night as the Germans concentrated on breaking the spirit of Londoners to the point where the Government would find it impossible to continue the war in the face of a collapse in civilian morale. And when the bombing of London failed to produce the expected surrender, and the offensive was turned on the big provincial cities, it only served to spread the resolve to hit back. Despite widespread damage the raids failed in their intention; heavy wastage in night-flying accidents reduced their effectiveness, and they ceased at last when Hitler ordered the large-scale transfer of units to the east for his impending attack on Russia. But they had meanwhile produced a highly significant by-product in the attitude of the British people to the bombing of Germany. Just as the years of attempted appeasement had had the effect of uniting the country against the Nazis when war finally came, so the blitz created a righteous indignation against the Germans themselves.

On 22nd June 1941, following the German attack on Russia, Churchill clearly foreshadowed a bombing offensive aimed specifically at the German people. 'We shall bomb Germany,' he said, 'by day as well as by night in ever-increasing measure, casting upon them month by month a heavier discharge of bombs, and making the German people taste and gulp each month a sharper dose of the miseries they have showered upon mankind.' The powerful emotional force of this argument had overcome the last vestiges of squeamishness.

This is not to attribute the existence and subsequent growth of Bomber Command to a desire for reprisals. With a Germany immune through her vast conquests from blockade, with our land forces weakened and deprived of contact, and with a young and independent air force in being and determined to play its part, a strategic bombing policy was inevitable. A nation fighting for its existence, facing the alternative of defeat and subjugation, uses whatever weapon comes to hand.

The British people were not hampered or divided by academic considerations and specious arguments about who started it – who started the war, who started unrestricted bombing, who first made war against peoples. They *knew* who started it. Accustomed to a measure of democracy, they could not believe that Hitler and the Nazis were not thoroughly representative of German desires and German ways. Otherwise the Germans would surely never stand for them. Here was an evil that must be destroyed. If it meant the complete destruction of Germany, so much the better for their children and their children's children.

To understand the bomber offensive, of which the Thousand Plan was the first real manifestation, it is essential to project the mind back to those years. The prevailing mood was on a higher plane than self-preservation, revenge or racial hatred. It was a mood of sacrifice. People felt they were taking part in a crusade. They felt, and were encouraged to think, that they had the whole of subjugated Europe, indeed of the Free World, behind them.

It has been said, as a kind of counsel's plea on behalf of the British people, that they were not properly aware of British bombing policy from 1942 to 1945 and must therefore be acquitted of guilt – if guilt there be – for the destruction of German towns and cities and the sufferings of the Germans. It was the fault of the politicians, of the Service chiefs, perhaps even of a single fanatic. One has heard this sort of thing before, from the other side, about a heavier and more convincing burden of guilt. The truth is that the British people were well aware, through the utterances of Churchill and others, of the plans for the devastation of Germany by bombing. It was a policy of which they thoroughly approved. Indeed, they themselves had demanded it.

3. CRISIS FOR BOMBER COMMAND

WHEN, IN SEPTEMBER 1940, the Luftwaffe was defeated in the Battle of Britain, the full significance of the victory was not at first comprehended. The diversion of scientific and industrial effort from defensive to offensive channels which might have been expected to follow came slowly. Until, in June 1941, Hitler attacked Russia, few people were confident that the danger of invasion was over. And throughout 1941 the threat from the German submarine and surface raiders to our seaborne supplies dominated the minds of all our leaders. This preoccupation, together with the demands of overseas theatres, meant that the considerable expansion achieved in Bomber Command during the year was entirely leaked away to other tasks.

By the autumn of 1941 a climate of disillusion surrounded

the bomber offensive. A statistical analysis of night photographs taken by the bomber crews themselves showed that in raids over the Ruhr, where many of the important targets were sited, not one bomb in ten fell within five miles of its target. From this startling revelation it was clear that small targets of military importance, and even closely defined industrial areas, which our bombers were still confined to, were impossible to hit regularly with existing facilities. This had two major political repercussions. One was the institution, in February 1942, of the area bombing policy, in which aiming points were to be chosen in large built-up areas, and not confined to important industrial targets within those areas. The other was increased pressure from the Admiralty and the War Office for a drastic review of Government policy for winning the war and a rapid reassignment of the bomber force. They argued that it was sheer obstinate stupidity to pursue an offensive that was so tragically wasteful of effort while there was such urgent need for a concentration of air power in direct support of the other Services. 'If we lose the war at sea,' said Sir Dudley Pound, Chief of Naval Staff, 'we lose the war,' and this was undeniable. The First Lord of the Admiralty demanded the immediate transfer of six and a half Wellington squadrons to Coastal Command and two further Bomber Command squadrons to Ceylon for long-range reconnaissance work, and warned that these requirements were by no means final. Further bomber squadrons should be thoroughly trained in the technique of homing on to enemy naval forces and of bombing moving targets at sea. These minimum immediate requirements were quickly followed by demands for the establishment of replica Coastal Commands in all overseas theatres and the transfer to them and to Coastal Command at home of further long-range bombers for anti-submarine and reconnaissance duties. Meanwhile the War Office were asking for the transfer of further squadrons to the Middle East for an offensive against Rommel's communications, and to the Far East for the defence of India. In both cases the demands included the specialized training of air crews for the tasks involved. The only possible source of aircraft and crews lay in the further denudation of Bomber Command.

In naval and military circles it was felt at this time that the only well-founded ground of criticism of the higher direction of the war lay in the control and direction of the Air Force.[1] Both Pound and Brooke, Chief of the Imperial General Staff, urged that it was the province of the Chiefs of Staff to advise on the allocation of aircraft as between the Services in the various theatres and for the bombing of Germany. It was quite unacceptable that the Air Force should continue to decide these allocations more or less independently. All other arms were subject to the overriding direction of the Chiefs of Staff. Why not the Air Force?

The attitude of the Naval and General Staffs was that the order of priority for the allocation of air forces should be:

1. The fighter defence of the British Isles.
2. The essential needs of the Navy.
3. The essential needs of the Army.
4. Anything left over – long-range bombing.

The Air Staff attitude was that the first two tasks were essentially defensive while the third did not and could not for a very long time involve major conflict with the chief enemy, Germany. The true function of the heavy bomber was to concentrate on strategic attacks against the heart of the enemy. In so doing it threatened the sources of all enemy strength.

There was, however, yet another argument which militated against Bomber Command's claims. Since Hitler had attacked Russia, and declared war on the United States following the aggression of Japan, the whole war strategy had become much more diffuse. It was very much more difficult to see the bomber offensive as the only possible Allied means of attacking Germany in the foreseeable future, especially in the light of its admitted failures of 1940 and 1941. It was time to end the scattering of bombs across the German countryside and

1. *The Business of War*, by Major-General Sir John Kennedy (Hutchinson).

concentrate all our armed forces on fresh strategic conceptions for winning the war.

The crowning humiliation for Bomber Command, in the eyes of its enemies, and even of some of its friends and of the general public, came on 12th February 1942, when the German battle-cruisers *Scharnhorst* and *Gneisenau*, together with the cruiser *Prinz Eugen*, passed unscathed through the Channel. Two hundred and fifty bombers, virtually the entire strength of the Command, failed to score a single hit. The fact that the day had been well chosen by the Germans for its appalling weather, and that conditions were hopeless for bombing, was not understood. Nor was it generally known that both battle-cruisers had been damaged, one of them seriously, by mines laid ahead of them by Bomber Command. The plain truth seemed to be that Bomber Command, whose much-advertised destruction of precision targets in Germany at night had been proved to be mythical, couldn't even hit a target 250 yards long in broad daylight on its own doorstep.

A two-day debate on the war situation followed within a fortnight in the House of Commons. In the course of this debate, many doubts were expressed by Members about the policy for the bombing of Germany, and whether the continued devotion of a considerable part of our war effort to the building up of the bomber force was the best use that could be made of our resources. Winding up for the Government, Sir Stafford Cripps, Lord Privy Seal and Leader of the House, reminded Members that the existing policy had been initiated when Britain was fighting alone against the combined forces of Germany and Italy; a bomber offensive had then seemed the most effective way of taking the initiative against the enemy. With the enormous access of support from Russia, and the tremendous potential of the United States, the original policy was under review. 'I can assure the House,' he said, 'that the Government are fully aware of the other uses to which our resources could be put, and the moment they arrive at a decision that the circumstances warrant a change, a change in policy will be made.'

This grave crisis in the affairs of Bomber Command coincided with the arrival, on 22nd February 1942, of Air Marshal A. T. Harris as Commander-in-Chief.

4. *HARRIS AND SAUNDBY*

IT HAS BEEN pointed out many times that 'Bert' Harris had no part in the decision to switch from selective to area attack, from the precision bombing of what were known as self-evident military objectives to the devastation of industrial towns; but it bears repeating again. The experience of 1940 and 1941 had convinced our leaders that this was the only way in which Bomber Command could be employed effectively. Plans for area attack took shape in 1941, and the formal directive from the Air Ministry preceded Harris's arrival at High Wycombe. Harris himself was in America at the time. It may be said, though, that in subsequent years, on the tactical and practical grounds that it was better to hit what we could rather than go on missing what we couldn't, he became the staunchest advocate of a policy that was often challenged.

The popular impression of Harris as a ruthless purveyor of brutality, a man filled with an implacable blood-hatred for Germany and for anyone who stood in the way of his plans for its wholesale destruction, is so wide of the mark that it needs some correction at the beginning. Harris had his weaknesses but he had the basic attributes of greatness. No doubt to some extent he was a man with an obsession; but as a man of vision he was second in Air Force history to Trenchard alone. He had absolute faith in ultimate victory over Germany through the power of the bomber. Just as there would have been no independent Royal Air Force without Trenchard, so there would have been no independent bomber offensive without Harris. Or anyway without Harris and Saundby.

Harris believed that involvement in land campaigns, especially Continental ones, served to reduce us to the level of the horde. To make a premature landing on the Continent, before the bomber had done its work, spelt disaster – as it had already done at Dunkirk. Our aim should be to destroy the industrial basis of Germany's war effort by bombing, producing a situation in which shortage of essential war supplies would sap the energy, effectiveness and morale of her armed forces and entire population. Harris, indeed, foresaw a situation, given a large enough bomber force, in which intervention on the Continent by land forces would amount to little more than police action.

Disruption and heavy civilian casualties in German industrial towns did not, in Harris's view, constitute terror bombing. Indeed, terror bombing as such was not likely to produce decisive results. On the other hand, the erosion of the enemy's power and will to resist could never be achieved by the destruction of key factories alone, even if they could be hit. They would always reappear elsewhere, and function for a time.

Germany, by unprovoked aggression on weak sovereign states at her borders, had pushed the frontiers of war far beyond her boundaries. Other countries, other peoples, were to suffer the horrors of war, not the Germans. Bombing was the answer to this presumption.

Harris had the ability to focus resolutely on one side of a question and to refuse to let his purpose be weakened by other facets. But he had the breadth of view when he wanted to employ it. A direct and forceful personality, he had no use for mincing his words or beating about the bush, or for anyone who did so. He had a gift for pungent language which he could not resist exercising, and this made him enemies. But he was the reverse of callous and brutal. In reality he was warm-hearted, although he did his best to hide it. He was filled with anger and remorse when he was obliged to sacrifice crews on operations in which he felt they could not be wholly effective, and it was in arguing the case against such operations that he made many of his enemies. He was resentful of interference, and felt that if he was going to have the responsibility of running the Command he must have the final say in the tactical control of his force, if not in strategic policy. As a commander he was never satisfied. As soon as he had achieved one purpose he was working enthusiastically on another. He never rested for one moment on his laurels.

The gift for pungent expression did less harm when it was employed orally. It was more likely to give lasting offence when put to paper. A typical broadside was provoked by the Government's refusal after the war to award a campaign star to the men of Bomber Command. When he received his Defence Medal he wrote that he would wear it proudly, although it put him and the men of his Command on a par with a fire-watcher who had spent alternate Thursdays playing whist in a dug-out in Blackpool. However much this sort of thing might be disliked it was no more than the truth, and it endeared him to his men. From the moment he took over, they knew he was ready to fight for them with all he had.

Harris was capable of a righteous anger terrible to behold. And he never dissembled. If he hated something, or someone, he never made any secret of it. He inspired in his officers a healthy terror. God help them if they made a mess of something and hadn't got a good reason for it. But if they genuinely failed in something and went to see him and put their cards on the table, he would be the first to think up a way of righting matters and getting them out of trouble.

Inevitably he took refuge in a cynical view of his role. One day he was driving from High Wycombe to an Air Ministry meeting in his canvas-topped Bentley. On his front bumper was a plate clearing the car from all speed limits. He was speeding on the Great West Road near Uxbridge when, in order to avoid an accident, he allowed himself to be overtaken by a police patrol.

'Do you realize you were doing more than ninety?' they asked.

'Have a look at the front of the car.'

'That's all very well, but you're liable to kill people at that speed.'

'I'm paid to kill people.'

This was his way of showing himself off as a ruthless commander, of fulfilling the image that had been thrust upon him. For those who took no notice of this sort of thing, and had real ability, he was a wonderful person to work for, supporting his staff in the same way as he supported his crews. His staff officers were in no doubt that the combination of Harris and Saundby was a great one. They had never served under better commanders, never worked so hard, never been so happy.

The nickname 'Butcher' hurt and surprised him when he first heard it, but he soon saw that for his crews it was a term of endearment, originating as 'Butch' among Commonwealth crews who used it freely as a nickname among themselves. For them, as for others, he became a symbol of Britain's determination to hit back at Germany. 'Five for the Butcher,' they used to say in the Pathfinder Force, when they had finished their sixty missions, and they really were doing these extra five sorties for Harris.

How did he achieve this astonishing respect, affection and loyalty? Unlike Montgomery, who believed in showing himself to his troops, Harris, due to the necessity for him to be at his headquarters to direct almost nightly operations, was hardly ever seen by his men. One of the most remarkable things about Harris was the way he succeeded in imposing his personality on operations from a distance. He did it, first, because the crews knew he was on their side. This began when he took over the Command. Previously, if crews failed to hit a target, there were always people ready to wag their heads and countenance the view that the crews must be lacking in resolve. Of course they could hit their targets – if they were really determined to do so. But Harris – and Saundby with him – was an expert. He had proved by his own experience in peacetime that targets were extraordinarily difficult to find at night, let alone to hit. Without radar aids to navigation and target finding he saw no prospect of improvement. He backed his crews to do the job if they were given the equipment.

Secondly, Harris gave the Command a sense of purpose. The

bombing of Germany was going to win the war. It might be contributory, it might be absolute, but it would be a decisive factor either way. This meant everything to men who, in any one tour of operations, faced almost certain death.

A man with as powerful a character as Harris could dominate people so easily that there was always the danger that he would frighten them into becoming yes-men. Those who, in order to deliver an expert opinion, had to stand up to Harris, generally found that it was necessary early in the association to have one good row with him. That was enough.

Robert Saundby had had his row with Harris twenty years earlier, in 1922, soon after Harris arrived to command No 45 Squadron in Iraq. Saundby, in addition to being senior flight commander, had the extraneous duty of President of the Mess Committee. One morning, without his knowledge, Harris gave orders for Saundby's office in the Mess to be moved. The result was that when Saundby went there he found it in chaos. He went straight to Harris and burst in upon him in a great rage. 'As President of the Mess Committee,' he shouted, 'and as your senior flight commander, I think I should be the first to know of any changes, and to learn from a Mess steward that I've been thrown out of my office without warning is absolutely monstrous.'

Saundby had been too angry to think of such niceties as closing the door, and the row could be heard all over squadron headquarters. Harris moved quietly behind Saundby and closed the door. 'Now,' he said, 'you'd better get it off your chest.' Saundby did. 'I think you're right,' said Harris. 'You'd better move back.'

Four years later, when Saundby returned to England, he got a letter from Harris, who was then commanding No 58 Squadron, the first night bomber squadron. 'I know you've got a couple of months of your leave to go,' wrote Harris, 'but I've just lost a flight commander and I'd like to have you in his place. Unfortunately I can't wait – I must have someone now.' Saundby's interests lay especially in navigation and night bombing, and he reflected that he might get a much less congenial posting if he let matters take their course. He admired Harris and was pleased to be wanted by him. The fly-fishing season, one of his greatest joys, was nearing its end. He decided to say yes.

For the next twelve months he worked harder than at any time in his life – up to the war. Harris was a slave-driver, and Saundby found himself flying three or four nights a week besides working in his office all day. But he was thoroughly enjoying himself, learning all the time about night flying and night bombing. It was in this period that he and Harris discovered for themselves how difficult it was to find targets at night, even in good weather and without the distraction of enemy action. 'Targets will have to be marked,' pronounced Harris, and he pressed for marker bombs. While in Mesopotamia, he and Saundby had improvised their own markers by fastening a white Very light to a 20-lb practice bomb so that the light fired as the bomb hit. It was a requirement that Harris continued for press for, but without success up to the war.

Harris was a great innovator, and he brought about many changes in equipment and method. Pilots had nothing more to guide them in instrument flying than a bubble and an airspeed indicator, and at night, in poor visibility, with no horizon, flying was too dangerous for all but the most skilled pilots, and too dangerous even for them in turbulence. Harris realized the need for a stabilized instrument panel, with an artificial horizon, and these were among the improvements he worked on and demanded. He had car headlamps mounted as landing lights, fitted on a swivel so that the angle of the beams could be altered during the approach, and he also called for an electrically-lit flare-path to replace the paraffin flares of the time.

If Saundby had a great admiration for Harris, and felt that after all their years together he understood him fully, Harris was no less appreciative of Saundby. He knew that in Saundby he had a man whose ideas were absolutely sound. But the two men were thoroughly dissimilar. It was true that Harris's bark was worse than his bite, but he had a bark, and he had a bite. Saundby, on the other hand, was perhaps the most approachable high-ranking officer there has ever been in any Service, a man able to put other men at their ease whatever their rank. Harris has described him as having less side than anyone he ever knew.

Saundby was a man of culture and sensitivity, tall and heavily built, with brown hair and moustache, extremely sociable, yet with a liking for his own company. It was in recognition of the leisure hours he had once spent at the contemplative sport of fishing that all targets in Germany bore the code-names of fish. Berlin was Whitebait – Saundby took a delight in calling this great capital city by the name of one of the smallest fish. Cologne was Dace.

As befitted one of the hardest workers in the Air Force, Saundby relaxed easily, whether hunting butterflies and moths in uniform in the Chilterns near High Wycombe, as he sometimes did, or having a drink and a chat in the company of junior officers for an hour or so at the end of the day, which he did frequently. In the first activity he protected his mind from obsession. In the second he provided the essential link in command between the body and the head.

What was Saundby's role? He had gone to Bomber Command as senior air staff officer in November 1940, and he stayed there until the end of the war. In this appointment, and from February 1943 as deputy C-in-C, he took charge of day-to-day operational matters, leaving Harris free to absorb himself in questions of high policy. His occupation of these two posts under Harris was one of the happiest chances of wartime personnel selection. Here was a man who drew affection and loyalty from his subordinates naturally and easily yet who was himself at his best when required to serve loyally under another. He and Harris were complementary, one man produced from an amalgam of two, the aggregate of their qualities amounting to something far greater than the sum of their parts.

In serving at Bomber Command for four and a half years Saundby undoubtedly earned the major credit for the building up of the bomber force, technically and in every other way. In seeing his task through he jeopardized his career. He was offered command elsewhere but refused it. He had built up the bomber force almost with his own hands and he was determined to guide it to maturity. When Harris told him that Portal had said that his refusal would affect his career, Saundby's reply was terse. 'I am not concerned with my career,' he said, 'but with winning the war and protecting our crews.'[1] Saundby rightly felt that on his personal knowledge and skills the safety of the bomber crews to a large extent depended.

Another factor in his loyalty to the Command was the health of Bert Harris. The strain of being responsible for what amounted to a major battle almost nightly for over three years was a frightful one. Apart from the very few nights when there was no flying, Harris hardly had a complete night's rest throughout that time. With weather and other hazards and uncertainties it occurred to him almost every night that he might lose a quarter or even a half of his entire force, losses which would be altogether crippling, quite apart from his concern for his crews. Harris himself has recorded his fearful apprehension about the weather, night after night, in conditions under which he could easily have justified himself if he had kept the entire force on the ground nine times out of ten. But while he was justifying himself, Britain would have lost the air war. The final responsibility, whatever the forecasts, rested squarely on Harris, and he had to take these decisions at least once every twenty-four hours. Failure to measure up to this responsibility would have held fatal implications for our own cities and destroyed our whole war strategy, completely aborting the invasion of Europe.

In addition to the overriding operational and administrative responsibility of running what became the RAF's biggest command, Harris found himself forced to conduct a public relations campaign, with the aid of stereoscopic photographs, to demonstrate to his own side the effectiveness of bomber operations. This political and social obligation was a tremendous additional strain, both on himself and on his wife. In just

1. Comment by Sir Arthur Harris.

over three years, he and Lady Harris entertained (and often put up and fed) over 5,000 people at Springfield, the Commander-in-Chief's solid Victorian house outside High Wycombe, in order to instruct them in what Bomber Command was doing and could do. The result was that Harris was so over-burdened that a failure in health was always a possibility.

The whole organization of bomber operations became so complex as time passed, with pathfinder techniques, radar spoofing, feint raids, intruding, mining, evasive routeing, all attuned to the weather and to the latest German counter-measures, that the departure of a man of Saundby's experience and background would have left a gap that only time could fill. During that time Harris would be bound to have to shoulder some of Saundby's responsibilities. It might prove too much for him. So Saundby stayed, and never for a moment regretted it, though at the end of the war he collapsed from a recurrence of an injury sustained in the First World War and was invalided out of the Service.

5. *'IF ONLY WE COULD PUT UP A THOUSAND . . .'*

BEFORE HE TOOK over at Bomber Command, Harris had been out of Britain for eight months leading the RAF Delegation in Washington, arranging and expediting the delivery of planes and other war equipment. It was Saundby's task to brief him on the current situation. Harris was in for some shocks.

'How many bombers have we got?'

'Available daily with crews – about three hundred and seventy-five. That includes the light bombers of 2 Group.'

'But we had over three hundred in 1939. Surely we've expanded more than that?'

'We added nearly twenty squadrons last year,' said Saundby, 'and lost the lot to Coastal Command and North Africa. The only bright spot is that we've now got forty or fifty heavy bombers – Stirlings and Halifaxes.'

'What about the Lancasters?'

'We'll be getting the first Lancasters next month. But only enough to equip two squadrons.'

'What about Lease-Lend? What about the stuff I've been getting from America?'

'All the heavies are going to Coastal. Most of the medium and light bombers are going to Russia and the Middle East.'

It was a dismal situation – two and a half years after the outbreak of war, and the front-line strength of the Command had changed hardly at all. There was actually a reduction in numbers since 1940, with a small improvement in bomb-carrying capacity due to the introduction of new types. Bomber Command remained the ugly duckling of the fighting commands at home, still the smallest of the big three.

When Saundby went on to describe the pressure being applied by the Admiralty and the War Office to divert practically the entire bomber force to tasks for which it was not designed and for which the crews had not been trained, at the expense of the strategic offensive against Germany, Harris exploded. In arguing his case he compared those who advocated the breaking-up of Bomber Command for the purpose of strengthening Coastal and Army Co-operation Commands and the overseas theatres to the amateur Socialist who wanted the total available wealth divided equally between all. Nobody would get anything worthwhile and in a very short time all would be squandered, while our only offensive weapon against Germany would be destroyed. 'One cannot win wars by defending oneself,' declared Harris. Manifestations of enemy power had of course to be contained, and our sea communications had to be safeguarded, but the application of air forces for defensive purposes should be restricted to the irreducible minimum necessary to survival. However, Harris was basically a man for deeds, not words, and he saw clearly enough that only one course of action lay open to him. Somehow, by the skilful use of the meagre force at his disposal, he had to achieve quick and spectacular results, impressing the War Cabinet with the potential of the bomber, reversing the tide and earning that share of the country's industrial backing without which the bomber force would always remain inadequate.

There was, too, another factor of crucial importance, one that Harris had been in the best possible position to evaluate. America was in the war, and although the Americans had not yet been able to bring their strength to bear in Europe, they were watching the strategic situation keenly. Agreement had been reached to treat Germany as the principal enemy and to defeat her first before concentrating on Japan, but powerful factions in America were opposed to this view. The notion of a combined bomber offensive, American and British, had received a severe jolt from the revelations of 1941. If the British were unable to do their part, for whatever reason, would an American air offensive be worth mounting, with all its risks? Were not the two interdependent? Harris recognized that only the magnet of success could ensure that when it came to it the American bombers were not diverted elsewhere.

In many ways Harris's predecessors had prepared the ground well. Ludlow-Hewitt, C-in-C on the outbreak of war, had developed a large, efficient and essential training organization within the Command. Peirse, who took over from Portal in October 1940, strongly supported by Saundby, had urged the development and provision of radar aids to navigation and blind bombing, and the first of these, known as 'Gee', was coming into squadron service, with an expected useful life of six months. (By that time the Germans would have learnt to jam it.) And the gradual re-equipment of the squadrons with the new four-engined bombers, although putting a brake on expansion during the conversion period, would ultimately double and treble the bomb-carrying capacity. But the effect of all these improvements lay in the future, a future whose very existence was problematical. Unless convincing evidence could be produced soon, the aircraft of the Command were doomed to diversion to a long list of defensive and inessential tasks.

Thus, in addition to the many problems of hitting targets at night, and to the growing threat of unacceptable losses through the expanding German fighter and anti-aircraft defences, there was a serious danger of the citadel of the bomber offensive falling virtually from within.

Harris's predecessors, for all the wisdom of their general planning, had lacked his practical experience of bomber operations. (Harris had been AOC 4 Group in peacetime and AOC 5 Group for twelve months in wartime.) Being mainly theorists, they believed in being careful not to over-saturate targets. Fifteen bombers, it was thought, were sufficient to wipe out a small oil target. Thus numerous targets at great distances apart could be attacked simultaneously, scattering the defences. This was an operational concept which Harris and Saundby believed to be false. Forces of this size could be picked off easily by alert defences. And with the weapons and aids of the time it was almost impossible to over-saturate even the smallest targets. In these opinions they were strongly supported by scientific analysis. A study was made at Bomber Command of the losses sustained during comparable raids on comparable targets in similar weather conditions and this gave a clear indication that the guiding principle ought to be concentration in time and space, concentration of the largest available force on a single target in the shortest feasible time-spread. Anti-aircraft defences could only engage a certain number of aircraft in any given period, and the number of fighters which could be controlled in one area was similarly limited: hence any additional aircraft flying across the area could not be directly engaged. The principle applied to routes as well as target areas. Concentration might also have the effect of confusing enemy defences by making it difficult to select one out of so many targets, and of cluttering up the detection devices and making it difficult to track even one selected target. These were the methods by which Harris hoped to saturate defences as well as targets and reduce bomber losses which otherwise threatened to stifle the bomber offensive quite as effectively as the threatened change in government policy.

The German air blitz on Britain had been mounted from

conveniently situated airfields in France and Belgium; this was in accordance with Hitler's plan, and it explained his reliance on short-range bombers. Such bombers were under attack only while over Britain itself. The problem confronting RAF aircraft was vastly more complex. To reach targets in the Ruhr they had to make a sea crossing of at least 100 miles, with another 120 miles across Holland before they entered Germany. These defensive advantages were fully exploited by General Joseph Kammhuber when he took over the newly formed German night-fighter division in July 1940, and he quickly set up three coastal night-fighter zones in northern, central and southern Holland, each zone containing ground-controlled interception by radar for the fighters and radar-controlled searchlights. Then at the end of 1940 he conceived the idea of a second line of defences to guard the Ruhr. An unbroken line of radar zones was stretched right across the Ruhr approaches, compelling RAF bombers to pass through one or other of the zones or embark on a very wide detour. In each zone a night-fighter was waiting to pounce. Immediately behind the radar zones were the searchlights, with which the fighters were expected to co-operate, and the flak. The whole system of second-line defence, which by the spring of 1941 stretched from south of the Ruhr to the Danish border, was nicknamed the 'Kammhuber Line'.

In the next twelve months the line was extended and deepened until by the time Harris took over at Bomber Command it had joined up with and embraced the original searchlight belts along the coast. The whole system was aided and abetted by a network of early warning radar stations along the coast, backed by large central plotting rooms which gave a picture of operations throughout each area. Germany, and especially the Ruhr, now had defence in depth; detours to avoid the Kammhuber Line were no longer possible, and as the bombers flew singly across the contiguous radar zones, one night-fighter after another was vectored into the attack. It was impossible to penetrate into Germany without running the gauntlet of these powerful defences; and all these hazards had to be faced a second time, for a period of at least an hour, on the return flight, with a hundred miles of sea still to cross. There remained the formidable flak, searchlight and local night-fighter defences of the main target area. This was what faced the young airman in Bomber Command as he set out at the beginning of his thirty operational trips over enemy territory.

To some extent Harris was an inheritor in much the same sense as Montgomery was in the Desert. Just as Montgomery had to liberate the Eighth Army from the stranglehold of inferiority complex and the philosophy of retreat, so Harris had to convince his crews that they were not doomed for ever to ineffectual sporadic raiding and crippling losses. As in the Desert, the reasons for past failures were clear, and new equipment and techniques were being developed which it was expected would turn these failures into success. Harris had also inherited the new area bombing policy. He had inherited the decision, based on our experience of the German bombing of our cities, to concentrate on incendiarism. (There was a limit to the damage which could be caused by a given quantity of high explosive, but the Germans had demonstrated how fire-raising took advantage of the combustible energy within the target itself.) But unlike Montgomery, who took over a rapidly expanding Army, Harris inherited a force at the nadir of its fortunes over which hung the threat of disbandment.

The most promising frozen asset taken over by Harris was the new radar aid called Gee. Between 100 and 150 aircraft equipped with Gee were ready to start operating, and it was in this new navigational aid that most of the hopes of improving the accuracy of our night bombing rested.[1] Harris indeed hoped that with the aid of Gee it would be possible to concentrate large forces of bombers over a single target in a short space of time, saturating the defences. He fired a question at Saundby.

'How many aircraft can we concentrate using Gee in a short raid of fifteen to twenty minutes?'

Although to some extent Saundby held a privileged position in his relations with Harris, he never departed from a few firm

1. For a short description of the Gee system, see Appendix A.

principles in dealing with him. One was never to say more, when asked for an opinion, than he could state with absolute confidence. When pressed it was better to say 'I don't know' or 'I'll find out' than to make any kind of pronouncement without being able to quote chapter and verse. In the case in question, however, Saundby had an expert on his air staff with whom he had worked almost throughout the war, first at the Air Ministry and then at High Wycombe. This was the Command Radar Officer, the tall, youthful, blue-eyed Wing Commander Dudley Saward. Saundby sent for him and took him in to see Harris.

Harris was continually hurling this sort of question at his officers, and Saward was ready for this one.

'If the entire force were equipped with Gee, we could safely put eight bombers across the target per minute. In fifteen minutes, say a hundred and twenty.'

'How do you know that?'

'It's a question of accuracy in timing and tracking. Gee will give the crews that.'

The Gee campaign opened on 8th March 1942 with the first of a series of attacks on Essen. Because only about a third of the force was Gee-equipped, nothing like the concentration suggested by Saward as feasible was attempted at first. A complementary technique, involving the employment of a flare-dropping force to lead the raid and a target-marking force using incendiaries to follow up, was evolved. In this way it was hoped to produce a concentrated area of fire into which the non-equipped aircraft could drop their high explosives. The limitations of Gee as a bombing device, however, were quickly exposed. In eight major attacks, all involving between 100 and 200 bombers, only one bomb in twenty fell within five miles of Essen.

Essen, with its powerful defences and ubiquitous industrial haze, was of course the hardest of all area targets to find and hit. Better results were obtained during the same period in a similar raid on Cologne, when 120 aircraft delivered their attack in the space of twenty minutes. But even here the damage was too little and too scattered, while the defences remained unsaturated by this scale of attack. Although Gee had many uses it could not solve the problem of target recognition unaided, and the bomber force was still much too small.

Another technique that needed proper developing and testing was that of fire-raising. This was tried out for the first time in force on 28th March 1942 against Lübeck, when 234 bombers devastated large areas of this very vulnerable target. For the second trial a month later another highly inflammable target – Rostock – was chosen. Like Lübeck, although outside Gee range it was an easily identifiable port, not too strongly defended. The town was raided on four successive nights and spectacular damage was done. In both these attacks – Lübeck and Rostock – the area bombing was accompanied by a pin-point attack on an important factory, a pattern which soon became standard procedure in an attempt to get the best of both worlds.

The success of these attacks inspired enthusiasm in Britain and shocked the Germans. But neither Lübeck nor Rostock, important as they were, was a vital, heavily defended industrial target, central to the German war machine. To those who cast covetous eyes at the bomber force these minor successes in small skirmishes seemed irrelevant. The big industrial centres would be a different proposition. Two more raids on Essen in April 1942, on much the same scale as the raid on Lübeck, failed to achieve concentration, and at Dortmund and Hamburg in the same month results were similar. Bomber Command had still to demonstrate its ability to hit and seriously damage important and well-defended targets in Germany, and it became increasingly obvious that against these targets a force of even 250 bombers was too small to achieve the concentration in time and space necessary to break down resistance and produce a high degree of devastation. Thus Bomber Command remained without a major victory, and to all appearances without the means to achieve one.

Meanwhile in other spheres the situation of the Allies was deteriorating. The entry of the United States into the war, so passionately longed for, seemed at first only to exacerbate the dangers on all fronts. The loss of Malaya and the fall of Singapore in February 1942 were followed by the invasion of Burma, the loss of the Dutch East Indies, and the imminent threat of invasion to Australia, India and Ceylon. Our own offensive in the Western Desert, designed to end the Axis threat to the Middle East, had resulted in dismal defeat. Supplies for Rommel were pouring across the Mediterranean into Tripoli and Benghazi, and there were strong indications of an imminent airborne invasion of Malta. In the first two months of 1942, 117 Allied ships totalling over three-quarters of a million tons were sunk in the Atlantic, the heaviest losses of the war so far, at a cost to the enemy of no more than two U-Boats a month. And worse was to come. Clearly the U-Boat war had to be won. Clearly Australia must be held, virtually at all costs. So must Egypt, Suez, the Levant and the route to the Caucasus. So must India and Ceylon. Demands for the reinforcement of these theatres seemed overwhelming. Meanwhile, on the Russian front, the Germans, profiting from their mistakes of the previous year, were about to develop a concentrated spring offensive, aimed at overrunning the Caucasus, gaining possession of Russia's main oil supply area and simultaneously opening the way for a link-up with the advancing Afrika Korps and for the domination of the entire Middle East. The temptation to apply every unit of air power to hold the enemy at bay seemed irresistible. Above all, the entire strategic situation still turned on the supply of shipping, partly on the rate of replacement, but immediately and urgently on the protection of existing tonnage.

Demands for the reassignment of the bomber force thus became vehement and clamorous. The Admiralty were agitating for their overseas Coastal Commands and for the employment of all other available bombers in the anti-submarine campaign; a most elaborate paper, written by Professor P. M. S. Blackett, head of the Admiralty's operational research section, supporting these proposals with a wealth of statistics, was presented to the War Cabinet by the First Sea Lord. The War Office were pointing to the breakdown of Auchinleck's Desert offensive as evidence of the RAF's failure to interrupt Rommel's lines of communication, the essential preliminary to success in the Desert war; all available heavy bombers ought to be sent to North Africa at once. The Japanese, too, could only be halted by bombing. The pressure on Churchill was so terrific that he felt compelled, in a cable to Roosevelt of 29th March 1942, to make an attempt to justify the continued existence of Bomber Command as an effective strategic force.[1] Everywhere the call was for more bombers – more and more long-range bombers. Harris and Saundby had their backs to the wall.

'If only we could put on something really big,' said Harris one evening at Springfield to Saundby. At Harris's suggestion, Saundby had gone to live at Springfield so that the two men could be in constant personal touch. 'One spectacular raid, big enough to wipe out a really important target. Something that would capture the imagination of the public.' In his restless impatience and frustration Harris could not keep still. 'A thousand aircraft!' he said. 'A thousand bombers over Germany! If only we could do something like that, we might get the support we need.'

It was not the first time that Harris had spoken to Saundby in this strain. As usual Saundby listened and said nothing. The front-line strength of the Command was now roughly 400 aircraft. If they threw in their reserves they might mount something like 500 heavy and medium bombers in all. The magic figure of a thousand was well out of reach, quite unattainable. Nevertheless the totals were improving. Saundby made a private resolve to go into the figures more closely next morning and see what could be done.

Saundby's careful, conservative arithmetic, relying on figures from many stations and units, took some days, and meanwhile Harris did not raise the subject again. It was a wild notion, beyond their strength and perhaps impracticable anyway. Meanwhile, as April passed into May, an urgent demand

1. *The Second World War*, by Winston S. Churchill, Vol. IV (Cassell).

was presented to the War Cabinet for the immediate transfer of 50 per cent of the bomber force, to be divided between the Atlantic, the Middle East and India, further transfers to be made as necessary. Under this continuous pressure from the Admiralty and War Office – whose needs were real enough – the War Cabinet wavered. Even Churchill, hitherto an enthusiastic advocate of the bomber offensive, had had his confidence undermined by the experience of 1941 and had become Bomber Command's severest – and most penetrating – critic. Only his determination to retain an offensive weapon to attack Germany had saved the Command for so long. The time had come when he might no longer be able to carry his colleagues in the War Cabinet with him.

It was a pleasant evening early in May at Springfield when Harris referred again to the need for a single bold stroke. For once there were no visitors, and the party at dinner had been confined to Harris and his wife, Saundby and Paul Tomlinson, Harris's personal aide. It was an informal atmosphere. The three men wore their basic uniform, but Harris had designed a plum-coloured velvet dinner jacket which they wore over the uniform trousers and shirt. If they were called out suddenly to the operations room or for some other emergency, all they had to do was to change their jackets.

The Air Ministry had wanted to put a guard on Springfield, but Harris wouldn't have it. Already, following the raids on Lübeck and Rostock, Lord Haw-Haw was talking about 'Hangman Harris', and reprisals, in the form of the 'Baedeker' raids on small cathedral towns, had been begun.[1] The Air Ministry were afraid that the Germans might put down a parachutist team to get Harris. But Harris didn't want his home to be turned into a fortress. That would have destroyed all the valued relaxations of family life. And in any case he believed that to fortify Springfield was to invite attention. Any commando force would surely look for a strongly defended headquarters for the C-in-C's residence, crawling with

1. Hitler spoke of taking Baedeker's guide and marking each British city off the guide-book as and when it was 'eradicated'.

sentries, bristling with ack-ack guns. They would hardly credit that this quiet Victorian façade, half-hidden by cedar trees, lacking so much as a flagstaff, could house the notorious 'Hangman'. The only defences Harris permitted were a number of rifles with which he and Saundby proposed to protect the women and sell their own lives dearly from the top of the stairs.

After dinner on this evening in early May, Harris returned once more to the subject that was tormenting him. 'It's the only way we can prove our theories about concentration,' he said. 'It's the only way to saturate the defences. And if we can't put on something big pretty soon it'll be too late. How long is it going to be before we can muster a really crushing force – something like a thousand?'

'We could do it now, you know,' said Saundby.

'Nonsense!'

'But we could.'

Saundby had been waiting for this moment. While Harris remained silent, Saundby spoke quietly and without emphasis, letting the words do their work. And from his pocket he produced the figures in support of what he said, figures he had taken great trouble to confirm.

'If we make use of the conversion and training planes, using instructor and if necessary pupil crews, I think we could put out a force of nearly double our front-line strength. Say seven hundred plus. If we can get the War Cabinet to support us, we ought to be able to call on all the bomber aircraft, together with their trained bomber crews, which have been transferred to Coastal Command in the past twelve months. That would add another two hundred and fifty aircraft and bring us within reach of a thousand.'

'A thousand, eh.'

Harris made no histrionic gestures. Perhaps he had known all along that Saundby would come up with something like this. The difference was in the set of his shoulders, the expression in his eyes.

'We'll try it. We've got to try it. We'll start working it out tomorrow.'

6. IS IT FEASIBLE?

IT REMAINED TO be seen whether it was practicable to put so large a force on to a single target, in the short space of time necessary if the desired concentration was to be achieved. There was no past experience to call upon. The largest force ever to raid London had been about 500, but this had covered a wide time-spread and achieved no real concentration. Such a scattered attack on a heavily defended target would cause insignificant damage and result in crippling losses. What would be the result of employing pupil crews, supposing they were forced to do so? It was true that, as part of their operational training, pupils were allowed to drop leaflets over France, but this was far removed from attacking a heavily defended target in Germany as members of a pioneering force setting out into the unknown.

It was clear at once to Harris that the risks involved in this operation were appalling. He would surely be the first commander in the history of warfare to commit his whole front-line strength together with his entire reserves and training backing in a single battle. Failure would mean, at the very least, the complete disruption of the training organization, a halt to any planned expansion and the curtailing of routine operations for weeks or even months. But almost certainly it would mean very much more than that. It would be the Command's last throw. Even their convictions and theories would be finally discredited and the Command would be broken up. They would have committed the most spectacular mass suicide of all time.

Against this it could be said with equal certainty that without some dramatic proof of its potential power, political decisions were about to be taken which would liquidate the force anyway. There was very little to lose and a great deal to gain. Success would mean not only a vindication of their theories and a profound warning to Nazi Germany of what was to come. It would convince public opinion of the overwhelming case for a bomber offensive as Britain's first instrument for winning the war. In this way Harris hoped to silence the objections of political opponents and of the other Services to the development of the bomber offensive, relying on the weight of public enthusiasm to bulldoze the idea through.

First, though, he had to be absolutely satisfied that the raid was feasible. An easily recognizable target was the first prerequisite. It would have to be a coastal city, or a city on an estuary with a good lead-in, like Hamburg. Or a city pinpointed by a winding river, like Cologne. A spell of good weather was another necessity. It would take at least three or four days to get the force together, carry out the raid, and disperse it back to its own airfields. A full moon was desirable, perhaps even essential. Yes, almost certainly essential. Better time the operation for the next full moon period. That was 26th to 30th May. It left about a fortnight to plan and execute the preliminaries to the raid. Just about right. Too long a delay would be bad for security.

The problems of operating so large a force would be greatly simplified by Gee. But none of the conversion and training aircraft was Gee-equipped, and only a proportion of the main force. A similar technique to that used at Lübeck and Rostock would probably have to be employed, Gee-equipped aircraft going in first to mark the aiming-point. This suggested a target within Gee range. The accuracy of Gee was good laterally – the operator could tell exactly what line he was on – but the reading of distance along that line was less reliable. This unreliability increased as the range increased, and would affect even medium-range targets like Cologne. But on the approach to Cologne lay the Rhine, snaking through the eastern outskirts of the city. If a flare-dropping force went in first to mark the way, using Gee, it could be relied upon to track across the city within plus or minus half a mile of its planned course. The release point as indicated by the Gee fix would be less accurate, but if a sighting could be made on the river in bright moonlight, a more accurate final check point could be found. None of this clarity at the point of bomb release would be available in the vast built-up area of the Ruhr.

If Harris had a predilection for any target at all it was Hamburg. It was highly combustible and easily identifiable, but outside Gee range. Essen, which was the biggest military target in Germany, and which Churchill was known to be especially anxious to see heavily attacked, was farther afield than Cologne, reducing the Gee accuracy, and was notoriously difficult to find. Harris discussed the question of target selection with Saundby, and Saundby sent for his specialist officers, beginning with Dudley Saward. The success of the operation, and to some extent the choice of target, depended on the progress made with the fitting of Gee.

Saward explained the position to Saundby. Most of the squadron aircraft had been modified to take Gee, but only about half had been fitted. The job was just about keeping pace with deliveries of equipment. Then there was the training of the Gee operators.

'Saward, I want you to do all you can to hurry forward the complete fitting of Gee in all front-line aircraft. How many could you have fitted within say a fortnight?'

'We could have four hundred ready, sir – virtually the whole force.'

'What about the training units? Could we equip some of those as well?'

'I'm afraid not, sir. They've never been modified for Gee and it couldn't be done in the time. It's a production-line job. But we could equip the aircraft of the conversion units – Lancasters, Halifaxes and Stirlings. They're modified and it would be a simple matter to fit the Gee boxes.' Saward hesitated, then decided to take the plunge. 'Is there some special urgency, sir?'

Saundby peered up at Saward over his narrow reading glasses, then took them off and began polishing them in a characteristic gesture. Security was vital and it was important that as few people should be told as possible. Yet there was much to be said for letting Saward, whose drive on the work of the Gee installations could be decisive, into the secret.

'The C-in-C proposes to put out a record number of aircraft shortly in a super raid.' He explained the political background, indicating that there would be no worthwhile expansion of the Command if the raid failed. 'Success in my opinion will be largely dependent on Gee. In fact without Gee we couldn't do it.'

'How many aircraft is it proposed to operate?'

'With the help of the other Commands,' said Saundby quietly, 'we hope to raise a thousand.'

Because of his close personal relationship with his staff officers, Saundby did not need to add that this information was for Saward only. That the Gee-fitting programme would go forward with the right sense of urgency was now assured.

The first successful trial of concentration had been the 120-bomber raid on Cologne in March. Cologne seemed the best bet from the point of view of Gee. And the more aircraft were fitted with Gee, the more sensible it seemed to be to build the success of the raid around it. But Harris, although enthusiastic about Gee as a navigational aid, had little confidence in its suitability for blind bombing. He felt that the proper course was to use Gee to the limit of its range as a navigational device and then identify the target visually in bright moonlight. On this principle Hamburg would be as easy to hit as Cologne. And Harris still wanted to attack Hamburg. But the question of the final choice of target could be left unresolved for the moment. Harris passed it meanwhile to the operational research section at High Wycombe for scientific analysis.

There was, too, another question that Harris wanted his scientists to consider, perhaps the most vital one of all. The greatest danger in operating a mass raid of this kind was collision. The spectre of the collision risk haunted both Harris and Saundby and they badly needed reassurance before committing themselves any further with their plans for the raid.

There were two main theoretical advantages to be derived from the planned concentration in time and space – the compression of the bomb pattern, and the saturation of defences.

But it would be quite pointless to succeed in reducing losses from enemy defences if they were simultaneously inflated beyond ordinary expectations by a high collision rate in the congested air space over the target, en route and at the bases. The question of the choice of target, which in any case in the final instance would depend on the weather, was secondary to the collision risk. Harris sent for his chief research scientist, the head of his operational research section, to get an opinion.

Dr B. G. Dickins, in his middle thirties, jovial and friendly in temperament, had been writing studies of the reasons for bomber losses for nearly two years. He was typical of many scientists in that he did not concern himself with the rights and wrongs of strategic policy. Harris, he knew, was convinced that the war could be won by bombing. Dickins never considered this question seriously. Whether the bomber offensive was right or wrong did not concern him. He was far too busy studying those aspects of it which were susceptible to scientific analysis to worry about the reason why.

It was in 1940, during the German blitz, that Sir Henry Tizard had hit upon the idea of examining the experience of our own bombers over Germany in an effort to translate this into new defensive techniques to combat the German raids. Dickins, then attached to Fighter Command at Stanmore, went to High Wycombe once a month to study raid reports and write appreciations of the cause of our bomber losses. The operational research section at Stanmore was so successful that it was eventually decided to form similar sections at all the main operational headquarters. With his experience of the previous months, Dickins was the obvious choice for Bomber Command. He and his section began at once to analyse all bomber operations, their ultimate purpose being to assist in getting the maximum number of bombers over their targets with the minimum of losses. They had three main sources of information: the sortie raid report, filed by the crews with the help of an interrogating officer after the raid; photographs taken at the time of bombing; and daylight photographic reconnaissance carried out subsequently by aircraft of the

PRU. Dickins soon became very close to both Harris and Saundby, who sent for him frequently and bombarded him with questions.

Dickins was on leave when Harris asked his question about the collision risk. When he got back he found that his deputy had been sent for and asked how many collisions would occur if 1,000 bombers were put over a target in the space of an hour. The information, as always, was wanted immediately.

Dickins found his staff gathering data that they thought would help them in their calculations. The first thing they asked themselves was – what did they know already? About half the force had been equipped with cameras and photo-flashes, and it was on the basis of pictures taken at the moment of bombing impact that the calculations had been made on the accuracy – or inaccuracy – of our bombing in the previous year. A further study of these and other more recent pictures disclosed that much additional information was available or could be deduced from them. The camera lens was open for a known period, and the photo interpreters were able, by plotting the photographs of the bombing run and the bomb explosion on charts, to pinpoint the bomber's position. They knew, from the sortie raid report, the time of the bombing. They knew the headings from the same source. The speed and height of the bomber were also established at interrogation. Thus from a study of these facts and photographs, available from many raids, they were able to build up a picture of the density of aircraft over a target at any one time. Using this data, and given the number of aircraft due to bomb a target within a specified time, they could estimate the likely spread of the force in time and space and calculate the collision risk.

Harris, hungry for reassurance, was soon on the phone asking for figures. There was no comfort for him. The first rough calculations suggested that, with the data given, the collision risk would be considerable. Harris and Saundby quickly changed their ground. They would have two aiming-points, splitting the force in half, routeing the two halves in on parallel tracks. Better still, they would have three aiming-points, and three parallel approach routes. Heights would be staggered. And the time-spread would be lengthened, from sixty minutes to ninety. These revised figures and factors were fed back into the calculating machine of the ORS and a fresh answer obtained. This time it was much more encouraging. Dickins was able to tell Harris that he estimated that there would be not more than one collision over the target per hour.

The staggering of heights, however, automatically posed another question of risk. With the new fire-raising technique there would be thousands of 4 lb incendiary bombs cascading through the sky as the force crossed the target. What was the risk of losses through aircraft being hit by falling incendiaries and HE bombs? Dickins and his staff concluded that this risk, less easy to calculate, was nevertheless a serious one, and aircraft at different heights were given different times for crossing the target. With this precaution, Dickins was able to estimate that the combined additional risks were infinitesimal compared with the certain losses from flak and fighters in an ordinary raid, losses which it was expected would be greatly reduced by the planned concentration.

But the idea of the raid, conceived by Harris and nurtured by Saundby against the trends of political opinion, still had to win political support if it was to develop further. Fortunately, quite outside the question of protecting the bomber force from disbandment, there lay many other factors of importance. Although in theory such an operation appeared to be practicable, the only way to test it was to launch it. The lessons learnt would be of enormous value. There was the inevitable impact on morale throughout Bomber Command. There was the stimulus to the whole war effort that the raid must surely inspire on all fronts. And there were the implications of the raid for the enemy. Harris's intention was to wipe out the selected target. No doubt after a single raid even of this magnitude a town could be patched up, but the impact of such a raid, and the inherent threat of further similar raids must have a profound effect on Germany's entire strategic thought.

The argument that the bomber offensive was the only means

of hitting at Germany, and must remain so for some time to come, still retained great force. A successful raid of this magnitude would surely clinch it. Harris went to see Portal, Chief of the Air Staff, to sound him out. Portal was keen in principle but guarded about the application. 'If you can produce a workable plan,' he said, 'I've no objection. But we shall have to convince the Chiefs of Staff of its usefulness. Such a raid is bound to attract reprisals and we must have the politicians on our side.'

The possibility of political opposition to the plan seemed intolerable to Harris. But there was one politician on whose support he felt he could surely count. Churchill in many utterances had committed himself to the increasing round-the-clock bombing of Germany and the German people, and Harris was determined to remind him of it. Chequers was only a few miles from Springfield, Churchill was always interested in what Harris was planning to do, and Harris was fairly frequently invited to dine there. As Minister of Defence Churchill approved all the plans of the Chiefs of Staff, so Harris had the ear of the one man whose support was indispensable. One Sunday evening in the middle of May Harris manoeuvred himself one of these invitations to dinner.

It was still daylight as Harris drove over in his canvas-top Bentley, and it was pleasant to push along through the country lanes, hedged in as they were by the lush greenness of early summer. These sessions with Churchill always lasted far into the night, and Harris drove the car himself rather than keep a driver waiting about for many hours. On these occasions Churchill never once pressed Harris to take any particular line of action, never once made any remark which could be construed as an instruction. Although he would often state some personal preference, he never interfered with the running of the air war. This is remarkable in view of the pressure he is said to have applied to leaders of the other Services. No doubt the RAF was fortunate in having a man like Portal at its head. He was much more successful than most other war leaders in handling Churchill. He never took Churchill's grousings too seriously, always avoided getting into direct collision with him, always succeeded in guiding him away from rash or unpromising schemes.

After dinner Harris came to the point. 'I'm thinking of mounting a single mass raid, something really big, a force of over a thousand aircraft. I can put up seven or eight hundred. The psychological figure of a thousand could be made up by aircraft lent to us for the one operation by Coastal and Army Co-operation Commands.'

Churchill's reaction was one of warm enthusiasm. More than anyone he had had to put up with the importuning of the other Services for the dispersion of Bomber Command. More than anyone he had seen from the beginning, even during the Battle of Britain, that only offensive action could win us the war. 'The Navy can lose us the war,' he had said in September 1940, 'but only the Air Force can win it.' And his promises to Russia on the effective bombing of Germany, now nearly twelve months old, lay unfulfilled. In naval and military circles he was regarded as a man obsessed with a bombing mania, the man chiefly to blame for the fact that the Navy were still short of long-range reconnaissance aircraft and the Army lacked the support of modern heavy bombers in North Africa.

'What's going to be the target?'

'We shall have to choose one that's easy to identify. I should think Hamburg or Cologne.'

'Can't you make it Essen?'

'Too risky. The whole raid might go astray.'

'How many are you going to lose?'

It was a question that Harris was ready for. 'We plan to concentrate the entire raid into the space of ninety minutes. The idea is to saturate the defences. I shall be very surprised if we lose more than five per cent of the force. Say fifty aircraft and crews.'

'I'll be prepared for the loss of a hundred.' Churchill was already thinking in terms of the political repercussions of failure.

The two men sat late discussing the raid, and it was three

o'clock before Harris drove back to Springfield. 'As I drove home,' he wrote afterwards,[1] 'I found myself humming "Malbrouch s'en va-t'en guerre". I suddenly realized that that tune always came into my mind whenever I had just left Churchill. The spirit of Marlborough did indeed breathe in his descendant and most emphatically he was going to war.' It was here that the temperaments of the two men were most in tune. Both were intent on going to war rather than have it come to them.

It seemed to Harris now that he had done all he could to ensure not only that the raid was feasible but that it would not be sabotaged by political objections. There remained the question of the final choice of target. Dickins and his staff had evaluated the results of every raid in the previous twelve months, and they were thus able to compare relative success or failure as between one target or group of targets and another. The day after Harris's visit to Churchill, Dickins appeared in his office with a detailed analysis. Harris waved it aside.

'Well?'

'First, sir, my advice would be to attack a target within Gee coverage. Given this limitation, Cologne is the best bet.'

'And Essen?'

'If you want to make sure of success, keep away from Essen.'

'What about Hamburg?'

'Raids on Hamburg have been fairly successful and as a target it's combustible and easy to find. But it's outside Gee range.'

'I still want to make it Hamburg.'

'Stay within Gee coverage,' advised Dickins. 'Go to Cologne.'

Harris decided that the draft operation order would specify Hamburg as the target and Cologne as the alternative, with full route instructions for both targets. But from this point on he had no doubt in his mind to which target, weather permitting, he would despatch the force. He had come to rely on Dickins's flair for finding out before a raid what to expect from it. He

1. In *Bomber Offensive* (Collins).

had not consulted his specialist officers for nothing. He would despatch the force to Cologne.

The appearance of Hamburg in the final operation order was little more than a security ruse. The number of officers in the know was kept to a minimum consistent with efficiency, but the choice of two widely separated targets, with Hamburg mentioned first, would offer its own protection if enemy intelligence got wind of the raid. In any case, no matter what the strategic or tactical advantages might be, the choice would be decided by what could be seen and what could be hit. As always the final arbiter would be the weather.

7. *'TO DESTROY THE CITY OF COLOGNE ...'*

CHARACTERISTICALLY, BECAUSE HE was never satisfied, Harris was already thinking in terms of striking a double blow while the force was assembled. The disruption to training and conversion, as well as to routine operations, would last about a week. If he sent the force out two nights running he would add only one day to the investment but probably double the dividend. The idea of a double blow, either against the same target or possibly a new one in the second instance, was therefore incorporated as part of the plan, the broad details of which were now firmly fixed in his mind. He had lobbied in the highest possible quarter and been assured of enthusiastic support. It was time to put the planning on an official level.

On Monday 18th May Harris drove to Whitehall and called on Portal, giving him brief details of the 'workable plan' Portal had asked for, and mentioning the possibility, if the first raid was a success, of an immediate follow-up raid of similar strength. Two days later, on 20th May, he received the go-ahead from Portal:

19th May 1942

My dear Harris,

You spoke to me yesterday about the 'Thousand' plan. I

mentioned it to the Prime Minister who warmly approved and tells me this morning that after speaking to the First Sea Lord about it he does not think there will be any objection to the co-operation of Coastal Command unless they have special operations on hand.

I therefore suggest that you should go ahead with your arrangements after discussing the matter with the other Commanders-in-Chief concerned, letting me know if there are any difficulties. Please let me know before the operation is actually staged so that I can tell the Prime Minister.

Yours ever,
C. Portal

Time was short if the motley force was to be assembled for the next full moon period in one week's time, and on the same day, 20th May, Harris wrote a letter to Coastal, Fighter and Army Co-operation Commands, to the five operational bomber groups, and to the two bomber training groups, Nos 91 and 92, laying out the details of the 'Thousand Plan', as it was now known, and asking for the maximum possible contribution towards it. The letter was remarkable for its clear statement of intention – to annihilate one of Germany's main industrial centres by fire. There were no euphemisms about factories and specific military objectives. The city of Cologne was to be wiped out in one night.

With his letter Harris attached a note to each individual commander in which he mentioned special requirements. Under a full moon, conditions would be favourable for a high loss-rate from catseye fighters, and Harris wanted attacks by Fighter Command and the light bombers of No 2 Group to harass selected night-fighter airfields, followed by fighter sweeps over the North Sea to cover the returning bombers. He was uncertain what Army Co-operation Command might be able to provide but hoped for a worthwhile contribution. In a personal message to Air Chief Marshal Sir Philip Joubert, C-in-C Coastal Command, he asked for a contribution of 250 aircraft. This was roughly the number that Bomber had lost to Coastal in the previous twelve months and it seemed no more than justice that they should be made available for this special occasion. Nevertheless, both Harris and Saundby had been doubtful whether the Admiralty, who controlled Coastal Command operationally, would allow them to provide more than a token force, and they had welcomed the news in Portal's letter that the First Sea Lord could see no objection. The figure of 250, a quarter of the total force, was very much the largest contribution requested from outside Bomber Command, and until final details were confirmed there remained in Harris's mind the fear that it might not be forthcoming and that the Thousand Plan would fall far short of its aim.

Joubert's reply to Harris, sent by return of post, removed the last lingering doubts about the willingness and ability of Coastal Command to come in and swell the figures past the thousand mark:

Dear Bert, 21.5.42.

I can go your 250 – your 2 Wellingtons and 2 Whitleys, the four torpedo Hampdens, 2 Beauforts,[1] and an assortment of Hudsons and OTU aircraft. If No 58 (Squadron) has not got its ASV by then they can join the party. We will use our own East Coast aerodromes, and we would like to come in about the middle of the show. I propose to use anti-submarine bombs to get the maximum blast effect. Is this all right?

Yours
P. B. Joubert

Harris now had a rough count of the likely availability of medium and heavy bombers for the raid:

No 1 (Bomber) Group	100
No 3 (Bomber) Group	160
No 4 (Bomber) Group	130
No 5 (Bomber) Group	100
No 91 (Bomber Training) Group	200
No 92 (Bomber Training) Group	120
Army Co-operation Command	Not known
Flying Training Command	21
Coastal Command	250
	1,081

1. Joubert was referring in each case to squadrons of aircraft.

It was the enthusiastic response of Philip Joubert at Coastal Command which carried the total, on paper at least, past the thousand mark.

The task of assembling the bombers, many of which, in the case of training aircraft of other Commands, had to be moved to advance bases on the east coast, was expected to take forty-eight hours. An operation order giving instructions for the move was issued by Bomber Command on 23rd May, and the move began two days later. Approximately 200 aircraft, from Flying Training, Army Co-operation and Coastal Commands and from the two Bomber Training Groups, were involved. The move was complicated by the necessity for radio silence: it was essential for security that the redistribution of aircraft to bases in eastern England should not be revealed to the enemy.

At the same time plans were laid, as requested by Harris, for the systematic attack of enemy fighter airfields along the route and in the target area before and during the operation. Light Bombers of 2 Group, Army Co-operation Command and Fighter Command were to provide this 'intruder' force, and Fighter Command were to provide further cover by carrying out sweeps in force as far as possible out to sea from the English coast, while Ansons and Blenheims of a Bomber OTU were to fly routine air/sea rescue patrols from daylight on. By these measures it was hoped to minimize the risk of interception for the bomber force and bring speedy aid to any returning bombers which came down in the sea.

The final operation order for the Thousand Plan was issued on 26th May. The raid was to take place on the night of 27th/28th May or any night thereafter up to the night of 31st May/1st June, when the moon would be on the wane. This gave a possible margin for unsuitable weather of five days. Harris hoped to have the operation behind him, and perhaps a follow up raid as well, long before the five days was up.

Once again the operation order summed up the object of the raid in an ambitious but simple phrase, this time of six words only: to destroy the city of Cologne.[1] 'The stage of the war has been reached,' the order continued, 'when the morale of the German people is likely to be seriously affected by an unprecedented blow of great magnitude in the West at a time when they are experiencing difficulties on the Russian front. We are in a position to deliver this blow from the air. . . .

'Apart from the effect on morale of such an attack, the unprecedented damage which will be caused is bound to have a considerable effect on the issue of the war.

'To produce the forces necessary, it is essential that every operationally serviceable aircraft is employed, not only from Bomber Command but also from Coastal, Army Co-operation and Flying Training Commands. OTU groups will also take part with aircraft manned by their instructional staffs.

'If every unit conscientiously plays its part in producing a maximum effort, it is estimated that a force of 1081 bombers can be employed in what will be the greatest air attack of all time.'

The emphasis on the susceptibility of German morale to shock attack will be noted. Also it will be seen that the support of Coastal Command had enabled Harris to keep his pupil crews out of the operation.

The raid was to be led by the Gee-equipped Wellingtons and Stirlings of Nos 1 and 3 Groups, who were allotted a time span of fifteen minutes to set the centre of the target alight. These were the pathfinders, though they were not yet styled as such, and they were to carry as high a proportion of incendiaries as possible. Their aiming-point was the *Neumarkt*, in the middle of the old town. They were to be followed in the next hour by the entire remaining force except the new four-engined bombers, the Lancasters and Halifaxes of Nos 4 and 5 Groups. These were to bomb the target in the last fifteen minutes, the whole raid being completed in an hour and a half. The other two aiming-points were a mile north and a mile south of the *Neumarkt*, crews being routed to their respective aiming-points

1. As already explained, Hamburg was quoted as the 'first choice' target in the actual order.

on parallel tracks. Zero hour was 00.55 – five minutes to one – and all aircraft were to turn for home by 02.25 whether they had bombed or not. This was to ensure that concentration was maintained and that stray aircraft were not caught out in daylight on the return trip across Holland. The minimum bombing height was 8,000 feet, but exact heights were left to the discretion of group commanders. On leaving the target area, aircraft were to turn south-south-west for twenty miles and then return parallel to their outward track, increasing speed and losing height and coming down to 1,000 feet for the run home over the North Sea. Most of this was designed to reduce the collision risk.

In order to allow the maintenance and servicing crews a full forty-eight hours in which to concentrate on preparing aircraft for the raid, there were to be no bomber operations the previous night. From 26th May, station commanders were to inform their group headquarters by noon each day of the number of aircraft available for operations. Each group would then pass a consolidated figure to Command.

The aggregate was comfortably in excess of a thousand when the biggest single figure in the addition was suddenly erased. At the last moment the Admiralty had intervened. After considering the implications of the raid, they gave orders to Joubert that Coastal Command was not in any circumstances to take part in it. Joubert was obliged to withdraw his offer of 250 aircraft. This cut the Thousand Plan down to about 800.

The defection of Coastal Command reached Harris and Saundby first as a suspicion, then as a fact. Harris determined to fight it: he had received the assurance about the attitude of the First Sea Lord, he had Joubert's written promise and he hoped that Churchill would force the issue. But he saw, too, that time was against him. The operation was due to take place in twenty-four hours. If there was going to be a political wrangle, it would last a good deal longer than that. The Admiralty had timed their intervention to a nicety. Without abating his determination to fight them for the future, Harris saw that he must be prepared to do without them this time.

Even if he could persuade Churchill to intervene, they would plead that it was too late now to move their squadrons in time for an operation in this full moon period.

Both Harris and Saundby had always felt nervous about the Coastal Command participation and had feared a let-down. It had been a mistake to rely on them. Harris would never have done so but for the fact that their contribution had seemed to offer the only means of producing the required number without calling on pupil crews. That he had always regarded as a last resort.

'Cut 'em right out,' growled Harris to Saundby, when he learned the news. 'Plan without 'em. I'm going to fight them, but either way they won't beat us. We'll get our thousand somehow from our own resources.'

In retrospect one cannot see the Admiralty's action as altogether reprehensible. The implications of the raid were plain. If it failed – if losses were high, as to them seemed likely – Coastal Command would sacrifice aircraft and crews that it could ill afford to lose. If the raid was a success, Harris would have made his point, and it would be harder than ever to get what the Admiralty regarded as a proper allocation of long-range aircraft for maritime operations. Either way the Admiralty would be the losers. Why should they act as pallbearer at their own funeral?

Saundby was left with the problem of bridging the gap. It looked an insuperable task, yet because of his earlier fears he was not unprepared for it. He believed that the instructions he had already given would produce a thousand bombers from within the Command if need be. Some of these aircraft might be manned by a further comb-out of the men on rest; scratch crews could be found from station, squadron and group staffs who would be only too eager to volunteer. But the bulk of the crew deficiency would have to be made up by using pupils.

The existing phrase in the operation order stated that OTU groups would take part with aircraft manned by their instructional staffs. To this Saundby added the phrase – 'though crews can be made up with personnel under training at the discretion of Air Officers Commanding'. This, he felt, would ensure that inadequately trained men were not thrown into the battle.

In order to make good the inevitable losses on operations, every Bomber Command squadron had what was known as an immediate reserve of two aircraft. These two aircraft were *in situ* on the squadrons and were brought into use when needed to bring squadrons back to full strength. On a nod and a wink from Command, this immediate reserve could be drawn on in every one of a total of thirty-seven squadrons. That added seventy-four to the total and brought it nearer to 900.

Terms like immediate reserve, in Saundby's view, were one's servant, not one's master. So was the reinforcement pipeline – from the Air Transport Auxiliary, who delivered the planes, back to the depots and the factories. Whenever an aircraft was taken on to squadron strength from immediate reserve, a replacement was indented for. Saundby had already told the squadron commanders to indent for replacement of the two immediate reserve aircraft brought on to strength, even though none had been lost. Thus, by a little guile, the squadrons got their hands on all available aircraft in the replacement pipeline.

So to the increased hazard involved in the decision to employ pupil crews was added the risking of every reserve aircraft that the Command could lay its hands on. But even this added only another thirty or forty aircraft to the total, so the Thousand Plan was a thousand no longer. Only 940 aircraft were listed in the revised operation order of 26th May. Even this figure was an optimistic one. Several of the aircraft involved in the move to advance bases, their crews hampered by the need for wireless silence, had force-landed at remote airfields or, worse still, crashed. And of those which completed the move on schedule – by far the majority certainly – not all were in a fit state to operate at long distance over enemy territory. Inevitably the standards demanded for operational flying were different from those required for short- or medium-range flights in and around the United Kingdom.

And now came the final frustration – the weather. On the

morning of 27th May, with approximately 900 aircraft and crews standing by at the ready, Harris went down to the underground operations room at High Wycombe soon after nine o'clock for his daily planning conference. Waiting for him were Saundby and his air staff officers, together with a short, gnome-like figure who, rather like the witches in Macbeth, was for the next few minutes to be promoted in importance as soothsayer and counsellor above all Harris's high-ranking operations staff, whose pronouncements would be listened to in awed silence and acted on without question by Harris himself. He was the Command Meteorological Officer, and his name was Magnus T. Spence.

In the campaigns of Bomber Command, meteorology was a much abused service which nevertheless did invaluable work. Described at the time as an inexact science, it was in those days less a science than an art. One of the supreme artists was undoubtedly Magnus T. Spence. A dour Scot, born in the Orkneys, Spence was a man of great precision of language, a man who thought carefully before speaking but who was never evasive or pedantic. At first it had seemed to Saundby that Spence had no sense of humour, and he waited a year before he saw him smile. The occasion was when Saundby asked him the origin of his Christian name. Spence gave his characteristic pause, and then came the smile. 'At the time when I came to be christened,' he said, his accent clipping the words like shears, 'my father was suffering from a severe attack of Norse mythology.' Saundby had penetrated the apparently frosty exterior and found a warm person underneath.

The difficulties of confirming the actual weather over an enemy country at a given time need no elaboration. They were nothing compared with the problems of accurate forecasting of the conditions over a particular enemy target fifteen hours ahead. This, daily, at Harris's morning conference, was what Spence was asked to do. The temptation was to use these difficulties as a shield, to explain that one had nothing to go on but an air reconnaissance several hours old and a few Resistance reports from Occupied Europe: definite pronouncements on such scanty information were impossible and it wasn't fair to expect them. But Spence never gave the slightest hint of this sort of attitude. The odds against his being right might be long, but he was always ready to face up to them, to give a firm opinion based on the best information available, without hedging himself round with escape clauses like a tipster. This was what Harris wanted. There was no question of his ever blaming his forecaster when things went wrong – as they sometimes did. Sudden and unpredictable weather changes over the target or at the bases were a continual source of disappointment and loss. But Harris knew he had been given the best available advice. The responsibility for the decision to despatch the force rested with him.

On the morning of 27th May, Spence's expression seemed even frostier than usual. Thundery conditions and heavy cloud existed over most of Germany, and Harris was forced to postpone the operation for twenty-four hours. The same thing happened on Thursday the 28th, and again on Friday the 29th. Harris's hopes of using the force twice in the full moon period began to evaporate. If this weather continued, the force wouldn't get off the ground at all.

The weather minima for the Thousand Plan were much sterner than for a normal operation. Harris could not send up a thousand aircraft to fly through thick cloud. The collision risk, which worried him enough already, would multiply tenfold. In addition to the need for bright moonlight, there had to be good weather over the target for the pupil crews to find it, and the weather had to be clear over the bases for the return.

The responsibility for holding the force in such prolonged inactivity bore heavily on Harris. He dare not disrupt the whole operational and training programme for more than another day or so. The security risk, too, mounted daily. In spite of the precautions taken to let only a handful of people into the secret, thousands of civilians near the bases must know that something unusual was on, quite apart from the countless ground crews and clerical staff together with about 6,000 aircrew. And even without some sort of security leak, the enemy must soon get suspicious of the long lull in bomber activity. To relieve the second danger, Harris decided on the morning of 29th May, after postponing the operation for the third time, to mount a raid that night on targets in France. He chose the Gnôme and Rhône works at Gennevilliers, near Paris, and coastal targets at Cherbourg and Dieppe. Minelaying was resumed the same night. A total of 150 aircraft took part in these raids.

As far as numbers were concerned, Harris felt he could now afford the losses that inevitably resulted from these raids. The delay had enabled the ground crews, working eighteen hours a day, to bring many unserviceable and under-equipped aircraft up to operational pitch. Day by day in that last week in May, as station by station sent up its tale of men – and aircraft – the total rose to 950, to 980, then to a thousand, and finally well beyond. At last the Thousand Plan was a reality. But two more things were still needed – an improvement in the weather, and the courage of the commander to give the executive order.

8. MOMENT OF DECISION

IT WAS TWENTY minutes past nine on the morning of Saturday 30th May when Harris walked from his office in the main air staff building at High Wycombe, down a narrow path between the beech trees and through the iron door into the hump of ground which betrayed the site of the underground operations room, completely hidden though it was from the air. With his peaked cap pulled well down over his ginger-grey hair, and his shoulders hunched characteristically in best blue – he never wore battle-dress – he strode into the operations room, accompanied by his personal aide. As he took off his cap and handed it to Tomlinson, the privileged few grouped themselves around him.

There was a ritual about Harris's morning conferences which has been described before. The scene has even been painted. Present in the lofty operations room, with its massive wall-boards of station, squadron and aircraft hieroglyphics, were, first, the normal ops. room staff, carrying on quietly with their duties; second, the senior representatives of all the major departments of the air staff; and third, the select few who gathered at Harris's desk. These were normally restricted to Saundby, 'Sam' Elworthy (Group Captain ops.), Dudley Saward and an intelligence officer. One other man – Spence – would join the group as Harris sat down. As befitted the trusted seer, Spence had his office immediately opposite the operations room and he had formed the habit of slipping in unobserved behind Harris. Now, as Harris settled in his chair, with Saundby standing on his right, Spence came forward with the latest synoptic charts and spread them on the desk in front of Harris.

Spence had been in his office since seven o'clock, collecting and collating weather information and discussing the overall picture by phone with the group meteorological officers to produce an agreed forecast. Now, as he unfolded his charts, he began his droning spiel. The weather over Germany, he said, was still unfavourable, dominated by large amounts of thundery cloud. The situation was blackest in the north-west, but was improving towards the south, where the cloud would disperse to smaller amounts during the night. 'There's a fifty-fifty chance,' said Spence, 'that the cloud in the Cologne area will clear by midnight.'

'What about the bases?'

'The bases on the whole will be clear. A few stations may be unfit through fog but the general picture is good.'

It was the first sign the whole week of any sort of improvement in the weather. Thundery conditions were persisting, and Hamburg was still under a blanket of cloud; whatever lingering partiality Harris may have had for Hamburg as the target was finally doused. But there was a chance, it seemed, for Cologne. An even chance, if Spence was right.

The winds which brought good weather over the bases generally tended to produce cloud over Germany. It was a recurring penalty, a pattern to which Harris was accustomed, but one which seemed to work continually in the enemy's favour. On the whole, as Harris knew well enough, bad weather over the home bases was the greatest threat – not so much of failure as of catastrophe. If he waited one more night – until the last possible moment, in fact, since the moon would then be on the wane – hoping for an improvement over Germany, he might lose the good weather over the bases. To attempt to land this huge force in adverse weather was to court disaster – it was absolutely essential to have a large number of bases free from low cloud and fog. Against this, if the target was cloud-covered the raid would be abortive. The enemy would be forewarned and the plan would be discredited.

The only alternative open to Harris, assuming that he regarded tonight as in all probability his last chance of despatching the force under the existing full moon – as in fact he did – was to wait another month for the next full moon. The time spent in assembling the force and keeping it idle night after night waiting for better weather would have been wasted. The tremendous fillip that the rumours of a big raid had already given to the entire Command would dissolve into reaction, leaving behind it frustration and bitterness. Indeed a dispersal back to normal might look very much like – and could possibly be – a failure of nerve on the part of the commander. And worse even than this, a month's delay would give time for the implementing of those political decisions which threatened to break up the force. Either way, tonight looked like being the last chance for Bomber Command.

All sound in the operations room seemed to be switched off, presenting a silent picture as Harris pondered. He pulled a carton of 'Camel' cigarettes from his patch pocket, flipped his middle finger expertly under it and drew out the protruding cartridge of tobacco. No one moved to light it for him – the ritual was too well established. He took a lighter from his other side pocket, lit the cigarette, then took a blunt, stubby cigarette-holder from his breast pocket and pressed the cigarette into it, finally fixing it firmly between his teeth. Then he leaned forward again, flattened the chart with his palm, and ran his fingers over the Low Countries and across the German frontier, stopping at a city on the Middle Rhine. Dudley Saward, peering anxiously over his shoulder, noticed that his index finger was bent back at the joint, the pressure on it driving the blood from the top of the finger-nail, leaving a half-circle of white.

Harris glanced up at Saundby and met his gaze momentarily. To the others, both men's faces looked expressionless. Their exact thoughts at that moment cannot, perhaps, be recaptured. But both men were students of military and naval history, and both recognized the decisive influence of the weather on all military and naval adventures. Both knew what happens when armadas fail.

Harris stabbed impatiently with his forefinger at the chart. '*Thousand Plan tonight. Target Cologne.*'

He rose from his seat, the cluster of specialist officers drew back and Tomlinson gave him his hat. Once again there was a ceremonial about every gesture. Then, without a word or a glance at anyone, he strode with bowed head from the operations room and out into the fresh air of summer.

It was, as Harris himself wrote afterwards, not perhaps the greatest gamble that a commander in the field has had to take in war. But it was a very considerable risk.

PART II

PREPARATIONS AT THE STATIONS

1. THE INCENDIARY FORCE

HARRY LANGTON was a London policeman, and everyone knows about them. Tall and long-legged, relaxed and even-tempered, patient and fearless, he was soon marked down for the CID. He had tried to join the RAF in 1939, but the Metropolitan Police had refused to let him go. Later, in 1940, he heard that aircrew volunteers were getting their release and he promptly applied again. In August 1940 he was accepted for pilot training, and when he was eventually called up at the end of that year his training was swift. Within a year he was on a squadron; but from the time when he donned uniform in late 1940 to the day of the Cologne raid, Sergeant Harry Langton had never managed to get so much as a single week's leave.

During initial training at Pembroke College, Cambridge, Langton had in fact managed to get himself excused one lesson. The lesson had been morse code. The excuse had been to get married. He had been back in the class-room again before lunch. But Langton was luckier than a good many young married Servicemen of his time. His wife was a trained nurse, and wherever he went she was able to take a job in a local hospital and stay with him or near him. Liz was a fine-looking girl, with a magnificent figure, possessed of an Irish-type beauty. Dark-haired and rosy-complexioned, with translucent blue eyes, her sharp, clear-cut features made her strikingly attractive. But her life as a respectable camp follower sometimes led to complications. One of the first bombs to fall on Cambridge hit the Globe Hotel, where she and her husband were living, and they both lost everything they had. The bed collapsed and the ceiling fell in, and what they didn't lose in the bombing and the fire disappeared in the looting that followed. Langton got his wife to the railway station and sent her home, then reported back for duty, minus uniform. He had had no authority to live out, which at that stage of his training wouldn't have been granted anyway, and he was at once put on a charge for being absent without leave. It was a chastening experience for a copper.

Langton went from Pembroke College to flying training at Marshall's in Cambridge, and straight from there to OTU at Lossiemouth. From Lossiemouth he was sent on fourteen days leave, and he and Liz packed their bags and travelled south, standing all the way from Lossiemouth to London, playing poker with a crowd of airmen in the corridor of the train and finally making their way to Langton's home in East Ham. Next morning Langton got a telegram to report to No 9 Squadron at Honington forthwith.

Liz got a job at the Wellhouse General Hospital in Bury St Edmunds, and although Langton was not allowed to live out, he called for her at the hospital on his off-duty evenings and they spent most of their time at their favourite pub, the Joiners' Arms, a quiet little inn in Garland Street. When he didn't call for her, Liz would know that he was flying, and in the early hours she would listen for a low-flying plane over the hospital – her husband's signal that he had returned safely.

No 9 Squadron had been one of the first squadrons to get Gee. They had been in the fire-raising party at Lübeck and Rostock, and they had been in most of the raids on Essen. Langton had shared in the squadron pride at being in the van, although it often meant heavier losses. In six months on the squadron Langton had had five different room-mates, the first four all going missing one by one. Although less than half-way through his tour, and with only a handful of trips as first pilot, he was senior in squadron service to all but three of the pilots. He had already been three times to Cologne – twice as second pilot and once as navigator.

When he had become a first pilot and captain, Langton had

had the good luck to take over a crew most of whom were already more than half-way through their tour. 'Tiny' Welsh, the six-foot-four navigator, was the most experienced, having done twenty-six operations when he joined Langton; the Cologne raid would be his thirtieth, the last of his tour. As deputy bombing leader on 9 Squadron he was one of the key men in the incendiary force. Langton's Wellington was scheduled to be the second aircraft off at Honington, the nearest base to Cologne, so they could expect to be one of the first crews on target. As yet they had no idea what the target was, but as the days on stand-by mounted, and the rumours of a big raid grew more persistent, they guessed that wherever they were ordered to go they would be in the van.

Two days before the raid, Langton's tail gunner went sick and Langton was given a replacement named Ken Pexman. Pexman had just been posted to Bomber Command and had only arrived at Honington that day; he had been a gunner on Defiants – night-fighters – but they had been withdrawn from service. He had never flown in a bomber or operated over Germany. He had hoped to get some leave before the transfer, but the sudden demand for extra crews had resulted in an immediate posting.

Ken Pexman had been a steel works wages clerk in Scunthorpe. Married four months earlier to a Scunthorpe girl, he was something of a dreamer, aesthetic-looking, with a poet's consciousness of life's brevity and of the ephemeral nature of happiness. Yet he was without solemnity, and was capable of the most buoyant high spirits and had a keen sense of humour. He had confided in his wife that he did not expect to see his twenty-second birthday. When he arrived at Honington it was only four days off.

*

At No 419 (RCAF) Squadron at Mildenhall there were sixteen Wellington III's, and sixteen crews to go with them, eight from each flight. That posed a problem for the squadron commander, Wing Commander 'Moose' Fulton, who was left without an aircraft. Mildenhall, like Honington, was one of the clutch of Suffolk airfields nearest to the target, and like Honington it housed a Gee-equipped squadron of 3 Group, which would automatically be a part of the incendiary force. This was a raid that Fulton had no intention of missing, and he soon cast a covetous eye on an old Wellington Ic which was used at Mildenhall as a trainer, and staked a claim to it. As squadron commander, of course, he could easily have earmarked a squadron aircraft for himself and detailed one of his crews to fly the Ic, but that wasn't Moose Fulton's way.

Fulton, a Canadian in the RAF, had arrived at Mildenhall to take over 419 Squadron when it was formed in December 1941, and very soon the squadron crews were aware that they were serving under one of the most remarkable leaders of men they were ever likely to meet. With one or two exceptions the crews were all Canadians, the chief exception being the squadron bombing leader, Flight Lieutenant the Hon. Terence Mansfield, who flew with Fulton and had ample opportunity to observe him and his methods. Fulton only had one principle for leadership. No one was ordered to do anything which he hadn't done himself or wasn't ready to do. He extended this principle to his flight commanders, both of whom had done more operations than any other crew on the squadron – always excepting Fulton. And these figures were not obtained by careful selection of the easier trips. Over every difficult target the crews were sure of being led by Fulton, with one of his flight commanders alongside, leaving only one of the squadron hierarchy on the ground.

There was no bluster about Fulton, no particularly dominating personality, no aggressive self-assurance, no heavy camaraderie. He was fundamentally a shy man, apt to blush to the roots of his red hair; but he knew everyone on the squadron strength by name and could have recited each man's family history almost as readily as his own. With his quiet, unobtrusive determination and his love and care for his men, he inspired a spirit and a feeling of confidence which people found unforgettable.

One of Fulton's finest moments came during the preparations for an operation that never took place. The target was to be the submarine pens at Hamburg, but since no bombs had then been developed capable of penetrating the concrete shelters from a height, a small force of twelve aircraft was to fly up the Elbe to Hamburg at low level and lob their bombs into the open mouths of the pens to explode inside. No 419 Squadron were to supply six of the aircraft. A high-level force would go in just ahead of them to draw off the flak.

Fulton held a meeting with his flight commanders and senior squadron staff. He believed that the chances of return were small, and he decreed that crews should be cut down from five men to four – pilot, navigator/bomb-aimer, wireless operator and rear gunner – and that as far as possible only single men should be selected. Fulton himself would lead the raid.

When the final order came through from Group, it contained a specific instruction that Fulton was not to take part. The station commander at Mildenhall, who briefed the crews, made this point at the briefing, to explain why Fulton was not going after all. The announcement was greeted by a spontaneous outburst of cheering that might have come from the pages of fiction. However, when the crews went out to their aircraft they met Fulton at dispersal, dressed in full flying kit, about to disobey the Group order and lead the raid. Fortunately the operation, after being laid on twice, was cancelled by Command.

For the attack on Cologne, 419 Squadron were to time their attack for five minutes after zero hour, aiming their incendiaries at the central aiming point, the *Neumarkt*, backing up the aircraft that had gone before and correcting any errors.

*

'Never again will I dive out of searchlights.'

That had been the conclusion of Sergeant Wilf Davis, a pilot on 218 Squadron at Marham in Norfolk, after a trip to Essen, a fortnight before the Cologne raid. His Stirling had been coned by searchlights over the target, and Davis had previously been told that the only way to escape when this happened was to put the nose of the aircraft straight down. He did this, diving to 3,000 feet and leaving the flak and searchlights far behind, but when he tried to pull out he found the controls locked and immovable against the weight of the airstream. The combined efforts of pilot and co-pilot could not arrest the dive, and under their appalled gaze the airspeed built up to 425 miles an hour. It seemed certain that the Stirling would break up; in any case it would shatter into a thousand pieces shortly as they hit the ground. Then at last they managed to pull out; but as soon as they levelled off, at 1,000 feet above the roof-tops and chimneys of Essen, the plane vibrated so severely that it seemed about to fall apart. Davis darted a quick glance at the airspeed indicator and saw that it now read less than 90. A Stirling simply wouldn't fly at 90. This must be the reason for the vibration – they were on the point of the stall. In a moment of near-panic he gave the order to bale out, then reversed it as he saw that he had mis-read the indicator. There must be some other reason for the vibration.

They had got home all right from that trip; the vibration had been caused by a broken propeller. But the incident had made a deep impression on the crew. None of them would fancy being in such a dive again. For those in the fuselage, the sight of the two pilots fighting unsuccessfully to pull back the control column had been a nightmare one. For the front gunner, watching the ground rush towards him, it had been particularly unpleasant. None of them disagreed with their pilot's resolve.

The man in the front turret that night had been Albert Smith, 'Smithy', at 29 the oldest as well as the most experienced man in the crew. A sergeant wireless operator/air gunner, Smithy hated the claustrophobic feeling of being penned up in the fuselage working the radio, and by mutual agreement he was always able to arrange it so that he occupied one or other of the turrets, front, mid-upper or rear. Fortunately there were always men, the reverse of Smithy, who preferred not to see too much. Smithy had been ten months on the squadron and had survived four bad crashes, three with bombs on board; to the other men of the squadron he seemed indestructible. Whatever happened, Smithy always got out, Smithy always got back. But Smithy, a true individualist who made up his own mind about everything, knew better. Gradually, over a long tour that had been unusually protracted by the four crashes and the conversion to Stirlings half-way through, he had seen so many men with his own conviction of personal immortality die that he knew well enough it could happen to him.

Smithy came from a humble Victorian terraced house in a Manchester suburb. He was a mass name from a mass area, unobtrusive and apparently colourless, yet he was a man with original opinions who gave them honestly and fearlessly when asked, one whose judgement was respected in any company. Of medium height and slight build, with fair, sandy hair, he was soft-voiced and impressively articulate, speaking without hesitancy and with no more than an agreeable trace of regional accent. He was a man who didn't say or do things just because others did or said them, nor did he deliberately take any contrary view. He had no sense of difference from his fellows, yet in any group of men in a crisis the clear-thinking Smithy stood out.

Smithy had done twenty-seven operations, and in that period he had seen every kind of human reaction to danger, to fear, to the certainty of death. He had had navigators who were brilliant on a night cross-country over Britain but useless over Germany. He had sensed the anxiety neurosis that had taken a co-gunner off flying altogether, and done his best to help. He had seen brave pilots lose their nerve. He was not given to praising extravagantly, neither did he condemn.

His present crew he trusted and liked. Wilf Davis, quiet and steady, of similar build and temperament to himself, was not normally the type to panic; the experience over Essen had been enough to unsettle anyone. And he especially liked the 23-year-old navigator from Cumberland, Joe Borrowdale; no one could call him quiet, he was too high-spirited for that, but he was alert and unflinching in the air. The one man Smithy knew little of was the new tail gunner; like Ken Pexman, of Langton's crew, he had previously been a gunner on Defiant night-fighters and had only just come to Bomber Command. But in one way this man was unique. He was in the Royal Canadian Air Force, his name was Howard L. Tate, Junior, he came from Dallas, Texas, and he was an American. Inevitably he was quickly dubbed 'Tex'.

*

Although, with Hamburg in mind, the operation order had coupled 1 Group with 3 Group as forming the marking force, in practice, with Cologne as the target, most of the first aircraft to bomb would come from the 3 Group bases in East Anglia. In addition to the squadrons already mentioned – 9, 419 (RCAF) and 218 – other squadrons with selected crews in the van would include 15 Squadron at Wyton (who would actually provide the first aircraft on target), 57 and 75 (NZ) at Feltwell, 101 at Bourn, 115 at Marham, 149 at Lakenheath and 214 at Stradishall. The aircraft types would be Stirlings and Wellingtons. The selected crews would be given early take-off times, and the remaining crews of all these squadrons would form a part of the main force.

2. THE MAIN FORCE

And when the air force saw it,[1]
It looked so sweet and fair,
They said 'That's what we're looking for,
We'll build our air force there.'

LARGE AREAS OF relatively unbroken, sparsely wooded country, within easy reach of the east coast, thinly

1. RAF Song.

populated and with no great industrial centres, made Lincolnshire, the second largest of the English counties, a natural choice when it came to bases for the bomber force. Of the four heavy bomber groups, two had most of their bases in Lincolnshire. No 1 Group, with headquarters at Bawtry, inhabited northern Lincolnshire, and No 5 Group, with headquarters at Grantham, was concentrated in the south. Many of the airfields were still under construction when war began, and by June 1941 another new airfield had been built at Elsham Wolds, in the extreme north-east of the county, six miles south of the Humber and four miles from the old market town of Brigg.

The airfield at Elsham Wolds was sited on the top of the chalk escarpment which runs like a rib through Lincolnshire from north to south – the bleak, sheep-grazing Lincolnshire Wolds. The road climbed steadily out of the village of Barnetby until, high on the plateau, the hangars, the prefabricated huts and the occasional buildings silhouetted themselves starkly against the sky. Highest of all, or so it seemed from the road, was the water-tower, black and uncompromisingly functional, standing to attention on its stilt-like supports like a sentinel.

At the end of June 1941 Hugh Constantine had been posted to Elsham Wolds to command the new station, with the rank of group captain. There had been no water when he arrived there, and no electric light, but under his urgings these things were provided in the next few days, just in time to receive No 103 Squadron when they arrived a week later.

Hugh Constantine was 33 when he took over at Elsham, one of the youngest station commanders in the Command at that time. Tall and massively built, with huge hands and a handshake of iron, he had played rugger for the RAF and Leicester and had had an England trial in 1934. He believed wholeheartedly in physical fitness as one of the main props of morale, and he played rugger regularly on the station at Elsham. Many a veteran operational pilot found himself tempted to flinch from contact when Hugh Constantine was running with the ball.

By May 1942, Constantine had been a station commander for eleven months and had formed his own ideas of what his task was and how best to approach it. To his great satisfaction 103 Squadron, although having no label of any kind, proved to be a truly Commonwealth squadron, a mixture of men from the Dominions as well as the United Kingdom, and Constantine believed that this brought a keen competition amongst crews which was not obtainable in any other way. He had always believed in the idea of a Commonwealth air force and regretted that politics had made the realization impossible. The mixture of nationalities brought its own problems, but Constantine, a disciplinarian, was always ready to deal with these when they occurred. It was not easy to draw the line between the essential letting off steam of high-spirited young men and the necessity for keeping a basic respect for authority, but Constantine learnt to do it.

There were no easy formulas for squadron *esprit de corps*; it was not something that could be effectively based on rigid discipline, a smart turn-out and respect for rank. Life had too many physical and emotional extremes, and the human material was too diverse. One of the best navigators on 103 Squadron, and one of the most valued morale-builders, an NCO named 'Dizzy' Spiller, was the scruffiest man on the station. He rarely wore his aircrew brevet or his chevrons of rank. He was only 21, short, round-faced and rosy-cheeked, and he had lost one of his upper front teeth during an argument after a party. It had been a lucky punch, because somehow the gap completed his personality.

Dizzy Spiller was a humorist, and one of his best jokes concerned an imaginary gremlin-like character whom he called 'Nebby'. When the flak got too close it was Nebby barking. The moon was Nebby's torch. Whenever a crowd of aircrew went into a bar with Spiller, an extra beer had to be bought and left on the counter, and a spare cigarette put by it – for Nebby. Anyone who came in and touched that beer or cigarette was greeted with howls of dismay. 'Don't touch that! That's Nebby's! Nebby will get you if you do!' Here was yet another of the euphemisms so dear to the men of the bombers, like going for a Burton, and getting the chop – phrases that somehow benumbed the perpetual horror of one of the most unpleasant forms of death.

These were the sort of men and conditions with which station commanders were continually dealing. Squadron commanders, obsessed with the immediate task on hand, were apt to be less tolerant, but for station commanders, maturity and human understanding were of more value than discipline and powers of punishment.

Few station commanders were as close to the men on their stations as Constantine was. He was too busy to do much flying himself, but he kept his hand in on the Wellington and flew just enough to remind himself of the operational problems and the physical and mental strains. In keeping his finger on the pulse of morale the people he especially relied on, after the squadron commander, were his wife, Helen, and the station medical officer. The doctor could usually distinguish a genuine case of anxiety neurosis from the more painful one of LMF – lack of moral fibre – and between them they were able to take a man off operations when it seemed the best thing to do in fairness to the squadron and the man, without attaching any sort of stigma to his name. Many an aircrew man got a quiet word from Constantine after a sticky trip.

'How do you feel?'

'All right thanks, sir.'

'Nerve all right?'

'Yes, thanks.'

'I can get you screened if you want, you know.'

In addition to their natural apprehensions, nearly all men had their own particular problems and personal worries, and when these became insistent they inevitably affected keenness and morale. This was where Helen Constantine came in. As an Australian herself she was able to break down the barriers that existed because of her husband's position naturally and easily. She persuaded her husband to take a small cottage in the village, and there, in an informal and relaxed atmosphere that she could never have created on the station, she gave bacon-and-egg parties and got to know all the squadron and station personnel. She knew all the aircrews as well as or better than her husband did, and understood the strains under which they were living. She knew, too, which ones were married, which of them had smuggled their wives into one of the local villages. That was something that was against aircrew policy, but it was something at which Hugh Constantine was generally prepared to wink, provided it didn't affect the man's nerve as a wartime flier.

Living out on an operational station was a snatched, stolen happiness, frowned on by authority and holding intolerable tensions for both man and woman. Squadron life played on the nerves of its adherents like a honky-tonk pianist, plunging from the treble of ecstasy to the bass of despair. Yet for many men it was the only married happiness they would know. A few days honeymoon leave, a few hectic weeks of separations and reunions, and then the warm bed that the husband had almost become accustomed to returning to still held only one occupant at dawn. The margin between grief and exaltation was such a narrow one. If an aircraft kept going for just a few miles more, the crash that had seemed inevitable could be converted into a safe forced landing followed by a reassuring telephone call to the anxious partner.

The work of bringing every available aircraft up to operational fitness went ahead with great enthusiasm at Elsham Wolds under Constantine's lead, until it seemed likely that there would be more aircraft than crews to man them. Two NCOs who had done a few trips as second pilot were promoted to first pilot and allotted crews, and Constantine made ready to go on the raid himself to make up the number.

On 27th May eleven more Wellingtons with crews flew in from No 22 OTU at Wellesbourne Mountford, near Stratford-on-Avon, as part of the planned move of training units to easterly bases. Constantine noted that the crews were the same sort of mixture of Commonwealth nationalities as his own. Many of them were trainees, but some of them were quite as experienced as his best squadron crews, and one pilot, a South African named Al Hamman, had already completed two bombing tours, one in the Middle East and one in the UK, and had the DFC and bar.

On 103 Squadron, one of the most typical crews was that captained by Clive Saxelby, 'Bix Sax', as he was known to his crew. Saxelby was a New Zealander, tall, pale, lean and casual, dark-haired and grey-eyed. He had trained as a pilot in New Zealand directly after leaving school, and he had come to Britain in 1940 when still only 18 to complete his training and to join No 75 (New Zealand) Squadron at Feltwell. He had begun that tour as second pilot to another New Zealander, Don Harkness, a 26-year-old regular airman on a short-service commission in the RAF. Harkness, reserved and serious almost to the point of the morose, was not physically strong but he was wiry, and he had quite exceptional courage. Saxelby would not easily forget the example Harkness had set, and he remembered especially an attack on invasion barges in August 1940; they had been co-operating with the Navy, and Harkness had made eleven runs over the target area with flares to illuminate the target for the Navy before going in to drop his bombs. With a cloud base down to 5,000 feet and a barrage of flak that was effective up to about 7,000 it had been a most dangerous task, and a frightening experience for the raw Saxelby. But Harkness had never wavered. The net result had been the destruction of many barges and a congratulatory signal from the Navy. When, a few weeks later, Harkness left the squadron at the end of his tour and Saxelby became a first pilot and captain – he was still only 18 – he tried to model himself on the slight, thin, sharp-featured Don Harkness, the most dedicated and professional airman he had known.

Saxelby had completed his first tour, put in a year as an instructor and then joined 103 Squadron at Elsham. He was not yet 21, but he was half-way through his second tour. Less than thirty miles away, and unknown to Clive Saxelby, Don Harkness was now a flight commander on No 158 Squadron at Driffield, on the far side of the Humber. He too was preparing to take a leading part in the big raid.

*

Flight Lieutenant Reece Read, a 28-year-old pilot on 101 Squadron at Bourn, on the St Neots-Cambridge road, had always wanted to be a doctor. But the end of his schooldays had coincided with the depression of the early thirties, there was no money in the family to finance him through university, and eventually he went to West Africa to work as a mining engineer. He was still there eight years later when war broke out.

Short and unremarkable in appearance and thus at first sight inconspicuous, Read soon impressed with his dogged perseverance and his sympathetic handling of people when he came home to join the RAF. He was marked down as a bomber pilot; there was nothing dashing about him, but he had obvious tenacity, and he would inspire great confidence in a crew. When he completed his training he was posted to 101 Squadron on Wellingtons, and early in May 1942, after five trips as a second pilot, he was made a captain and allotted a crew. Since then he had been on three bombing trips to French ports, but he had never operated as a captain over Germany. 101 was one of the Gee-equipped 3 Group squadrons, and although Read would not be one of the first to take off he would be early on target.

*

Air Vice-Marshal Jack Baldwin, Air Officer Commanding No 3 Group, based at Newmarket, had bombed Cologne before. But that had been a long time ago – almost exactly twenty-five years, in fact, during the First World War.

Baldwin was a man of vigorous physique and personality who had retained a youthful outlook on life in spite of having reached his half-century. In many ways – the right ways – he had never quite grown up. A cavalryman before transferring to the RFC, his life's interest – after flying – had been horses, and it was said that even Trenchard had recognized this obsession and connived at a posting for him between the wars to overseas stations where he could revel in his beloved polo.

When his active flying days were over, Baldwin's love of horses was inevitably promoted to first place, and he decided to leave the Air Force as soon as he could retire on full pension, devoting his life to farming and the breeding of polo ponies. When the opportunity came, it was August 1939. He did not believe that war would come, and he left the Service. The RAF, perhaps with their tongue in their cheek, let him go. Twelve days later he was attending York races when he got a telegram recalling him to duty as AOC 3 Group, based at – of all places – Newmarket. Somebody who knew him must have picked that one.

Baldwin had the typical background of the commissioned officer of the early twentieth century. Public School – he was at Rugby – and Sandhurst. It was in off-duty hours at Sandhurst in 1910 that he used to ride his motor-cycle – a mode of transport forbidden to cadets in those days – down to Brooklands, near Weybridge, where he learnt to fly at his own expense, financed by his own earnings as a free-lance mechanic on the aerodrome. No doubt learning to fly, and working as a paid mechanic, would also have been forbidden at Sandhurst if anyone had happened to think of it. Baldwin was the type of young man who delighted in the unusual. But the open manner in which he flouted petty restrictions disarmed superiors. Despairing contemporaries, punished for offences hardly more serious, averred that Jack Baldwin could get away with anything.

Baldwin had attended a conference of group commanders called by Saundby at the outset of the planning stage. He had realized that here was an operation which would amount to an entirely new dimension in air warfare. The concentration of aircraft, the saturation of the target, the collision risk – all these were facets of a new technique of which, as a group commander, he felt he ought to have first-hand experience. He saw it clearly as his duty to go on the raid. And anyway, he *wanted* to go on it.

More than thirty years' experience of the Service had taught him that it was fatal to mention this sort of intention to anyone. He would only draw on himself a direct order from Harris that he was not to go. There would be no getting round that. The only course open to him lay in taking the action and justifying it afterwards.

There were, of course, people whom he would have to let into the secret. His deputy at Group would have to know, so would the station commander at Marham, the station from which he proposed to fly, so would the commander of the squadron whose aircraft took him. But these men would simply be carrying out his orders and would not be personally involved.

All that Saturday at Marham the ground crews and armourers were working without rest to get the aircraft of two squadrons – the Stirlings of 218 and the Wellingtons of 115 – ready for the night's operation. When they had finished there were nineteen Stirlings and eighteen Wellingtons bombed up and positioned in front of the control tower, against the normal absolute maximum – never attainable in practice – of sixteen per squadron. Not a single bomber at Marham would be left on the ground.

During the afternoon Wing Commander Paul Holder, a tall, quiet South African, commander of the Stirling squadron, had a phone call from the station commander, Group Captain 'Square' McKee. McKee was a thick-set New Zealander whose breezy enthusiasm and ubiquitous presence had worked the station up into a lather of efficiency in the previous few days.

'The AOC wants to fly with your squadron tonight,' said McKee. 'Who shall we put him with?'

'He'd better come with me.'

The only other person Baldwin told was his daughter Pamela, who was staying with him at Exning House for the week-end. Pamela, tall and dark, was a WAAF officer, stationed at Upwood, now on week-end leave. She divided these short leaves between her father at Newmarket and her mother at the family home at Stamford. Baldwin did not believe in married men having their wives with them on operational stations and he practised what he preached.

Exning House, an ornate Victorian mansion faced in red brick, was the home of Lord Glanelly, a leading racehorse owner and the man who for many years held first claim to the services of Gordon Richards. At Exning House Baldwin was able to keep up his interest in horses, riding on the Heath every morning before breakfast. On this particular Saturday morning he allowed his daughter to ride in his place. That, she knew, meant a liverish air vice-marshal for most of the morning. But by lunchtime his good temper was restored, and she listened to his casual mention of the raid he proposed to go on. 'It's a target I bombed in the last war,' he said, 'and I'm going to bomb it in this.'

Pamela Baldwin had been brought up against a background of RAF stations, home and overseas. At Cranwell, where her father had been Commandant, she had been in her teens, an impressionable age at which she had met and admired the young cadets, most of whom, it seemed, had been killed in the first two years of the war. But she had learned not to make a fuss. That was the cardinal sin. She thought now of the fresh, eager faces of these young men, she thought of her mother, and she thought of her father, who perhaps would not return from tonight's raid. But she said nothing. Any remark, any fear expressed for her father's safety, would have earned the rebuke that hundreds of aircrew, not all of them young men, were flying over Germany almost every night. Whatever happened, she was too well schooled in Service tragedies to make a fuss.

Dinner at Exning House that night was a strange meal. Father and daughter sat at opposite ends of the long mahogany table, their dinner cooked and served by Lord Glanelly's staff. They talked of routine things, family matters, but of nothing too close to either of them and not at all about the raid. Meanwhile, at Marham, the officer and airmen aircrew were having their pre-flight meal in the Messes. The atmosphere away from the airfield had a leisurely tranquillity. Officers who had just finished their evening meal were strolling on the lawn in front of the Mess in the evening sunshine. Some of them were watching a tennis match. Others had gone to their rooms for a final clean-up before the raid.

After coffee at Exning House, the staff car crunched up the gravel drive and stopped at the door.

'Good-night, Pamela. Don't wait up for me. See you at breakfast.'

*

Jim Wilkie was 16 when he went to the recruiting centre in Manchester in June 1940 to volunteer for the Royal Air Force. A pale youth, with dark brown hair that was curly rather than wavy and clung tenaciously to his scalp, he was working as an office boy in his home town of Altrincham, Cheshire, marking time until he could get into uniform. A product of the local grammar school, he had succeeded, among the complexities of English society, in reaching the age of 16 without any complexes at all. He got past the recruiting centre and was sent to Padgate, but there his junior insurance card caught up with him, and a fatherly warrant officer patted him on the back and led him gently out of the gate, telling him to come back in two years' time.

His first attempt had failed, but only through the damning evidence of the insurance card. He at once left his job, thus getting rid of the card, worked locally on a farm as a casual labourer and applied again, this time to the Liverpool recruiting centre. When they asked for his birth certificate he told them he had been born in India, which was true, and added with not quite the same truth that registration of births had been less strict in India and that anyway his birth certificate had been lost. His story was accepted, and soon afterwards he was called up and began training as a pilot. He actually got his wings on his eighteenth birthday, 18th July 1941.

Early in 1942 he was posted to 50 Squadron at Skellingthorpe, a satellite of Swinderby, three miles out of Lincoln. He had done three operational sorties on Hampdens when the squadron was converted to Manchesters. After his conversion course, Wilkie came back to the squadron with an entirely new crew, but this involved a conflict of loyalties, particularly over his former navigator, the cheerful, smiling Alan Bee. They had been through training and the Hampden operations together and had become close friends. Eventually the older loyalty won and Alan Bee came back into the crew.

Like most bomber crews they had quickly achieved harmony, perhaps as much as anything because of their dissimilarities. Alastair Benn, the mid-upper gunner, was an Australian. Eddie Finch, the front gunner, hair thinning and face beginning to crease, was twice Wilkie's age and the only married man. Finch's special pal was the youthful rear gunner Doug Baird. These two men, the old and the young, supplied a mutual need that could not be dismissed in purely Freudian terms. Finch, a hardened Cockney, always took care of Baird. He would sit on the floor of the crew-room, a cigarette sticking out of the corner of his mouth, absorbed in a game of poker – but he wouldn't allow Baird to play.

In mid-May, when about a third of the way through their tour, the crew were sent on leave. On 22nd May they were recalled. The other crew-members were 'Toby' Tobias, the second pilot, and Jock Campbell, the wireless operator. Campbell had completed his thirty-second trip before going on leave and he was surprised at the recall. Eventually he was told that, depending on aircraft availability, he might be asked to do one more trip.

All through that week Wilkie and his crew were one of two spare crews for whom there were no aircraft. Then on the Saturday morning the two crews were flown to Coningsby to pick up two spare Manchesters. They were going on the raid, Campbell included. When they went out to their aircraft that evening they were well before time, and they sat around on the grass at the dispersal point, watching the sunset. Wilkie noticed that Alan Bee, usually so talkative and animated, was strangely quiet. Did he perhaps regret coming back into the crew? Did he have some premonition? He noticed, too, that the homing pigeons were fluttering unhappily in their baskets. Wise birds, perhaps they too were concerned about their future.

*

Leslie Baveystock, a second pilot, also on 50 Squadron, viewed the week's preparations at Skellingthorpe with some disquiet. He had been given a short week-end pass and his wife was coming up from London to spend it with him in Lincoln. Les and Bette Baveystock had met in their teens – he had been 17 and she only 15 – and they had married six years later, in 1938. There had never been anyone else for either of them. Their last leave had been marred by the illness of their 18-month-old daughter Jill, who had developed pneumonia, but now Bette's mother was looking after Jill, who had recovered, and Bette and Les were looking forward eagerly to their week-end together.

All through the week Les Baveystock – 'Bavey', or 'Bave', as he was known, even to his wife – watched the tantalizing progress of the squadron's servicing teams, tantalizing because if the raid was going to be something really big, as everyone said, he would like to go on it, and conversely because his week-end pass, although not yet cancelled, was obviously in jeopardy. By Saturday morning, fifteen aircraft and crews were listed on the squadron board. Flying Officer Leslie Manser, Baveystock's pilot, was still not among them. But during the morning Manser and his crew were called to the flight office. There they ran into Jim Wilkie. Both crews were to collect Manchesters from Coningsby, and to stand by to fly them that night. Baveystock was told that his leave was cancelled.

'Do I have to go to Coningsby?' asked Baveystock.

'Why?'

'My wife's coming up from London by train this afternoon. It's too late to stop her now. She'll be expecting me to meet her. So if I could just slip into Lincoln for an hour to let her know. . . .'

'All right. Just for an hour, then. And not a word about the raid. Be back here for briefing at six o'clock.'

Baveystock went off to Lincoln while Manser and Wilkie and their crews went to Coningsby. The London train steamed into Lincoln at two o'clock, and a blue-eyed, fair-haired girl, young and attractive, peered out of a window half-way down the train, looking for her husband. There he was, in uniform, waving to her – but not somehow with quite the joyous abandon she had expected. She guessed at once that things might not go quite as they had planned.

'What is it? You're flying!'

'Yes.'

'Oh-h-h. . . .'

'It's something pretty big. More important than usual. But I don't know much about it and I can't tell you anyway. How's Jill?'

'Wonderful.'

He took her to a hotel near the station where he had booked a room. 'I'm sorry, Bette. It only came up this morning. I couldn't let you know. But I'll be back for breakfast in the morning, and then we'll have the whole day together.'

He was glad she did not complain. She never had. He had been in a reserved occupation and had had quite a struggle to join up, but she had never reproached him for it, not even at his OTU at Cottesmore, where five pilots out of sixteen on his course had written themselves off and thirty-eight men on various overlapping courses had been killed while they lived out together.

'Come out to Skellingthorpe this evening. I'll be able to slip out of camp for an hour after briefing. If this weather holds we can have a walk and you can give me all the news.'

'Where do I get the bus?'

'I'll show you. Now I really have to go.'

What a cheat it was, she thought, what a sell. She meandered back to the dreary little hotel and tried to settle in. It was the longest and emptiest afternoon she had ever known. But at last the time came to catch the bus to Skellingthorpe. Bave was outside the gates to meet her. She had rarely seen him so excited. 'It's something really big, all right,' he said, 'and it'll be a piece of cake. Nothing to it, not to worry.' She was infected with his confidence, enjoyed the walk through the country lanes.

'What's the pilot like?'

'He's a young chap – younger than me. Only about twenty. I've never flown with him before. Commissioned type. But he's friendly and he gets across. When I first met him I thought he was a bit effeminate, but he isn't – just quiet and natural. I like him, and he's a good pilot.'

At eight o'clock they headed back for the camp. They said good-bye out of view of the camp gates.

'Take care.'

'Of course I will. I'll see you at breakfast, so don't worry. But if by any chance I don't show up it'll probably be because I've been diverted somewhere. There's a risk of fog. So don't phone the camp, will you – that's taboo. Wives aren't supposed to be here.'

Back inside the camp, Baveystock found an aircrew acquaintance who was not going on the raid. 'Look,' he said, 'my wife's in this hotel at Lincoln.' He gave him the name. 'If we don't get back on time, find out if we've been diverted, will you? And if we're missing, tell the adjutant?'

'OK, Bave.'

It was not a premonition, just a normal precaution, like carrying escape money, or a Mae West. But another man in Manser's crew *did* have a premonition. He was the wireless operator, Pilot Officer Norman Horsley, a strong, fair-haired Yorkshireman with a round, open face. Horsley, like Jock Campbell in the other spare crew at Skellingthorpe, had finished his tour. Then had come the news that he was to do one more trip with Leslie Manser as pilot.

Horsley was a very cool young man, quick to sum people up. At first, like Baveystock, he had thought that this fair-skinned, rather too handsome young pilot, with what seemed a weak, almost girlish mouth, was a bit of a cis. He soon saw his mistake. The first time he flew with him he noticed how Manser brought his crew's attention to mistakes and omissions, without mincing his words, but quietly and without fuss. His regard for Manser grew. Here was a chap who surprised you.

Another man in the crew who would testify to Manser's competence and capacity for leadership was Flying Officer

Richard Barnes, better known as 'Bang-on' Barnes because of his accurate navigation. Barnes was himself a pilot, but having flown with Manser as a second pilot on Hampdens he had asked specially to stay with him and do a full tour as a navigator.

Horsley was nevertheless pessimistic about his chances on this raid. It must surely be tempting fate to do this extra trip. And the aircraft they had flown over from Coningsby that afternoon had not exactly inspired confidence. It was, he thought, a clapped-out old machine, probably used for training at Coningsby, and it was very dirty inside – a sure sign that it was not an operational aircraft. It had no mid-upper turret and the rear escape hatch was permanently screwed in. But they had tested it thoroughly and it had seemed airworthy.

Horsley went back to his room after lunch, had a sleep, and then tidied up his kit, just in case he didn't get back. It was something that in thirty trips he had never done before. The premonition that he wasn't coming back grew stronger. He sorted through all the letters in his locker. Some of them were from girl friends, a few were precious to him. But they would make embarrassing reading for any party detailed to go through his kit. He tore them up.

Beyond his premonition, Horsley did not worry. He never had. And he felt no particular fear. When someone said go, he went. The premonition did not extend to details about survival. He took that for granted. Somehow he would get away with it. The rest he dismissed with a shrug.

*

Seven miles north of Skellingthorpe another 5 Group Manchester squadron, No 49, was preparing for the raid. The station was Scampton, one of the best-known in the Command. Also at Scampton was No 83 Squadron, still partly equipped with Manchesters but in the process of converting to Lancasters. Perhaps the most interesting character on either squadron was a 23-year-old Manchester pilot named Philip Floyd. Floyd was an intellectual, a man who had done outstandingly well at his grammar school at Minehead and won a county scholarship to Cambridge. Talented, high-principled, intolerant and introverted, he had a haughty manner which aroused resentment wherever he went, and he made few friends. Even with his brother, four years his junior, he had established no contact. Most people dismissed him as an intellectual and social snob. Brought up in a staunch Methodist and traditionally pacifist background, he had turned to theology at Cambridge soon after the war started, intensifying his pacifist pursuits, and the news of his sudden decision to join the RAF had shocked and astonished his family. What lay behind it none of them knew, though they traced it to the end of the 'phoney' war, with which it roughly coincided. Wrapped up in himself though he seemed to be, the last man to talk about himself and his problems was Philip Floyd. Perhaps that accounted a good deal for his apparent aloofness.

At his OTU at Upper Heyford, Floyd had met a navigator named John Valentine, four years his senior, a qualified accountant, perceptive, unprejudiced, married, mature. Valentine had penetrated Floyd's shell, recognized that here was a man who had been tormented by his conscience, a man who had had the courage to discard a rooted and inborn pacifism and take up the fight against Germany. Such a thing was not done easily; it would leave its mark on any sensitive man. Inside Philip Floyd there was clearly a dynamic but undeveloped personality searching for expression. As with most apparently proud, conceited, disdainful people, Floyd's difficulty in human relationships was largely attributable to shyness and nerves.

No pressure was put on trainees at the OTUs to crew up together; they were left to sort themselves out into natural groups. What Valentine had first noticed about Floyd was his loneliness, and he had gone out of his way to get to know him. That was the kind of man Valentine was. Soon they were flying together, soon a friendship developed between them, based on mutual respect and confidence. When the time came to go to a squadron they went together, as part of a crew.

*

Air Marshal A. T. Harris at his desk at High Wycombe with his Senior Air Staff Officer, Air Vice-Marshal R. H. M. S. Saundby

FOUR OF THE PLANNERS

Dr B. G. Dickins
Operational Research Section

Wing Commander Dudley Saward
Command Radar Officer

Group Captain Magnus Spence
Command Meteorological Officer

Group Captain S. C. Elworthy
Operations

A Hampden of 408 (RCAF) Squadron

A Lancaster I of 83 Squadron

A Wellington III of 115 Squadron

Lillian Fiddian

'Bave' Baveystock

Liz Langton

George Gilpin

When Geoff Gane, a 21-year-old New Zealander, heard he was posted to No 12 Squadron at Binbrook, he knew instinctively that his days were numbered. Some men had a flair for knowing these things. Already an old friend of his had been posted missing from 12 Squadron. But there was more to it than that. He knew with chilling certainty that a night would come when he and his crew would not get back to Binbrook, when they would be shot down over Germany.

For the majority of men there was the protection of a belief in personal immortality. It was the other fellow who got shot down. For most men there were moments of foreboding, but they were generally able to shake them off. There were always a few men, though, who had a conviction of personal disaster. With some men it was of long standing, almost dormant within them; with others, it came upon them suddenly. Sometimes it lay heavily on an entire crew. Most of them came to terms with it; these men, perhaps, displayed the highest form of courage.

Geoff Gane, or 'Kid' Gane, as he was called, seemed an unlikely candidate for a mystic. His round, chubby face and large blue-grey protuberant eyes, framed in incredibly long lashes, seemed more suited to the schoolroom than to uniform. Excitable and voluble, with a vivid imagination and subject to severe attacks of nerves, he felt he would make a good gunner if he could somehow control his temperament. Now here he was, tail gunner in a Wellington, shortly to set out, like hundreds of others on the projected raid, on his first operational flight.

Any lurking hopes Gane had of escaping what he felt to be his destiny had been dispelled when he arrived at Binbrook. It was a well-planned pre-war station, with permanent administrative buildings and accommodation, but to the newcomer the atmosphere was depressing, almost macabre. The old hands kept up their spirits, fortified by comradeship, their sensitivity blunted by the stresses of war. They had tossed their courage into the common pool, and they drew on it as required. But the new men, outsiders at first until they proved themselves, not yet absorbed into the squadron image, had to manage for a time on their own. Day by day the news of losses from the previous night's operations ticked out on the tape in the intelligence room. Every few days the impact became close and personal through empty beds in the block. For 'Kid' Gane the squadron atmosphere at Binbrook, oppressive with irksome, petty regulations as well as with death, seemed akin to that of the morgue.

Then had come the week's confinement to camp, nerve-racking and irritating, but infectious with a sense of purpose and revitalized by a painful gestation akin to the miracle of birth. Gane had been crewed up with a 19-year-old pilot named Bruce Shearer, an Australian from Brisbane, and this had pleased him, though he thought his pilot incredibly young. The crew was made up by two more New Zealanders and another Australian, and Gane was greatly comforted at being with men of a similar background to his own. Whatever lay ahead of them, if they could face it so could he.

Bruce Shearer was of medium height, dark-haired and good-looking, with the fresh but ruddy outdoor complexion of the Queenslander. Quiet and reserved in temperament, he was not a typical Australian emotionally, though the independence of mind was there. Perhaps his upbringing had contributed to this. He had lost his parents as a child and had been brought up with special care by an uncle and aunt. He approached his task as captain of aircraft seriously and was anxious to prove himself and to lead a first-class crew. So far he had done five operational trips as second pilot, and this raid would be his first as first pilot and captain. None of his crew had any operational experience at all. Eddie Ansford, the thoughtful, unsmiling observer, and 'Mac' McKenna, the wireless operator, were from New Zealand. Bruce Brown, the bomb-aimer and front gunner, solid and steady, had been a taxi-driver in New South Wales. Like a good many other men pressed into squadron service for the raid, their first trip over Germany was going to be their last.

*

The Thousand Plan was made possible by the ubiquitous Wimpey, the crews' name for the Wellington, from J. Wellington Wimpy, the character in the Popeye strip. They made up the bulk of the force, 600 of them in all, of every mark and modification from Ia to IV, from every kind of formation and unit, flown by every Allied nationality from Czech to Pole. The Poles, indeed, formed three squadrons in No 1 Group, 300 at Ingham, 301 at Hemswell and 305 at Lindholme, all in northern Lincolnshire, with their own OTU at Bramcote. Amongst these Polish crews were some of the real veterans of military flying – men who had flown in the Polish Air Force for twenty years or more and boasted total flying hours of 15,000 plus. One such pilot, Flight Lieutenant Hirszbandt, OBE, DFC, of 305 Squadron at Lindholme, had been born in Warsaw in 1899, twenty years before most of the young British and Dominion crews taking part in the raid. Hirszbandt was a university-trained engineer and had been a major in the Polish Air Force at the time of the German attack. After the surrender he had escaped from Poland and joined the RAF. His family, if they were alive at all, were still in Poland. Such men, aggressive and fearless, contemptuous of opposition and even of death, could be forgiven for hating.

3. THE TRAINING UNITS

IN SPITE OF the instruction that as few people as possible were to be told what was afoot, it was inevitable, in a tiny country that was already packed with airfields, that news of unusual movements should be the subject of gossip in many of the smaller provincial towns. One man, recalled from leave, dropped into the Coach and Horses at Banbury on his way back to the OTU at Chipping Warden and was assured by the knowledgeable locals that he wouldn't be wasting his time much longer in training: he would be taking part in the bombing of Germany. The transport of bombs, by day or by night, was not easily camouflaged or hidden.

The man behind the counter at the NAAFI at Cottesmore, in Rutland, was always well informed. It was a part of his job. It was always useful, for business reasons, to know what was going on, who was posted in, for instance, and even more important for the collection of accounts, who was about to be posted away. But on this Saturday morning he had a special question for the wives of the aircrew men on the station when they called to do their week-end shopping.

'Is your husband going on the big raid?'

'What?'

'This big operation.'

'What operation?'

'The big raid on Hamburg.'

The woman thus addressed spoke slowly and quietly, surprised and puzzled, yet only mildly so. Dark-haired and petite, the wife of a trainee pilot, she was of a serene, even temperament and was not easily shaken.

'Hamburg? But this isn't an operational station.'

The man at the NAAFI winked knowledgeably, a gesture which suggested that he knew a great deal more than he did, and Muriel Ramsay went on with her shopping. Whatever it was, her husband would be able to reassure her when he came home to lunch.

Home for the Ramsays – temporarily – was a farmhouse at Cottesmore that was actually within the airfield boundary. The airfield had swallowed up the farm, but farmhouse and outbuildings had been allowed to remain, initially as a station commander's residence. When Tom Ramsay, or 'Mac', as he was known, was posted to No 14 OTU at Cottesmore for operational training, he looked around for possible living-out accommodation and his eye fell readily enough on the imposing Glebe House Farm. It was a large house, more like a country residence than a farmhouse, with fine mullioned windows, and when he called he found a woman named Helen Jordan living there alone with her five children. Her husband had been at Cottesmore but had been posted away, and she was glad of the

Ramsays' company. They had their own lounge and bathroom, and use of the kitchen, and the house was large enough for a second couple – their name was Richman – to have a sitting-room and a bedroom without inconveniencing anyone.

Tom Ramsay had been 30 when war broke out, and as an architectural draughtsman, which was a reserved occupation, he had had some difficulty in joining up. Although both he and his wife were Londoners, their home then had been in Leeds. Tom Ramsay was the kindest of men, with a quiet disposition, modest and retiring, honest and just, a man who never lost his temper or his poise. To balance this, though, he had an obstinate streak. It had been this obstinacy, this refusal to take no for an answer, that had finally enabled him to get into the Air Force as a pilot, despite his age and occupation. And it was a streak that was at work, too, on this warm but thundery Saturday morning in May.

The Ramsays enjoyed their life at Cottesmore. There was the Ram Jam Hotel, on the Great North Road, where they often spent their evenings. And there was Oakham, seven miles away, where they sometimes loitered in the antique shops to try to pick up something for the home they had kept on in Leeds. This morning, while Muriel Ramsay cycled across the airfield to the NAAFI, her husband was travelling into Oakham by bus. On an earlier visit with Muriel he had seen an unusual jug in one of the antique shops which had caught his fancy. Muriel had hated it, and they had done nothing about it at the time. She had said it looked evil. But Ramsay was determined to have it, even against Muriel's wishes, and this was the reason for his trip to Oakham today.

He wasn't thinking of the jug in terms of a talisman or good-luck charm, nor did the thought occur to him that, with his first operation probably facing him in a few hours' time, this might be his last chance to get it. He wasn't thinking on these lines at all. Yet both ideas must have got together somewhere in his subconscious. How else to explain this illegal sortie into Oakham, against his wife's wishes, when the whole station was nominally confined to camp?

He brought the jug home shamefacedly but without subterfuge. It was quite a large jug, holding perhaps three pints, shaped in the form of a head, with a nose and a chin jutting out from one side and a handle protruding from the other. It was the face of a man – Muriel, indeed, had said it was the face of a devil. The expression, with creases round the eyes and teeth bared, suggested pain, and a sort of strangled hatred, a hatred which Muriel cordially returned.

'Someone must have thought a lot of it, Mu,' said Ramsay persuasively, when he showed her the jug over lunch. 'Look at the way it's been repaired.' She had noticed the riveting before, when the jug was in the shop at Oakham, and she did not dispute what her husband said. 'I just don't like it,' she said. 'I think it's evil.' But her husband was the sort of person it was impossible to quarrel with, or even be angry with, and she accepted the jug reluctantly as a new possession.

'The man at the NAAFI said something about a raid tonight,' she said, after placing the jug high on a shelf, almost but not quite out of sight. 'What did he mean?'

'We're night-flying,' said Ramsay cautiously. 'That's all, so far as I know.'

'He said something about you all going to Hamburg.'

'He's mad. He ought to be reported.'

Tom Ramsay knew well enough, far better than the man at the NAAFI, that something big was afoot, that Hamburg was rumoured as the target, and that he was going to be a part of it. But he had been told to tell his wife he was night-flying, and so far as he was aware the raid was still a well-kept secret. It was his duty to deny it. And because he had never told Muriel a lie in five years of married life, or indeed ever, she accepted what he said and dismissed the idea altogether from her mind.

*

The most experienced airman going on the raid from Cottesmore was a man well known to Ramsay – Squadron Leader Donald Falconer, the commander of 'A' Flight. Thick-set,

number of days of the 'Practice' was said to be indefinite, and crews were advised to take a 'reasonable amount' of personal kit, which at the maximum should be no more than a small suit-case or half a kit-bag.

Married men at the training units mostly had their wives with them, and the order about personal kit gave them a chance to get in a quick trip to their digs to break the news to the women. Half an hour to pack – that was what they were mostly allowed. For the majority of them that meant five minutes packing and twenty-five minutes in bed, in the desperate knowledge that this might so easily be the last time – although nothing of course was ever said.

Pilot Officer David Johnson and his wife Denise – 'Dinny' – were one of those perfect young married couples often visualized but rarely seen. Everything about them, their meeting, their courtship, their marriage, had an idyllic quality. They had met on holiday at Thorpe Ness when they were both 18. He was six-foot-three, slim and athletic, with high cheekbones and a strong, prominent nose, dark-haired, with a small moustache to lend maturity. Not long since he had been captain of his school at rugger and a competitor at the junior tennis championships at Wimbledon. She was a foot shorter, perfectly proportioned, with shoulder-length fair hair worn in the page-boy style of the time. He was gay but not irresponsible; she was a fatalist. They both lived very much for the day; within a few hours they found they were living for each other. They took such a delight in each other's company that they spent every available minute of that holiday together, under the disapproving eye of her aunt, with whom she was staying, and his parents, with whom he was on holiday. Both families objected to such a close relationship, on the grounds of their youth and careers. As a photographer's, artist's and fashion model she had exceptional prospects, not only in her career but in marriage; he was apprenticed to Daimler's in Coventry and was studying for an engineering degree. Two other less tangible factors were present to intensify their mutual attraction and add piquancy to the stimulus of parental opposition – he was a trainee pilot in the volunteer reserve; and it was the summer of 1939.

At the end of that holiday they became engaged. With parents still disapproving, she left home and took a job in Coventry to be near him, and they spent all their free time together. When war broke out he was called up immediately, and she followed him to his initial training at Cambridge. Just before he was posted to flying training three months later they were married, still without parental consent. They were only 19. Since then she had lost count of the airfields to which she had followed him.

But in spite of all the fears and temporary separations there had never been any kind of shadow across their happiness. He was of a calm, even disposition, she was not the worrying kind, and the stresses which had sent many a pilot's wife home to her family a nervous wreck were borne much more easily by a girl with a belief, however vague, in predestination. Life was now, not tomorrow, and they lived every moment of it. It wasn't that tomorrow never came; that wasn't it at all. They were optimistic and they believed in the future. It was just that they never thought about it.

Early in 1942 David Johnson was posted as a staff pilot to the Central Gunnery School at Sutton Bridge; he found digs about a mile from the airfield. Now, with two other pilots from the School, all of them with scratch crews, he was to fly down to Feltwell in a Wellington Ia to take part in some sort of practice – that was what they called it. Most people had other ideas. He might be back in a week, he might never come back at all. All he knew was that he had to see Dinny before he went.

They had their few precious minutes together, and then he was gone. And when he said good-bye, it was not just to Dinny alone. Not any more. He said good-bye, too, to Clive, their 6-months-old son.

*

At Driffield, in addition to No 158 Squadron, there was a blind approach training flight and a target-towing and gunnery flight, both staffed by screened personnel, both using Whitleys.

The Whitleys were serviceable enough for local flying, but there was a lot of work to be done on them if they were to be got ready for a long operational flight. And to make up a full crew for each aircraft, several spare trainees had to be found from other stations. The work went on all that week, and with the uncertain promise of some secret and special operation in the offing, nervous tension on the station rose perceptibly, especially amongst the screened personnel. One man who seemed unaffected by it was the commander of the blind approach training flight, a 21-year-old squadron leader named John Russell. Born in Oban, Argyllshire, tall, slim, curly-haired and boyish, John Russell was one of the most colourful personalities on the station. Already he had been awarded the DFC. Artistic and high-spirited, his style and manner were more that of the fighter than the bomber pilot, and he had managed to keep his hand in operationally by begging to be allowed to take part in an occasional sortie over enemy territory – and somehow getting his way. One almost felt that a refusal would not have stopped him – indeed there were rumours of a lone operation against orders. Thoroughly reliable in his work, John Russell had retained that adventurous streak which outsiders took for rashness and irresponsibility. He was neither of those things, but he was as yet untamed.

*

'I'm posted to Snaith, Yorkshire. That's not too bad, it is?'

The diminutive, energetic sergeant pilot from Alresford in Hampshire had always known what he wanted. First, when he left school at the age of 14, it had been cars. Then in 1936 he had joined the Air Force as a trainee flight mechanic, transferring later to the trade of fitter; and when the war came he remustered to airman pilot. Early in 1942 he was posted to No 27 OTU at Lichfield to graduate on Wellingtons. It was at Lichfield that he met Lillian Fiddian, a WAAF who worked in the fabric section.

The Wellington was of geodetic construction, the surfaces being fabric instead of metal. Other responsibilities of the fabric section included dinghies and dinghy equipment. One morning the crews were taken round to examine the survival gear, and among them was Freddie Hillyer. At once his eye fell on a young girl of striking freshness, alert and petite, who, in variation of the old song, was sucking milk through a straw. He wandered rather sheepishly across to her, and grinned, and she shared the bottle with him.

For many women the curly, tousle-headed Fred Hillyer, slim and wasted as a jockey, quietly spoken but with a warm Hampshire accent, would have aroused the protective instinct. The intuitive Lillian Fiddian saw deeper than this, saw that this young man had an inner strength and a secure background that she herself lacked. She knew right from the beginning that he was the man for her.

The posting to Snaith was a blow, but they had been expecting something like it. At first she felt frightened at the prospect of his going, but the surroundings at Lichfield had become friendly and comforting since they had absorbed the ambience of her attachment to Fred Hillyer. She was thrilled and proud for him that he had completed his training and was about to do what he wanted to do, to fly on operations over Germany.

Hillyer's course at Lichfield ended a few days before the big raid and as many crews as there were aircraft available were held back to take part in it. Hillyer and his crew were among the men who were not retained and they went on leave. At this stage the choice seemed purely capricious – no one knew yet about the raid. Hillyer went home to Alresford, but within a day or so, on Friday 29th May, the tray that carried his morning tea also held a telegram. He was to report immediately to RAF Station Wing, near Leighton Buzzard.

After six years in the Service Hillyer was sceptical about recall telegrams, and he was in the Bell Hotel at Alresford that lunchtime when he heard his name called.

'Fred! You're wanted – by the police!'

The RAF orderly room staffs were taking no chances. They had telephoned the local police. Soon Fred Hillyer, complete with kit-bags, was on his way to Leighton Buzzard. When he finally got to Wing he found himself amongst an assortment of aircrew of varied experience, hardly any of whom he had met before, all of whom were talking in excited tones about a possible big raid. Only a handful were from Lichfield – his own crew and one other. Some of the men were in the middle of their training, others were instructors with an operational tour behind them. The trainees were nudging as close as they could to the veterans, picking up tips about flak, fighters, searchlights, ditchings, bale-outs, escape and evasion. Hillyer discovered that Wing was the headquarters of another bomber OTU – No 26. The two crews from Lichfield – Whiting was the other pilot's name – had been sent for to man two spare Wellingtons. He learned, too, that his aircraft was waiting for him at a nearby satellite field called Cheddington, and that they were all to operate from a new airfield at Graveley, twenty miles away.

Hillyer got into conversation with an instructor named Ford, a flight sergeant with the DFM, whose high colour belied his abstemious habits and quiet temperament. At 31 Ford was older than the average pilot; he had been a motor salesman in civilian life. Ford gave Hillyer several useful tips, one of which described what to do if he got caught in searchlights. 'Dive down the beam,' said Ford, 'and then pull out. That usually shakes them off.'

All Hillyer's crew had turned up at Wing. Smith, the rear gunner, the only married man, was the oldest; short and tubby, he sat in his turret smoking his pipe in spite of repeated warnings from Hillyer. The youngest was the bomb-aimer, a 22-year-old pilot officer named Cyril White, the only commissioned man in the crew. Cyril White was the son of a parson, but he had had his own beliefs disturbed during a theological course at Oxford, and he had decided not after all to enter the Church. He had joined the RAF.

Next morning Hillyer and his crew were taken by road to Cheddington. They were not returning to Wing, so they took their kit-bags with them. They were met at Cheddington by a flight sergeant fitter. 'Your machine's just had an overhaul,' he said, 'and it's virtually ready. Would you fly it to Graveley? They'll complete everything outstanding there. I can't give you any fuel here but you've got enough to get to Graveley.'

Hillyer discovered that there was 5 lb of boost on one engine and only 2 lb on the other. The brakes were faulty, and the compass hadn't been swung. There were several other minor defects. But even these unpromising details didn't altogether dampen the enthusiasm of Hillyer and his crew. Hillyer warmed up the engines and they started off. The uneven boost made for an erratic take-off, but once airborne it didn't matter. Graveley, astride the Great North Road near Stevenage, was a short hop and they were soon in the circuit. Clearly it was a new field – huge runways, few administrative buildings and only one hangar. Traces of the previous occupiers of the land were still visible; the dispersals backed on to a row of recently evacuated chicken-houses. Hillyer landed carefully, treating the brakes gently, and he and his crew went for a meal. They were told that their machine would be refuelled and that they would take off that evening for a target in Germany.

No ground servicing seemed to be available, but as a former NCO fitter Hillyer was not unduly concerned. He inspected the engines, borrowed a landing compass and enlisted the help of some Army gunners from a nearby gunpost to turn the Wellington through the various headings necessary for the calculation of compass deviation. He corrected most of the minor unserviceabilities, but he could do little about the boost.

A petrol bowser came round and filled the plane up with fuel, but half an hour later the driver came back to say that there wasn't enough fuel to go round and that it would have to be rationed. One hundred and twenty gallons of precious fuel were taken out. Then the armourers came round and loaded the incendiaries. The business of getting the aircraft ready took the entire day.

No doubt Hillyer and his crew were fortunate at being so fully occupied. When an airman's life was suddenly disrupted in this way, when he was dumped in a strange and cheerless land, he was apt to remember the arithmetic that most of the time he managed to forget, the figures that told him that he had no chance, and he felt the chill certainty of death. It was at times like this that an airman cursed his luck. He knew well enough the part luck played in his expectation of life. Like cards, there was a certain amount of skill involved, but a great deal of it was luck. And just the same as at cards, if you felt your luck had run out, it always did.

Cyril White found a quiet corner and sat down to write a letter home. 'Since I last wrote,' he said, 'I have been on three different aerodromes. I can't tell you where I am now and you mustn't tell anyone at all. I can tell you this, it's a big job. . . . There's a grand possibility, a really big one, that I shall never come back.'

In the circumstances it was remarkable that Hillyer and Whiting and their crews kept up their spirits to the extent they did. Not only were their surroundings unfamiliar and their comforts meagre; they had no accommodation of any kind. When Hillyer took off from Cheddington that morning he had carried the crew's kit-bags in the aircraft. There was nowhere at Graveley for them to settle in and unpack. Yet they could hardly take their kit-bags with them to Cologne. When the time for take-off approached, they carried their kit-bags to one of the empty chicken-houses and dumped them inside. Then they wrote out a notice and nailed it to the hut. 'This belongs,' they wrote, 'to the crew of O for Orange.'

What would happen to that pathetic notice, and to the precious belongings of the five men who pinned it there? Would they get back to claim it?

*

'What's it like on ops these days, John?'

At No 11 OTU at Bassingbourn, many of the instructors had been off operations for at least a year. For them the news that they were to take part in a big bombing raid on Germany came as a shock. The bombing of Germany at night in early 1941 had been practically unopposed. In the course of the year the defences had been strengthened, and now they were clearly formidable, judging from the numbers of bombers that failed to return whenever a deep penetration was attempted. This looked like being a very different party from the old days, and the veterans turned to the man who had come most recently from a squadron – the 20-year-old Sergeant John Bulford.

Bulford was a quietly spoken young man with jet black hair, bushy black eyebrows and small, black, deep-set eyes, not a person of great animation, but one who at once created an impression of stolid power, with obvious qualities of leadership. A man of lucid mind and expression, he could turn those penetrative eyes inwards at himself without undue danger of introspection. Somehow he had missed a commission at the outset, but his superiors had no doubt that he was commissioning material, and they had already hinted to him at Bassingbourn that after two or three months on the unit, and assuming he did well, his application would be forwarded with favourable comment. This meant a lot to Bulford, who was ambitious and wanted to get on.

He reassured his fellow instructors where he felt reassurance was necessary, but he did not omit to warn them of the very different reception they must expect nowadays over enemy territory. Inevitably, when it came to the allocation of crews, the older instructors got the more experienced men, but Bulford got a screened rear gunner and wireless operator, and the only pupils he was given were two New Zealanders, both recently arrived from initial training in their native country.

Bulford had that aura of loneliness that sets a man apart from his fellows. He was undemonstrative, and not unduly sensitive to atmosphere. The excitement before the action left him unmoved. He was confident of his ability to find the target, even with a trainee navigator, and he took the prospect of the raid in his stride.

★

Sergeant Jack Paul, a tall, solid Midlander of slow speech and determined mien, heard the first whisper about the raid on the top deck of a bus bound from Didcot to the No 15 OTU base at Harwell, on his return from honeymoon leave. Two or three men from the camp were travelling on the same bus. He was nudged to attention, then treated to a loud and significant whisper.

'Something queer's on.'

'What is it?'

'What do you think's been arriving at the camp? Bombs! Lovely great big bombs!'

Jack Paul had spent his honeymoon at Stratford-on-Avon. He had been married a week. He had completed a bombing tour on Wellingtons in the Middle East and was now an instructor. Calm and unexcitable, he felt a queer flutter in the stomach at this suggestible whisper. When he got to Harwell he discussed it with his close friend Jack Hatton. Hatton, an ex-Cranwell apprentice, now 26, had the typical veneer of the regular airman of his time – the casual, light-hearted exterior beneath which lay the firm confidence generated by thorough training and physical fitness. Dark-haired, with a thin, dark moustache and strong white teeth, he relaxed easily in off-duty hours and had a prodigious memory for RAF drinking songs. Now, with the regular airman's inoculation against rumour and counter-rumour, he shrugged his shoulders and laughed. 'We'll know soon enough what's happening. How did the wedding go? When's Joyce coming?'

'I'm cycling into Didcot tonight to fix something. Joyce is coming up by train on Sunday. The flap ought to be over by then.'

Paul cycled into Didcot that evening on a tandem which he had bought in anticipation of pleasant summer evenings in the Oxfordshire countryside. He booked some lodgings, then went back and wrote to his wife. 'I'm not quite sure whether I'll be on duty on Sunday or not,' he told her, 'but I'll send you a telegram on Sunday morning telling you what train to catch, and I'll meet you at Didcot.' He had made the journey only just in time; next day the whole station was confined to camp.

*

Several of the instructors at No 12 OTU were on leave when news of the raid reached Chipping Warden. They were quickly recalled. For them the most disquieting feature was that the men not on leave had already formed themselves into tight little groups of five – the crew of a Wellington. To find their own names on the detail they had to search through a supplementary list of stand-by aircrew who in emergency might be required to make up the number in any of the listed crews.

One of the men thus left in uneasy suspense was a sandy-haired regular airman named Ronald Grundy. Grundy's ambition had always been to be a pilot, but his application in 1935 at the age of 19 had been turned down. Later he had joined as a ground wireless operator, then taken an air gunner's course. By the autumn of 1940 he had completed an operational tour.

At Chipping Warden he had been offered a commission, but he had refused it for two reasons. First, he was married and his wife was expecting a baby; he had digs in Wardington, not far from the camp, and he feared a posting on commissioning. Secondly, he had applied for training as a pilot; a commission as a wireless operator/air gunner might prejudice his chances.

It was very difficult in wartime to get reliable advice on these personal things. No one could promise anything, still less put it on paper. A man simply had to back his hunch. Ever since 1935 Ronald Grundy had had an abiding ambition – to be a pilot. He still put it first, even before a commission.

On the Saturday afternoon, a few hours before the raid was due, he heard that a wireless operator in a pupil crew had been taken ill and that he was to fill the vacancy. This was exactly what he had been afraid of. He knew the plane he was to fly in – it was an old drogue-towing Wimpey with a winch in the rear of the fuselage, making it difficult to pass to and from the rear turret. But it behaved all right on air test. He knew the pilot vaguely; his name was Bob Ferrer and he came from Stetchford, Birmingham. Ferrer lived out with his wife in the same block of council cottages in Wardington, and the two wives had got to know each other.

The rest of the crew were Canadian. The navigator, Albin Lucki, of Polish extraction, had been teaching in Canada when he volunteered for the RCAF. With his corn-coloured hair and startling, piercing, Prussian-blue eyes he made an immediate impression on Grundy. Kenneth Buck, the 19-year-old front gunner and bomb-aimer, had also impressed his personality on Grundy by that evening. Rugged, athletic, thick-set, forthright and outspoken, he was an obvious extrovert. The one man Grundy saw little of was Mackenzie, the rear gunner, but he took the trouble to check on the crew's training record at Chipping Warden and found that they had all done well.

4. THE HEAVIES

THE LAST FIFTEEN minutes of the raid would be the most concentrated of all. In this period more than 200 heavy bombers from Nos 4 and 5 Groups – about 130 Halifaxes, and 75 of the new Lancasters – would arrive over the target. Some of the Lancasters would be operating over Germany for the first time. This section of the force, not only the most concentrated but carrying the greatest weight of bombs, was expected to deliver the final knock-out punch.

The most northerly of all the bomber bases was the 4 Group station at Middleton St George, in the Pennines, on the Yorkshire/Durham border. It housed a Halifax squadron – No 76 – with its own conversion unit. On that Saturday afternoon, twenty-one aircraft were being loaded with 1,000-pounders and incendiaries for the raid. The same thing was happening five miles to the south-west at Croft, a hutted satellite of Middleton, which also housed a Halifax squadron with its own conversion unit.

A good many of the things that happened on a squadron

were almost unbearably tragic. Others were uproariously funny. Paddy Todd, an Irishman from Belfast, dark-haired and round-faced, of less than medium height but not short, had a wonderfully expressive face that seemed to be ready for anything. It was the set of the mouth that did it, and of course the eyes and the eyebrows. But even the most solemn expression soon broke up into a grin. Paddy Todd loved squadron life and wouldn't have left it for the world.

Todd had joined No 205 (Ulster) Auxiliary Squadron in 1935 and had been mobilized in 1939. From the outbreak of war he had flown as a wireless operator/air gunner with Coastal Command on patrols and convoy escorts. Early in 1941 he had completed his tour; his posting had been to Canada, as an instructor. This was no good to Todd, and he had said so. He was one of the boys – mostly one of the good boys: he believed in discipline, and he obeyed orders, except of course when he didn't quite agree with them, when he would find a way round them if he could. If he couldn't, he wasn't afraid to speak out. It was no good arguing with an Irishman, and you couldn't put a chap like Paddy Todd in irons. He would only laugh at you. So when he refused to go to Canada, his punishment was an immediate posting – to No 78 Squadron. Three days later he found himself on York station with his kit-bags, bound for the airfield at Croft. They had flung him just about as far as they could. But he wasn't a bit depressed about it, and as he stood on York station he couldn't resist chuckling to himself. He had got exactly what he wanted. And when he got to the squadron, and the gunnery leader sent for him and promised him a month's training and familiarization before sending him on operations, Todd looked upon such molly-coddling as an insult. He handed his log book to the gunnery leader with an insolent grin.

'Wipe your nose on that.'

Two nights later he was flying over Germany.

Todd had a sense of humour and the ridiculous that was almost Chinese; everything in life was basically comical. This perhaps explained his apparent genius for finding funny books,

books that made you laugh out loud. He always took a book into the air with him, and when he wasn't actually in the turret, chuckles and guffaws of laughter could always be heard from him. He radiated honesty, too, but like most wartime aircrew he wasn't averse to a little honest fiddling. There were always opportunities of 'winning' something. After a crash-landing on a strange airfield, when the aircraft had burnt out, he had rescued and won a parachute. The silk of the canopy was a valuable commodity in wartime, especially with the women.

For more than five months that parachute had remained in Paddy Todd's locker. He hadn't known what to do with it. Now something had happened which made him anxious to rid himself of that damning evidence. He was up for a commission. The SPs were always suspicious of aircrew, always on the prowl, always uncovering some petty crime. All it wanted was for someone to give an order for a general search of lockers, and he would be caught. That would certainly cost him his commission.

The long wait with no operations in the last ten days of May gave him plenty of time to brood on his problem. Meanwhile the excitement at Croft increased daily. The serviceability state reached its highest peak, and the conversion unit was working overtime, getting every available pilot ready. 'Bomber' Harris was up to something, that was clear. Todd and his friends in the Sergeants' Mess had a high regard for Harris. Things had changed a lot since he took over. He didn't suffer fools. He had cleared away the dead-wood, got rid of what they termed the 'nancy-boys', the smooth-talking men in smooth battle-dress who rarely seemed to fly. He had given them good leaders, increased their confidence, showed them what they could do if they tried.

Almost every pilot at Croft had converted on to Halifaxes under a squadron leader named Peter James, the man who was working overtime to get everyone fit for the raid. James was 6 feet 2½ inches tall, with very long legs, and feet that splayed out. His dark hair, close-cropped at the temples, clung easily to his scalp, he had a frank open face and an engaging smile, and he was one of those fortunate men who could maintain the aura of seniority and command and at the same time pass as one of the boys.

Conversion flying was hard work, involving continual circuits and landings, four hours at a time, with four different pilots taking their turn. Then when the morning session was over the aircraft were serviced and fuelled ready for night flying. This was how Peter James spent his operational rest. Few men were more relaxed and even-tempered, yet there came a time when he was biting his lip until it bled.

On 18th May, 78 Squadron were given a new squadron commander, a solid, ponderous, weather-beaten man named Sam Lucas who combined a love of beer and good company with an artistic background. Peter James had the task of checking him out on the Halifax. Lucas, a photographic specialist, had done very little flying since the war started. But he was determined to lead the squadron on the big raid, and throughout that final week he was still practising night landings with Peter James.

To Paddy Todd the general absorption with the raid spelt opportunity; he made up his mind at last what to do with his loot. Tubby Porter, the flight engineer in his crew, had given him the idea. Tubby hated the Germans so much that every time he flew over Germany he poured the contents of the Elsan down the flare-chute. Why not take the parachute with him and dump it overboard? In the general excitement on the night he would be able to smuggle it on board without attracting attention. Most of his crew knew about it anyway, though that didn't include his skipper, the tall university graduate Bob Plutte. Pluto would have made him give it back straight away. He had a lot of time for Bob Plutte. But on the night of the big raid he would dump the parachute over the target. That was the answer to his problem.

All went well at Croft until mid-afternoon, when a Halifax about to take off on test swerved badly off the perimeter track, flattened a bicycle and collided with another Halifax at dispersal. A flight sergeant who was on the spot attacked the resultant flames with a fire extinguisher, but the dispersed Halifax was badly damaged and the offending aircraft was a write-off. The flight sergeant, who had worked for many days and nights on these two machines, was almost in tears when Sam Lucas arrived on the scene. 'Look what the madman's done!' he raved. Then his eye caught something else, even more outrageous and personal. 'And what's more – look at my bloody bicycle!'

*

Many of the men who later became famous far beyond Bomber Command were amongst the crews of the heavy-bomber squadrons. Willie Tait was commanding No 10 Squadron at Leeming, twelve miles south of Croft; three weeks earlier he had taken over from Don Bennett, missing in an attack on the *Tirpitz*. (Bennett escaped through Sweden, and by a coincidence it was Tait who afterwards led 617 Squadron in the raid which sank the German battleship.) Many of the men who later formed 617 were on the raid. Hopgood and Maudslay, killed in the raid on the Mohne and Eder dams a year later, were on 106 and 44 respectively. Calder, first man to drop the 22,000 lb 'Grand Slam' bomb – on the Bielefeld viaduct – was at Middleton St George on 76. Fauquier, later to be 617's last wartime commander, was leading No 405 (RCAF) Squadron at Pocklington, near York. His squadron had just been converted on to Halifaxes by No 1652 Conversion Unit at Marston Moor; commanding this conversion unit was a young squadron leader named Leonard Cheshire. Although most of the squadrons ran small conversion flights, a central conversion unit for the Halifax had become essential, and Cheshire had been running it – under protest, because he hated being taken off operations – for seven months.

Guy Gibson had just taken over 106 Squadron at Coningsby. The squadron was in the process of converting from Manchesters to Lancasters, but despite the many difficulties this caused they were getting ready to put up eleven Lancasters and five Manchesters. It was their first operation in the Lancaster.

Guy Gibson had no crew as yet and was not taking part.

One of Cheshire's senior pilots at the conversion unit was a flight lieutenant named Stanley Wright. There was no more loyal officer in the Air Force, yet twice in twelve months Wright had caused inconvenience to the Royal Family, and on the second occasion had actually endangered their lives. Tall and Brian Aherne-ish, Wright had first earned His Majesty's (entirely impersonal) displeasure by force-landing in his Whitley on the Royal Estate at Sandringham. On the second occasion, in March 1942, His Majesty's displeasure had been less impersonal.

The King and Queen were due to visit the RAF station at Leeming, where Wright was commanding the 10 Squadron conversion flight. During the morning, Wright sent one of his pupils up solo in a Halifax. While he was airborne, a Whitley crashed and blocked the main runway. Wright had to call his pupil on the R/T and tell him to land at Croft. After lunch he drove over to Croft to collect his aircraft and pupil. But meanwhile, at Leeming, an experimental mine with which Don Bennett was planning to attack the *Tirpitz* had fallen off a Halifax as it came in to land. It was some time before the mine could be rendered safe and moved, and the arrival of the King and Queen had to be delayed. The whole programme, unknown to Wright and his pupil, was put back more than an hour. Thus when Wright flew his pupil back from Croft late that afternoon, the Royal visit that he thought was over was still in progress.

Wright began a fast run over the airfield, beating up the open tarmac between the two main hangars. As he swooped low towards the tarmac he saw something loom up in his windscreen that looked like a full-dress parade. It *was* a full-dress parade. Wright's instinctive reaction to pull out of the dive only made the beat-up more impressive. King George VI and Queen Elizabeth were in the middle of their inspection.

Next morning Wright was sent for by the station commander. 'You're posted. The adjutant will give you the details. I want you off the station today.' The posting had been to

Marston Moor. It had been good-bye to all his friends, and, more significant when he heard the news about the big raid, good-bye to his trusted crew.

Wright expected to be able to find his way to and from the target easily enough; what he felt would be needed were experienced gunners. He especially dreaded surprise attack from the rear. When he was given his crew, three of them, navigator, wireless operator and tail gunner, were spare men straight from training. They were keen chaps, good chaps, but inevitably raw. The only crew-man of experience was the flight engineer, Lowman, who was with Wright on the conversion unit. He regretted that unwitting beat-up of Their Majesties more than ever.

Wright's apprehensions about attack from the rear were to prove all too well founded.

*

The fluctuating and inconstant progress of Bomber Command in the previous twelve months was recorded in microcosm in the log book of Flight Lieutenant George Gilpin, a Yorkshireman of ruddy complexion who before the war had been in the property business in Leeds but who looked much more like a farmer (and afterwards became one). Gilpin had begun his operational career on 61 Squadron at Syerston exactly a year earlier, in May 1941. The squadron had then had Hampdens. Gilpin had completed a routine ten trips as navigator and followed this with eight trips as pilot before the squadron changed to Manchesters in January 1942. He had done twelve trips on Manchesters to complete his tour by April 1942, and then the squadron had changed again, this time to Lancasters. With a squadron leader named Rupert Gascoyne-Cecil, Gilpin was given the job of running the conversion flight, training new pilots on the Manchester and converting squadron pilots to the Lancaster.

Like the vast majority of Bomber Command aircrew, Gilpin was a man who carried out his work conscientiously and in accordance with both the spirit and letter of the order yet who would have ridiculed any tag of heroism. He was doing his job to the best of his ability, but he was doing it in the knowledge that the bombing of Germany was a long-term business and that it was in everyone's interest that he and his crew should survive as long as possible.

The war was a welcome change from property. There was no getting away from that. For the millions, war was monstrous, shameful, abhorrent, pitiless. For a few tens of thousands, war was a liberation. Flying in wartime was an unforgettable experience, however much it frightened you at times. And being frightened was rather like the chap being hit over the head with a mallet; it was so wonderfully uplifting when it stopped. In any case, no one really expected to survive the war, so every day lived could be counted as a bonus, a daily stimulant which gave a continually heightened perception.

No 408 (RCAF) Squadron, the other squadron nominally at Syerston, had been dispersed to a nearby satellite at Balderton, so there was plenty of room at Syerston, and the station had been chosen to accommodate the five Hampdens of Flying Training Command from the gunnery school at Jurby which were to take part in the raid. Three of the five Hampdens left Jurby on 25th May, together with three Ansons and two Blenheims carrying maintenance crews. But the standards of navigation at a gunnery school, adequate for local flying, were not perhaps up to squadron level. Only one of the Ansons and the two Blenheims reached Syerston before dark. Most of the others had force-landed after missing their way.

Eventually four of the Hampdens made it, and two more arrived from Manby, making six in all. The crews, many of them normally considered too old for operational flying, arrived in a spirit of high adventure, thrilled at the prospect of operating over Germany. The Messes were now packed out and the atmosphere was tense, rowdy and expectant. Unfortunately all the Hampden crews had arrived short of essential flying clothing and equipment, all the aircraft were unserviceable by operational standards and all revealed an excessive consumption of oil. It seemed extremely doubtful whether they would be able to go.

In the next three days, while the raid was postponed from day to day, all squadron aircraft were made ready, while work proceeded on the Hampdens. The two aircraft of the conversion flight were also got ready, and the station commander, Gus Walker, told Gascoyne-Cecil and Gilpin that they could go if they could each find a crew.

The first question to be decided was who was to have the Lancaster and who the Manchester. Gascoyne-Cecil, feeling that he could hardly send his deputy in an aircraft known to be so much inferior, decided that this was not the time either to pull rank or for magnanimous gestures: it was a clear case for tossing up. Gilpin won the toss, and he did not need to name his choice.

That's grand, thought Gilpin, but how to find a crew? Some of his original squadron crew were with him on the conversion flight and he had already earmarked them, but all squadron personnel were committed. Bit by bit he managed to fill all the places except one – bomb-aimer. John Beach, his navigator and former school contemporary, could drop the bombs, but the bomb-aimer also acted as front gunner, and he wasn't keen to do the trip with an empty front turret. There was only one answer: over a jug in the Mess at lunchtime he would have to buttonhole one of the chaps from Jurby. Some of the Hampdens were reckoned to be unserviceable and he ought to be able to get a gunner.

At first the task proved impossible. All the Jurby men were still hoping to go. Gilpin and his crew combed the station without success. Then came the news that the Hampdens were scrubbed. Gilpin went straight to the Mess and pounced on a man in his thirties who wore the aircrew half-wing – a Flying Officer D. H. Brewer. In his eagerness Gilpin did not notice that it was the badge of a navigator. But Brewer, who had never been in a Lancaster in his life, let alone in a power-operated Lancaster turret, agreed to go.

PART III

BRIEFING AND INTRUSION

1. *BRIEFING*

THERE WAS STILL time, of course, for a nervous commander to dither. All that Saturday a drama was being enacted over which Harris could exercise no control – the drama of the weather. It was normal procedure for a final decision, based on the latest weather information, to be taken by Harris late in the afternoon. The executive order had been given by phone after the morning conference, and by midday it had been confirmed by signal, but the countrywide activity that had been set in motion could still be arrested on a word from Harris.

The one o'clock forecast was not reassuring. Over Cologne there was still much residual cloud. It was tending to clear, but probably only to about seven-tenths. Other parts of Germany were worse. Half the bases in Lincolnshire were expected to be unfit through fog by the time the bombers were due to return. Harris read the forecast impassively and directed Spence to come in again with the latest news after considering the 16.00 hours synoptic chart.

By five o'clock Spence had prepared his most detailed forecast of the day. Conditions over the bases at take-off would be good except for local thunderstorms. There would be thick cloud up to 15,000 feet along the route to Cologne, with more thunderstorms, and the icing index would be high, but conditions would tend to improve for the return flight. Over Cologne itself Spence predicted that the cloud would begin to disperse by midnight, and he hoped for large breaks over the target area. Visibility would deteriorate over eastern England as the night progressed, particularly in Lincolnshire and Yorkshire, but only about a quarter of the total number of bases would be affected. From all this it was clear that a small miscalculation, either about the time or extent of the cloud dispersion over Cologne, or the timing of the deterioration over the bases, could still wreck the raid.

Harris, however, did not change his mind. As Saundby left the C-in-C's office he ran into Dudley Saward. 'What's going to happen?' asked Saward. 'Is it going to be all right?'

'I hope so,' said Saundby. He gave a somewhat guilty grin. 'I expect it will be. The C-in-C always has the luck of the devil.'

All day at the bases the work on the aircraft had continued. Saundby and Elworthy kept in touch with the group commanders, the group commanders rang their stations, and visited them wherever they could. Across the fens and lowlands of East Anglia, on the exposed plains of Lincolnshire, on the moors and the wolds of the north, and between the Chilterns and the Cotswolds, the work went forward. The very names of the airfields provided a battle order whose recital was as thrilling as a list of regiments. Elsham Wolds, Binbrook, Lindholme, Snaith, Breighton, Ingham, Grimsby, Hemswell – this was the clutch of bases comprising No 1 Group. Marham, Mildenhall, Lakenheath, Feltwell, Stradishall, Alconbury, Honington, Wyton, Oakington, Bourn – these were the 3 Group bases in East Anglia. And of No 4 Group, in Yorkshire – Driffield, Dalton, Leeming, Linton, Pocklington, Croft, Marston Moor and Middleton St George. Of No 5 Group – Scampton, Syerston, Skellingthorpe, Waddington, Woodhall Spa, Balderton, Bottesford, Coningsby. And of the OTU groups, from north to south: Finningley and Bircotes; Cottesmore, Lichfield, Bramcote, Graveley; Wellesbourne Mountford and Stratford; Chipping Warden, Pershore, Bassingbourn and Steeple Morden; Moreton in the Marsh and Edgehill; Upper Heyford, Abingdon and Stanton Harcourt, Harwell and Hampstead Norris. Fifty-three airfields where wires were buzzing, where station and squadron commanders were continually on their internal phones, nagging the lives out of their engineering staffs; where, during the day, most of the aircrews carried out their night-flying tests before going to their bunks for a rest, and to write, perhaps, that last letter; where maintenance and servicing teams, riggers and fitters, radar, signals and electrical mechanics, sweated in the stuffy aircraft and in every workshop and hangar, while bowsers filled petrol tanks by the thousand and cranes lowered the bombs from the bomb-dumps for the armourers to tow to dispersal and haul under the gaping bellies of the bombers. Four-thousand-pounders, 2,000-pounders, 1,000, 500 and 250-pounders, and above all, incendiaries, 4 lb and 30 lb incendiaries, thousands and thousands of them, canister after canister bound for the same address – an address still undisclosed. For clerks, for telephone operators, for drivers, for cooks – for everyone, RAF and WAAF, man and woman, it was the longest day. Incredibly, by teatime they had more bombers ready on many stations than the squadrons had crews to man. Station and squadron staffs volunteered to fill the gap, the example being set in some cases – as at Elsham Wolds – by the station commander himself. Even so, such was the enthusiasm and skill of the ground teams that not all the bombers got ready for the raid could be manned.

There were Lancasters, Halifaxes, Stirlings, Manchesters, Wellingtons, Hampdens and Whitleys. There were four Canadian squadrons, three Polish, one Australian, one New Zealand, one Rhodesian and countless individual Commonwealth airmen in the squadrons of the RAF. There were certainly at least five Americans, all in the RCAF. Flight Sergeant R. J. Campbell, a twenty-three-year-old wireless operator/air gunner from Pawling, New York, had joined in mid-1940 because he wanted to get into the war on the ground floor. He was flying in a Halifax of No 405 (RCAF) Squadron from Pocklington; his pilot, Squadron Leader Keith Thiele, came from Christchurch, New Zealand, his navigator from Ottawa. Campbell had done more than twenty raids; round his neck he wore the medallion of St Christopher. Thirty-one-year-old Sergeant Charles Honeychurch came from Brooklyn; he was a graduate of Erasmus High School and had spent two years at Brooklyn

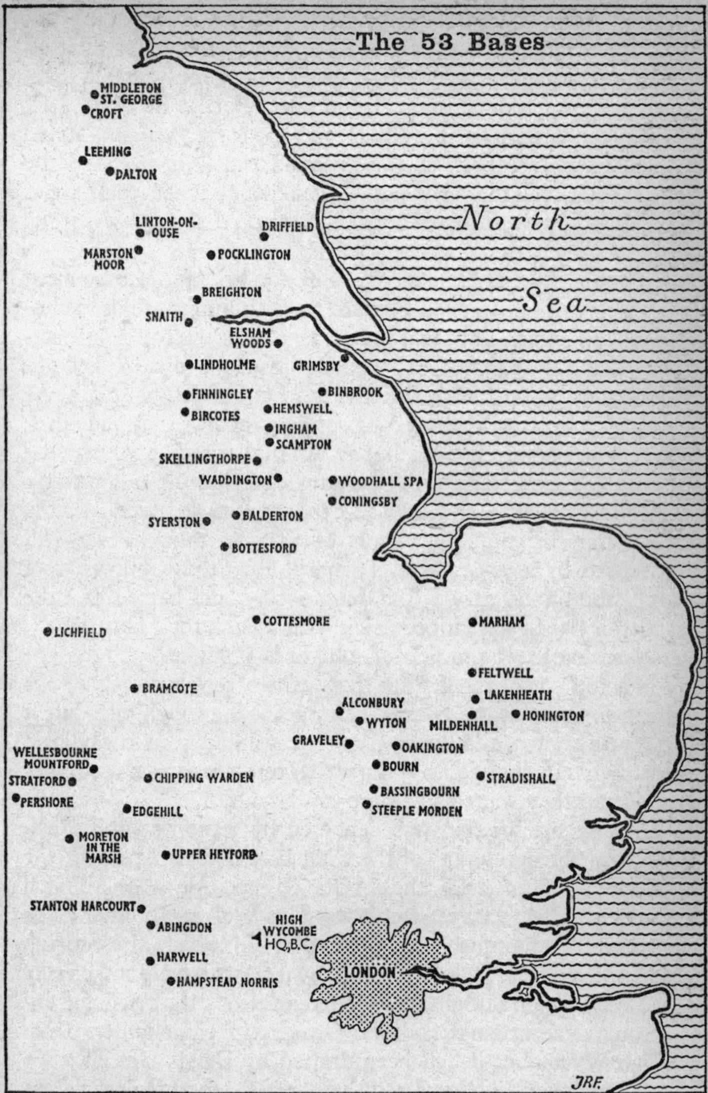
The 53 Bases
North Sea
MIDDLETON ST. GEORGE
CROFT
LEEMING
DALTON
LINTON-ON-OUSE
DRIFFIELD
MARSTON MOOR
POCKLINGTON
BREIGHTON
SNAITH
ELSHAM WOODS
LINDHOLME
GRIMSBY
FINNINGLEY
BINBROOK
BIRCOTES
HEMSWELL
INGHAM
SCAMPTON
SKELLINGTHORPE
WADDINGTON
WOODHALL SPA
CONINGSBY
SYERSTON
BALDERTON
BOTTESFORD
COTTESMORE
MARHAM
LICHFIELD
FELTWELL
BRAMCOTE
LAKENHEATH
ALCONBURY
HONINGTON
WYTON
MILDENHALL
GRAVELEY
OAKINGTON
WELLESBOURNE MOUNTFORD
BOURN
STRATFORD
CHIPPING WARDEN
STRADISHALL
BASSINGBOURN
PERSHORE
EDGEHILL
STEEPLE MORDEN
MORETON IN THE MARSH
UPPER HEYFORD
STANTON HARCOURT
HIGH WYCOMBE
ABINGDON
HQ, B.C.
HARWELL
LONDON
HAMPSTEAD NORRIS
JRF.

College. Flying Officer Frank Roper was a Lancaster pilot on No 207 Squadron at Bottesford. Twenty-one-year-old Sergeant Bud Cardinal came from Fort Worth; he and 'Tex' Tate, the American in Wilf Davis's crew at Marham, styled themselves members of the Royal Texan Air Force – the 'RTAF.' In all there were more than 6,000 airmen, unaware as yet that they were about to make history, yet slowly awakening to their strength.

Then at last, at six o'clock, came the briefing, the moment the aircrews had looked forward to with a mixture of excitement and dread. They had waited a week for the truth, suspecting all the time that ahead of them lay some suicidal daylight raid, and the tension had built up to an intolerable pitch. As they filed into the briefing rooms, filling them as they had never been filled before, generating an atmosphere of appalling suspense and expectation, the curtains covering the target maps were drawn aside, and they saw the familiar red tape running east from Britain. The whole of Europe, though, was still obscured by a large sheet of paper. Then the windows were shut, the blinds drawn, the doors locked and barred and the sheet of paper was ripped aside with a conjuror's flourish.

'Gentlemen, the target for tonight is Cologne.'

The uproar of relief from those at the front soon leaked the truth to those at the back. The target was a tough one, but it was well known, and they weren't being asked to go in daylight. Instinctively, though, they knew that this was to be no ordinary raid, and they waited for more revelations.

Mostly the briefing was delivered by station commanders, many of them veterans of the First World War. At Croft, the briefing officer was the AOC Group, Air Vice-Marshal Roderick Carr. At Syerston it was Gus Walker. In other cases it was left to the squadron commander. Willie Tait, shy, retiring and apologetic as ever, briefed his own crews tersely and crisply at Leeming. All stations had a letter governing the briefing from Group. The original had come to group commanders from High Wycombe; it had been drafted by Harris himself.

'I think you've all guessed that there's something special on tonight,' said the station commander at one station. 'I can tell you now what it is. We're bombing Germany, one city in Germany, with more than a thousand aircraft.'

He could get no farther. There was a tiny punctuation mark of astonishment, and then the whole briefing room exploded into an uproar as hardened aircrews jumped to their feet and threw their hats in the air. This was what they had all been waiting for, and the cheering was frenzied and spontaneous. Even the station and squadron commanders were taken aback at the vehemence of the reaction; how much more astounded were the American observers who were present at more than one station, their preconceived notions about the phlegmatic British confounded by this access of near-hysteria.

The detailed instructions for each squadron and training unit differed according to the briefed aiming-point, height and approximate time over target. Aircraft were routed from their bases to the Dutch coast virtually direct; some from the northern bases would cross The Wash and finally leave the English coast near Cromer, but by far the majority were routed to cross the English coast in the region of Aldeburgh, Suffolk. With Cologne lying on about the same latitude at Southampton, all the crews would be making good a course slightly south as well as east. Some of the bases in East Anglia were no more than 300 miles from the target. Others, in Yorkshire and the Midlands, were over 400. The Dutch coast would be crossed south of Rotterdam, in the region of Goedereede and Ouddorp on the island of Over Flakkee, and the route across Holland and into Germany would touch good pinpoints at Eindhoven and Munchen Gladbach. Crews were recommended to pick out the Rhine north of the target and follow it into Cologne. After bombing they were to steer south-south-west for twenty miles to Euskirchen, then turn for home on a track parallel to their outward track, taking them across northern Belgium rather than Holland. A gradual loss of height after bombing was also recommended, coming down to about a thousand feet over the North Sea to keep below the threatened build-up of cloud over the bases.

The most important briefing was that given to the Gee-equipped incendiary force of Nos 1 and 3 Groups charged with setting fire to the first aiming-point, the centre of the old town at the *Neumarkt*. These were the fire-raisers, the pathfinders, and the whole success of the raid would depend on their correct target identification and accurate bomb-aiming. Starting at 00.55 hours, they would have the target to themselves for fifteen minutes. Other than this fairly broad time span, there was no attempt to give individual crews an exact time on target.

Apart from the Lancasters and Halifaxes, all other aircraft were to bomb in the next hour, their attacks being spread over this period as evenly as possible. The remaining aircraft of Nos 1 and 3 Groups – those not in the marking force – would have the same aiming-point, the centre of the old town. Aircraft of 4 Group, and the training planes of 91 Group, would aim a mile to the north of the *Neumarkt*. Aircraft of 5 Group, and the training planes of 92 Group, would aim a mile to the south. In this way the devastation would be spread over the largest possible area. Crews were ordered to drop their bombs between rather than in existing fires, spreading and increasing the conflagration in the immediate locality rather than wasting bombs on areas already blazing well. They were warned, too, not to be diverted from finding and bombing their aiming-points by dummies, or by real conflagrations elsewhere.

'Cologne,' said the briefing officer at one station, 'is one of the most heavily defended cities in Germany, and one of the most important. In and around Cologne are more than five hundred heavy and light anti-aircraft guns and about a hundred and fifty searchlights, which work in close co-ordination with the gunners. But with this very large force, the belief is that all ground defences will be saturated and overwhelmed. The same should apply to night-fighters. Your track will take you close to several night-fighter stations, but intruder aircraft from Fighter and Army Co-operation Commands and 2 Group will be attacking these stations before and during the raid. Even so, look out for night-fighters. Tail gunners, be careful what you fire at. There will be a large number of friendly aircraft over

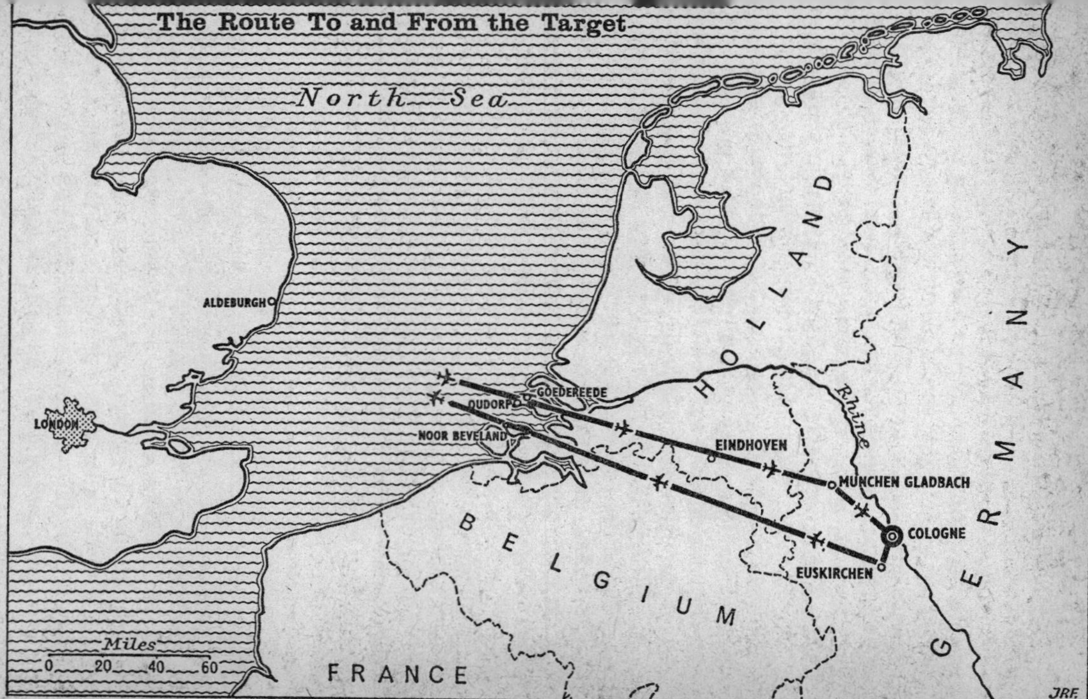
The Route To and From the Target
North Sea
ALDEBURGH
LONDON
GOEDEREEDE
OUDORP
NOOR BEVELAND
EINDHOVEN
MUNCHEN GLADBACH
COLOGNE
EUSKIRCHEN
Rhine
HOLLAND
GERMANY
BELGIUM
FRANCE
Miles
0 20 40 60
JRF.

Cologne. Don't mistake our own twin-engined bombers for Ju 88's.

'The key to the success of this raid is saturation, which itself depends on getting these thousand aircraft over the target in the shortest feasible time-spread. Tonight's attack is to be concentrated into ninety minutes. This means accurate timing, not only for the saturation of defences but to avoid collision. Exact heights are just as important. Follow your briefed timings and courses. If you don't, this raid, instead of being the costliest in history for the enemy, could be the costliest in history for us.

'Now I'll come to the collision risk.' Here the crews, already attentive, sat forward apprehensively, eager for reassurance. Ever since the figure of a thousand had been introduced at the start of the briefing, this was the spectre that had haunted them. Mid-air collision was a hideous experience, one which few men had been known to survive.

'The boffins are confident,' went on the briefing officer, 'that the risk is negligible.' There was a murmur of scepticism, which died away as the briefing continued. 'They have assessed the chances' – here the briefing officer paused for a moment, to give full effect to his statement – 'at one in a thousand.'

They were being given the bull. That was the instant reaction. A thousand aircraft milling about over a single target at night, beset by searchlights and flak, jinking and weaving, twisting and turning, diving and climbing under fighter attack, jam-packed together along a narrow route, struggling to get back under difficulties into over-crowded circuits and bases – and the long-haired boys at Command had decided that there would be only one collision! At more than one briefing, certainly at Syerston, and certainly at Skellingthorpe, the entire room rocked with derisive laughter.

'Have the boffins worked out,' asked a wag from 50 Squadron at Skellingthorpe, 'which two aircraft it will be?'

There was another gust of laughter, and then the briefing officer, judging his audience correctly, replied in similar vein.

'I have it on the highest authority that it will be a Tiger Moth and an Anson.'

When the laughter had subsided the briefing officer continued. 'I am assured that the saturation of defences achieved by the high concentration of aircraft will vastly over-discount any risk of collision. But the figure of one collision is based on the assumption that aircraft keep to the recommended approach and departure routes and heights and run up to or near their allotted aiming-points. So it's up to you.

'I do want to impress on you all that this is no ordinary occasion. This is the first major bomber battle in history. In the opinion of the C-in-C, the whole future course of the war may be altered by this raid. For the first time the force employed is adequate to annihilate an objective of vital importance to the enemy at one stroke. All our calculations from our own experience of German bombing show that if a high proportion of this force attains the objective and bombs with care and reasonable accuracy, the weight of incendiary and high explosive is sufficient to destroy the objective entirely as an industrial centre and to achieve an effect which will spread apprehension, despair and panic throughout Germany.

'At best the raid may bring hostilities to a more or less abrupt conclusion. It could finish the war. The enemy may well be unwilling to accept this kind of punishment as our bomber force and that of the United States builds up. At worst it must have the most dire moral and physical effect on the enemy's war effort as a whole and force him to withdraw vast forces from his exterior aggressions for his own protection.

'Remember that, however big the raid, the final outcome depends on each man's effort and determination as an individual. The C-in-C has himself sent a message for you to remind you of this, and I'll read it to you. Here it is.

' "*The force of which you form a part tonight is at least twice the size and has more than four times the carrying capacity of the largest air force ever before concentrated on one objective. You have an opportunity, therefore, to strike a blow at the enemy which will resound, not only throughout Germany, but throughout the world.*

' "*In your hands lie the means of destroying a major part of the resources by which the enemy's war effort is maintained. It depends, however, upon each individual crew whether full concentration is achieved.*

'"*Press home your attack to your precise objective with the utmost determination and resolution in the foreknowledge that, if you individually succeed, the most shattering and devastating blow will have been delivered against the very vitals of the enemy.*

'"*Let him have it – right on the chin.*"'

2. *INTRUSION*

PLANS FOR INTRUDER operations against German night-fighter bases, called for by Harris in the operation order, had crystallized over the previous few days. The German night-fighter force was a formidable one and included over a hundred Me 110's, besides Ju 88's and Me 109's that normally operated by day but which could be employed at night. Under conditions of full moon and no cloud, the greatest danger to the force – assuming that the scientists were right about the collision risk – would be catseye fighters. Conditions that were perfect for visual bombing – conditions which approximated to daylight – could result in an orgy of destruction by the German fighter pilots. A comparatively small force of these, operating along the route to and from the target, could break up the force on the way out and complete the débâcle on the way home, so that losses might run into hundreds. It was absolutely essential to pin down the bulk of the night-fighter force, either by direct attack on its bases or by keeping it occupied on diversions.

The bulk of the intruder force was to be provided by Blenheims – of No 2 Group, Bomber Command, and of Army Co-operation Command, fifty Blenheims in all. There would be two squadrons from 2 Group, Nos 18 and 114, operating from Wattisham and West Raynham respectively. They would be reinforced by two squadrons from Army Co-operation Command: No 13 was pulled out of Army manoeuvres to

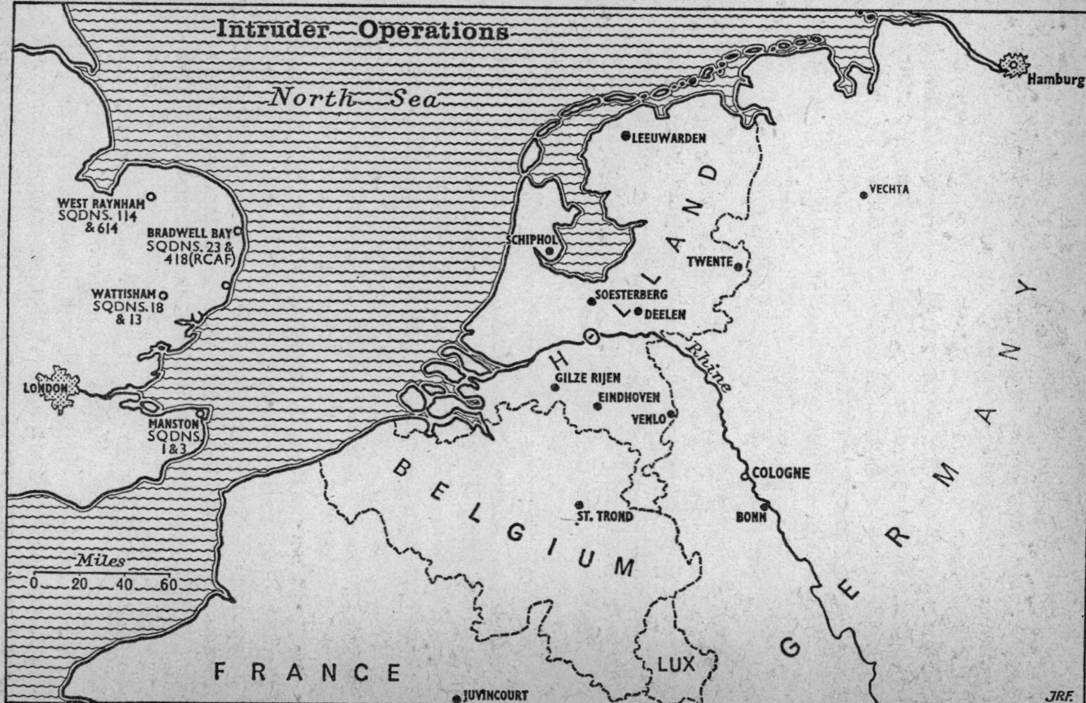
Intruder Operations
North Sea
Hamburg
LEEUWARDEN
VECHTA
WEST RAYNHAM
SQDNS. 114
& 614
BRADWELL BAY
SQDNS. 23 &
418(RCAF)
SCHIPHOL
TWENTE
WATTISHAM
SQDNS. 18
& 13
SOESTERBERG
DEELEN
HOLLAND
Rhine
LONDON
GILZE RIJEN
EINDHOVEN
VENLO
MANSTON
SQDNS.
1 & 3
COLOGNE
BONN
BELGIUM
ST. TROND
GERMANY
Miles
0 20 40 60
LUX
FRANCE
JUVINCOURT
JRF.

join No 18 at Wattisham; No 614 was brought down from Scotland to join No 114 at West Raynham. Both these squadrons were ready to operate from their temporary bases by 28th May.

The task of the Blenheims would be to bomb the night-fighter airfields at Bonn, on the Rhine near Cologne; Vechta, 115 miles north-east of Cologne near Osnabruck; Twente, 90 miles north of Cologne; Venlo, on the Dutch/German border 30 miles east of Eindhoven; Juvincourt in northern France; and St Trond in Belgium, 35 miles east of Brussels. Twenty-four Blenheims were to operate from Wattisham and twenty-six from West Raynham.

The aircraft joining in the intrusion from Fighter Command would be Bostons, Havocs and long-range Hurricanes, thirty-eight aircraft in all. Their task would be not only to bomb the bases but to keep enemy night-fighters engaged while the bombers were on their way to and from the target. The squadrons taking part were Nos 23 and 418, flying Bostons and Havocs from Manston and Bradwell Bay, and Nos 1 and 3 Squadrons, operating Hurricane IIc's from Manston. These squadrons, too, had Venlo and St Trond among their targets, plus Eindhoven, Gilze Regan, Schipol, Deelan and Soesterburg in southern and central Holland and Leeuwarden in the north.

First to take off, beginning at 22.45 so as to precede or overtake the outriders of the incendiary force, were the Bostons of 418 Squadron bound for central and northern Holland from Bradwell Bay, five Bostons to Soesterburg, thirty-five miles south-east of Amsterdam, and four to Leeuwarden in the extreme north. Some carried 250 lb instantaneous and delay bombs, others carried 40 lb anti-personnel bombs. The experience of the four who went to Leeuwarden was typical. There was no attempt to fly together; the weather wasn't good enough. They crossed the Frisian Islands at various points; some passed over Terschelling and approached Leeuwarden from the north, others went straight in over Vlieland and Harlingen. They found the airfield obscured by ten-tenths cloud, and even after diving beneath the cloud they had difficulty in locating it. One Boston, piloted by an American named Lukas, spent half an hour making runs over the area looking for the target; he could not have been more conscientious. Finally he found it and dropped his bombs, four 250's, on the centre of the airfield, where he saw the bursts. Another pilot dropped his 40 lb bombs in a shallow dive, aiming at the runway intersection, but as he pulled up to regain height he flew straight into cloud and missed seeing the results of his attack. One crew failed to find the airfield at all and dropped their bombs on the harbour at Harlingen. All this no doubt had useful nuisance value but it was not likely to ground an efficient and determined force.

The remaining Bostons and Havocs took off at about 23.00. Of five Havocs briefed to attack Eindhoven, two bombed the runway but three failed to locate the airfield. Five more Havocs which went to Gilze Regen, thirty miles west-north-west of Eindhoven, reported that the target had been successfully bombed; runways had been cratered and buildings damaged, yet the airfield remained active and Me 110's were still able to use it. Of the two Boston crews briefed to attack Deelan, one saw no sign of activity on the airfield but bombed and hit the runway; the other was shot down near the airfield with the loss of pilot and navigator, the gunner being taken prisoner. Four more Bostons went to the Amsterdam airfield at Schipol, where all encountered intense searchlight and anti-aircraft opposition. One of these Bostons, coned in the searchlights, used up so much petrol that eventually the crew returned to base without dropping their bombs. The other three crews reported that they had bombed the airfield. One of the successful pilots, a Dutchman named Van Riel, saw four night-fighters working in pairs and co-operating with the searchlights over Amsterdam.

The Blenheims from West Raynham, aligned for the deepest penetration, crossed the North Sea as low as the failing light permitted and climbed to their bombing height of 2,000 feet when they crossed the Dutch coast, flying on to their targets along flak-free routes specially planned for them. Most of them reached their targets about midnight, just under an hour before the main attack was due to start. The first of seven briefed to attack Bonn found the airfield lights still on, but these were extinguished when the first bombs fell, making it difficult for the following-up aircraft to locate the target. At Twente, five miles from the Dutch/German border near Enschede, the first pilot on the scene saw an enemy night-fighter in the circuit being signalled to land by Aldis lamp. The flare-path was on, and this and the funnel lights helped several Blenheims to deliver their attack before they were extinguished. Sixteen of the twenty-six Blenheims from West Raynham reported successful attacks, but the others either failed to find their targets or were forced for various reasons to turn back. As a result of these failures the attack on the most distant target, Vechta, near Osnabruck, was virtually abortive, only one Blenheim getting through to the target, and there was doubt about the effectiveness of the raid on Twente. One Blenheim from West Raynham was shot down and all its crew were killed.

Of the twenty-four Blenheims at Wattisham, eight went to St Trond, of which six reported successful attacks from low level in perfect weather. There was no ground or fighter opposition, the flare-path was on, and bombs fell amongst buildings as well as on and near the runway. One of the pilots who bombed St Trond while the flare-path was still lit was a Squadron Leader H. G. Malcolm, who six months later was to win a posthumous VC in a famous suicide raid in North Africa. Six crews who went to Venlo all reported successful attacks, yet here again the operations of night-fighters, at an airfield commanding the final approaches to Cologne, were not prevented. Eight crews reported attacking Juvincourt, and one dropped his bombs just as a night-fighter was landing, claiming it as probably destroyed. A ninth Blenheim detailed to bomb Juvincourt may have delivered its attack, but it was shot down near the French coast, crashing into the sea with no survivors.

Last to take part in the intruder operations were the long-range Hurricanes, which took off at intervals from midnight on, their task being to patrol the airfields along the latter part of the route to Cologne – Gilze Regen, Eindhoven, St Trond, Venlo. But the German night-fighter pilots proved elusive. The only man to engage a night-fighter was a Canadian, Warrant Officer G. Scott. Scott took off from Manston at 00.55 and reached St Trond forty-five minutes later. The great raid had started, St Trond had already been attacked by the Blenheims, but the airfield was brightly lit. Scott passed to the south-west at 1,500 feet, looking out for the aircraft that he guessed must be in the circuit. Suddenly he spotted the navigation lights of an enemy plane – a Ju 88. It was about a thousand feet below him, flying north-east in the direction of Venlo or perhaps Cologne. Scott gave chase at once and dived into the attack. At 500 feet he was dead astern of the German plane, and after firing two short bursts he saw his tracer beating into the Junkers' fuselage. Then a blinding white flash came from the port engine. The next moment Scott was caught in a long stream of white smoke from the fighter and he had to break off to avoid collision. Immediately after the attack the airfield lights at St Trond were doused and a red Very light was fired, piercing the sudden darkness like a torch. The Ju 88 pilot must have been able to transmit a warning to the controller at St Trond, and Scott did not see the aircraft crash. He continued to patrol the St Trond area for nearly two hours, but the only other aircraft he saw was a Blenheim. He claimed the Ju 88 as damaged.

Another pilot of the same squadron who was briefed to patrol Venlo saw no sign of airfield lighting or activity, so after twenty-five minutes he set course for Eindhoven and Gilze Regen. On the way to Gilze Regen, after over-flying Eindhoven, he saw a British bomber blow up and three others come down in flames. All seemed to be returning from Cologne. At his patrol height of 1,500 feet the Hurricane pilot saw nothing of the enemy fighters that must have been responsible.

The intruder attacks, many of them delivered with daring and accuracy, by men of the highest calibre, had unfortunately had little effect on the operations of the German night-fighter force. The bombing of airfields with 250 lb and 40 lb bombs, except where large numbers of planes were crowded together, rarely produced more than temporary inconvenience. A handful of bombs across an airfield, however well placed, could not prevent a small fighter like the Me 110, requiring only a short take-off run, from getting airborne, or from landing afterwards. German reports suggest that very few of the bombs that were dropped did significant damage. The intruder force, flying through uncertain weather but helped in many places by lighted flare-paths, had suffered from the same inadequacies as had hampered and frustrated the main bomber force throughout the war so far. No navigation or bombing aids; resilient, dispersed targets, difficult to find at night, even more difficult to put out of action when found; inadequate weapons, inadequate numbers. It was the old unhappy story of the years of preparation; good men lost, and very little achieved.

The bombers would still have to fight their way through to the target, absorb all that the ground defences could hurl at them and then fight their way out.

PART IV

THE RAID

1. MARKING THE TARGET

THE SUN WAS sinking over the fens as the crews of the marking force drifted down to the flight offices. All were talking excitedly about the great revelation that had been made at briefing. Soon the crew rooms were noisy with activity as each man pulled his flying kit from his locker and struggled into it. It was warm enough on the ground, but it would be cold at 15,000 feet. Shuffling out in their flying-boots, dragging their parachutes and flying helmets after them, they flopped down in untidy groups on the grass in front of the crew rooms and waited for the transport to take them out to their aircraft. When the lorry came they climbed in to the accompaniment of a cacophony of moans and exhortations, with a flow of *risqué* wisecracks directed at the WAAF driver. She grinned, she was used to it, it meant nothing. Everyone knew that she was reserved for that pale, humourless air gunner in 'B' flight, that she would be waiting for him tonight when he got back. If he got back. 'He's a quiet one, he is!' they shouted. 'What's he got that we haven't got?' The jests were charged with innuendo but somehow stopped short of the ribald. Soon the lorry moved off to dispersal, drowning further repartee.

The light was fading rapidly now, and the flare-path lights twinkled. Beetle-like tractors were towing aircraft stern-first into position. Petrol bowsers were topping up fuel tanks. The lorries carrying the aircrews dumped their disorderly cargo at the farthest points of the field. Soon, as the human figures were swallowed up by the huge, lumbering aircraft, the semblance of order was restored. Now for a few moments the bombers stood silent and sinister, pregnant with their load.

Then it began, first the pistol-crack of ignition, stuttering into a machine-gun rapidity as engine after engine roared and rumbled into life, then the thunderous reverberation as bomber after bomber strained against its chocks and the engines raced. For a time the noise seemed almost hysterical; then it eased to a steady, throbbing heartbeat, breaking into a score of purposeful crescendos as signal lamps flashed green and one by one the Stirlings and the Wellingtons answered the roll-call, moving heavily forward before accelerating between the flares, tugging themselves off the ground, tucking up their wheels and circling for height, navigation lights still on. Now the noise attacked the ear at a dozen different frequencies and from a dozen angles, from the dispersals, from the perimeter tracks, from the runway, from overhead, combining into one great orchestrated din. Then slowly the sound began to ebb as one by one the bombers turned east and set course for Cologne.

No 9 Squadron at Honington, 57 and 75 at Feltwell, 101 at Bourn, 419 (RCAF) at Mildenhall – these were the five leading Wellington squadrons of 3 Group; also in the vanguard were four Stirling squadrons, 15 at Wyton, 149 at Lakenheath, 214 at Stradishall and 218 at Marham. Several crews in 1 Group, too, were timed to be over the target in the first fifteen minutes. The first men to take off were the squadron commander and the senior flight commander of No 15 Squadron at Wyton, Wing Commander J. C. Macdonald and Squadron Leader R. S. Gilmour. They were airborne at 22.30, and they set course into a clouded night sky that was still refulgent with the memory of sunset. But perhaps the most impressive scene was being staged by 57 and 75 at Feltwell, where two flare-paths had been laid 300 yards apart and where the Wellingtons were being despatched personally by the station commander simultaneously from both runways, with the entire station staff assembled at various vantage points on the edge of the field to see them off. Eleven Wellingtons got away from Feltwell in the first eight minutes. Altogether there were forty-seven Wellingtons on this station alone – twenty from No 57, twenty-three from No 75, and four Ia's from Flying Training Command (among them David Johnson's from Sutton Bridge), the only aircraft from this Command, indeed the only aircraft from any Command outside Bomber, to fly that night to Cologne.

Ten miles due south, at Mildenhall, Moose Fulton and the Hon. Terence Mansfield were waiting behind sixteen Wellington III's to take off in their vintage Ic. Fifteen miles to the south-west, at Honington, Harry Langton, the ex-policeman, was second in line in his Wellington III. Fifteen miles to the north, at Marham, an air vice-marshal was climbing into a Stirling.

*

That Saturday in Cologne had been a mild but pleasant day, dry but overcast. For most people it had been a day of work and of week-end shopping, followed by a walk in the park and a quiet evening. Tomorrow was Sunday. That at least for most of Cologne's 800,000 citizens would be a day of rest. Many people were planning to go to a race-meeting at Riehl, on the northern outskirts of the city.

*

The weather in eastern England had improved steadily during the afternoon, and the thunderstorms which had been active most of the day had died out towards evening. But at some of the more westerly bases, heavy rain was falling as the aircraft took off. And as far as anyone knew, Cologne still lay under a blanket of cloud and would remain so at least until midnight. Would the cloud disperse in time? Could Spence possibly be right? If it failed to clear before the incendiary force arrived, there would be no conflagration at the central aiming-point and nothing to guide the many hundreds of less-experienced crews to follow. Bombs would be scattered over a wide area and the attack would be a failure.

And over the North Sea a new hazard presented itself, the hazard of icing. It was particularly severe for the crews at the northernmost bases, the squadrons of No 4 Group in Yorkshire. At Driffield, where nine Wellingtons and eight Whitleys took off about 23.30, all the crews found climbing difficult under a heavy weight of ice and four Wellington and four Whitley crews were forced to turn back. Another sortie had to be cancelled through the illness of the pilot. The contribution from this station was thus cut in half; if this proved to be the general pattern it would be disastrous. (Characteristically, among the pilots at Driffield who pressed on in spite of the icing were Don Harkness and John Russell.) At the same time the force was being further eroded by unserviceability; in spite of the tireless efforts of the ground crews at all the bases, many of the older machines, labouring under an unaccustomed load and asked to climb to unwonted heights, were developing faults which made continuing the sortie inadvisable and sometimes impossible. In this early stage of the operation, of a total of 1,046 bombers that actually took off from the bases, more than a hundred crews had already been forced to turn back.

Airfield after airfield that had lapsed into an uneasy and morbid silence was alerted to assist in the sheepish return of one of its flock. There was always an awkwardness between air and ground crews at these times; both felt they were under suspicion. But when the 'boomerangs', as they were known, were back, and the silence returned, the air was still vibrant with the memory of that mass take-off. The men on the ground were left to ponder through the night hours, to hope, to fear and to wait. Very few men – or women – could sleep. Even Harris and Saundby were not immune from the Command-wide insomnia. Commanders who can't rest don't last; yet this was one night when sleep would not come. All through the slowly passing hours their thoughts went round in circles, alternately elated by hopes of success and tormented by fears of failure. Only these two men could fully appreciate how much depended on the result of the raid, how great would be the prize of success and how bitter the penalty of failure.

Already there had begun that litter of human tragedies which must inevitably pollute and yet sanctify all major operations of war. At Binbrook, No 12 Squadron had put up twenty-eight aircraft and crews, more than any other single squadron; but they had only achieved this figure by promoting second pilots specially for the raid, to carry out their first operation as first pilot and captain. Most squadrons had been forced to do the same; so, to add to the trainee crews from the OTUs were scores of fresher crews from the squadrons. First of these fresher crews to fall was captained by Sergeant G. H. Everatt of 12 Squadron, who crashed in Norfolk twenty-five minutes after take-off, apparently through engine failure. His Wellington caught fire and he and all his crew perished.

Meanwhile, on the other side of the North Sea, although the direction and scale of the main attack were not yet known, the defences had been alerted by the intruder force and by radar warning of the bombers, and the first casualties through enemy action were about to be registered. First to be shot down was Don Harkness, the man so much admired by fellow New Zealander Clive Saxelby when they had bombed invasion barges together nearly two years earlier. Because of the heavy icing encountered by all the Driffield aircraft, Harkness had been unable to climb his Wellington above nine or ten thousand feet, but he had refused to turn back. Thus it was that his plane, as it crossed the Dutch coast south of Rotterdam, was picked out by searchlights and easily seen by two patrolling German fighters crossing the Easter Scheldt and approaching the island of North Beveland. The fighters pounced, and against them the Wellington, still struggling for altitude, had no chance. An eye-witness on the island saw the fighters attack, saw the Wellington plunge downwards, then watched it disappear into the Easter Scheldt, at the point where it joins the North Sea. The bodies of the crew, Harkness excepted, were washed ashore on North Beveland in the ensuing few days. Hopes were held out by the Dutch that the pilot might have escaped, but the body of Don Harkness was finally recovered on the last day of 1942.

Harkness had been one of the most experienced men on the raid. At the other extreme was the early loss of a training crew from No 23 OTU at Pershore, the most westerly base employed for the raid. Aircraft from Pershore had nearly an hour's flying before they even crossed the English coast, and their take-off times were put forward accordingly. One Canadian pilot, Sergeant W. R. C. Johnston, with a crew of three Englishmen and an Australian tail gunner named Broodbank, was another victim of the fighters patrolling over the north and south islands of Beveland, on the Dutch coast. The crashing Wellington was seen by the town secretary, Wouter Verhoeff, who immediately alerted the fire service and a doctor and hurried to the scene. The plane, with a full load of incendiaries still on board, was burning fiercely, but the rescuers found the pilot well clear of the wreck. His parachute was open around him, but he was dead. Either he had been thrown out or he had baled out too late. There was no sign of the rest of the crew, and the Germans organized a search of the area, suspecting that the four missing men had made good their escape. Next day, about 200 yards from the main wreckage, they found the tail section in a potato field, untouched by fire. The body of the dead Australian gunner was still in the turret. That left the three Englishmen unaccounted for. The search of the area revealed nothing, and there was no trace of the missing men in the wreck. Eventually, when the smouldering cinders had burned themselves out, the Germans sifted the ashes and turned up three identity discs. Sergeant Johnston and his crew had lost their lives within an hour of leaving the English coast on their first operational flight.

Another early casualty was Pilot Officer Reece Read, the mining engineer who had always wanted to be a doctor. Read, of 101 Squadron at Bourn, was on his first trip over enemy territory as captain of aircraft. Soon after take-off the engines began to run roughly, and he was unable to get full climbing power. One by one the crew called him up to comment on it, and Read knew it would be a popular decision to turn back. But if everyone who suspected some small mechanical fault gave up, the target would get away lightly. A little unhappily, but sure that his decision must be right, he carried on.

At first the engines seemed to settle down. But nearing the Dutch coast the trouble returned. The starboard engine suddenly lost revolutions and power, and they began to lose height rapidly. Soon the port engine went the same way. Read called the gunners out of their turrets, and when the plane nosed forward into a steep dive he gave the order to bale out. Eveyone got out safely.

The next thing Read knew was that he was on his hands and knees in a half-waterlogged field and his mouth and nostrils were choked with mud. He had no recollection of leaving the plane, and indeed his amnesia stretched back before the bale-out, so that he couldn't understand what he was doing in this strange quagmire of a field. It was the steady drone of bombers passing overhead that jogged his memory. Why hadn't he turned back? There had so obviously been something wrong with the plane. But surely it had been important to press on. The chaps overhead now were pressing on. Not all of them would get back, either.

A few weeks later, Read heard of the death of his brother, killed in a flying accident. He had encouraged his brother to join the RAF. He went to pieces for a time, then realized that he must find something to occupy his mind. He began to study medicine. The misfortune of being taken prisoner was for Reece Read the beginning of the fulfilment of a life's ambition.

Harkness, Johnston, Read – these were some of the men who fell at the first hurdle. The main defences of the Ruhr had not even been reached, let alone penetrated. But for the van of the incendiary force the moment was fast approaching.

*

All the way across the North Sea, all the way across central Holland, the leading crews flew above a blanket of thundery cloud, with very few breaks except over the Dutch islands, where most crews managed to get a pinpoint. Over the Continent the cloud was still thick and impenetrable. Soon it was after midnight, and still there was no sign of the promised dispersal of cloud. To starboard lay a towering switchback from which the flattened tips of thick anvil-heads protruded, formidable as an Alpine range. In all other directions, to the rear, to port and dead ahead, stretched this soft carpet of grey-white, infinite as the wastes of ocean, blotting out the earth, turning the sky into a segregated, circumscribed, partitioned world. But over this world, unifying it and fixing its boundaries, shone the early yellow light of a full moon, reporting for duty as promptly as any Serviceman, exactly as briefed. If Spence's predictions about the cloud could be half as accurate, all would yet be well.

And suddenly, sixty miles from Cologne, with less than half an hour to spare, the crews saw the great tongue of cloud beneath them falter and fall away, discovering the ground in astonishing clarity under the steady floodlight of the moon. Magnus T. Spence had been right. A lake gleamed momentarily, then turned pitch black, a dark blot on the paler countryside. The cloud had disappeared as if by some feat of legerdemain, just as the first of the thousand were entering the air-space of Germany.

Macdonald and Gilmour, in the two Stirlings of 15 Squadron, were the first to break through the Kammhuber Line and approach Cologne. They were making their run towards the city at 15,000 feet from almost due west, and to comply with their briefing they would have to swing to port so as to approach from the north. But at this stage of the raid there was no collision risk, and both men were more concerned with fixing their position. Through Cologne the Rhine ran virtually north and south, but immediately south of the city the river twisted into a huge S-bend. They steered for this and it gave them their pinpoint. Before reaching the Rhine they turned north and began their run up towards the centre of the city, keeping the Rhine on their right. Their next pinpoint would be the twin central bridges, first the Hindenburgbrücke, then the Hohenzollernbrücke. A mile due west of the first bridge was their aiming-point, the *Neumarkt*, in the centre of the old town.

As yet the reaction of the defences was desultory. Below them the intense moonlight was throwing the entire city into braille-like relief, like a model. Individual streets could be traced their entire length, honeycombed by buildings, while railways ploughed wide furrows right round the city and in one instance probed deep into the old town from the north-west, passing the cathedral before swinging east across the Hohenzollernbrücke and away. The old city itself, bounded by the

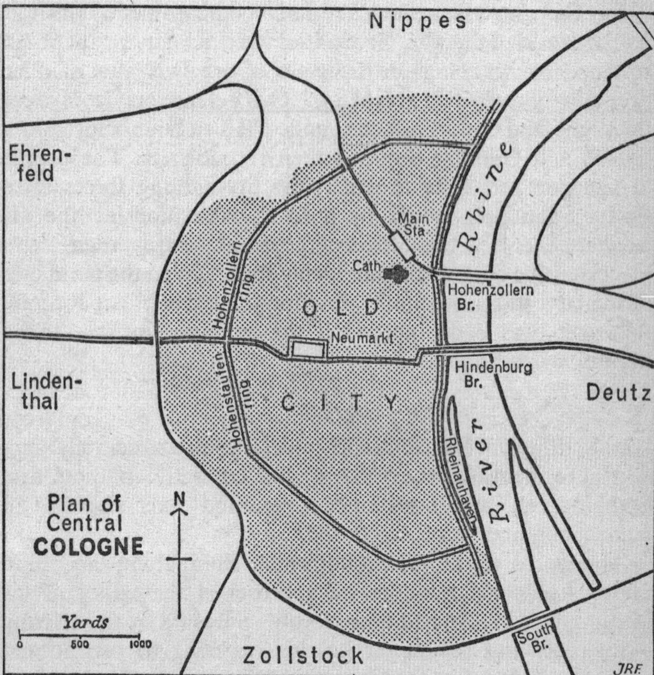

straight line of the Rhine to the right and the curving arc of a railway to the left, stood out boldly, like a jewel in its setting, as though specially marked out for attack. Macdonald and Gilmour were looking down on a sight that might never be seen again if the raid went well – the intricate fretwork of the old city of Cologne.

It was forty-seven minutes after midnight when they dropped their bombs. They were eight minutes early, but there seemed no point in waiting until the ground defences became more accurate and put them off their aim. Their sticks of incendiaries, 4- and 30-pounders, sprinkled across the *Neumarkt*, would light a beacon for the squadrons to come.

But Cologne was no novice to aerial bombardment. This was its 107th raid of the war. Great cities were hardened rather than softened by bombing on the scale of previous attacks. The preliminary alerts had reached the civil defence services before midnight, and the sirens had sounded half an hour before Macdonald and Gilmour dropped their incendiaries. The people of Cologne had gone to earth; the fire-fighting forces were ready. Soon they would be hard at work, dousing the incendiaries. As the two Stirlings turned westwards, their crews saw extensive dummy fires suddenly spring up on the perimeter of the city, in open country, inviting the unwary. An accurate follow-up was badly needed if the aiming-point was to be illuminated beyond all doubt.

*

'Don't drop your incendiaries unless you're absolutely sure you have identified the aiming-point correctly. If these first bombing runs aren't accurate, a thousand other aircraft will come along and be off target too.'

The words of the briefing officer at Honington were still in Harry Langton's mind as he approached the target in his Wellington III. He had been deeply impressed by the briefing – he could not remember hearing anything so precise and emphatic before. In the past they had mostly raided as lone wolves, flying at what height they liked. Tonight they had been given a definite route and a definite height, and Langton and his crew had kept to them both. Even the timing was to be more exact, and Langton, finding himself ahead of schedule, had circled off the Dutch coast for a minute or two until he caught a glimpse of the river of traffic coming up behind.

The incendiaries scattered by Macdonald and Gilmour had

not yet gained a hold, and the approach to the aiming point was confused by the dummy fires. Ignoring these dummies, 'Tiny' Welsh directed Langton towards the centre of the old city.

'Throttle back will you, Harry? We're still a few minutes ahead of our bombing time.'

Because of this throttling back it was a very long run-up, the longest Langton had ever known. Johnnie Johnson, the wireless operator, had moved from his set to the astro-dome to look out for fighters and to help keep track of other bombers. John Haworth was in the front turret, Ken Pexman, the new man from the Defiant squadron, was in the rear. The flak was being hurled at them with increased violence, but Langton, his own experience as a navigator over Cologne still fresh in his mind, took no evasive action. He had learnt on that earlier occasion that with the smallest movement of the control column, the slightest lifting or dropping of the nose, whatever the navigator was trying to hold in his bombsight completely disappeared. So while Tiny Welsh continued with this very long bombing run, giving instructions to Langton throughout, Langton held the Wellington perfectly steady, realizing the navigator's problems, and between them they brought the aircraft into a perfect bombing position.

'Steady. Steady. Bombs gone.'

Welsh, down at the bomb-aiming position in the nose, saw the incendiaries splash across the old city, saw a gleaming succession of platinum flashes which slowly turned to white and then to red as the flames began to take hold. The aiming-point was beautifully illuminated.

They were conscious now of many other aircraft in the sky around them; they had been overtaken during that slow bombing run. Welsh gave Langton a course to steer for Euskirchen, the briefed turning point for the return flight. But now the flak was more intense than ever. Two aircraft quite near them fell earthwards, streaming flame. Suddenly there was a loud crack to the left, and as Langton looked out he saw the port engine cough up a vivid expectoration of flame. As the engine spluttered to a stop, Langton feathered the propeller and turned at once for home.

'Give me a course for Manston, Tiny. If she stays up we can try and make Honington from there.'

By the time they reached Antwerp it was clear that they would never get to Manston. Langton ordered the crew to prepare for ditching, and all the hatches were opened. Then it became equally obvious that they wouldn't even make the Belgian coast. They were below 500 feet and still descending. Langton peered ahead for a place to land. A quarter of a mile ahead he could see what looked like a marshy field, just what he wanted, but between him and the field lay a farmhouse and two lines of trees. He tried to avoid the trees but the Wellington stalled and dropped straight into them. Langton, who was not strapped in, was catapulted through the open hatch above him.

Welsh, in the second pilot's seat, was also thrown out, but less violently, and when Haworth and Johnson emerged from the broken fuselage they found Welsh supporting himself against the starboard wing. All three were bruised and dazed and they could see nothing of Langton or Pexman. Langton in fact had been thrown thirty yards from the plane and they couldn't find him. But when they went to the rear of the plane they found Ken Pexman, half in and half out of his turret, killed instantly in the crash. His premonition about his twenty-second birthday had been right.

Liz Langton, in the hospital at Bury St Edmunds, would listen for her husband's plane in the early hours in vain. But Harry Langton, limbs broken and head little more than a mass of pulp, was not dead. Two years later he was repatriated in an exchange of wounded prisoners, and he subsequently made a full recovery.

*

Over Cologne, the main attack of the incendiary force had been developing as Langton left the target area. There were a few early arrivals from the 1 Group bases in the north, but the bulk of the marking was done by the aircraft of 3 Group.

Moose Fulton's squadron was there, although Fulton himself, 50 miles an hour slower in the old Ic, was well behind the rest of his crews. He was somehow able to coax the old Wimpey up to 17,500 feet, and from there he was able to make a complete circuit of the target without risk of collision, pick his spot carefully and drop accurately at a point about 400 yards north of the centre of the old city.

Already the flak and searchlights, although extremely active, were exhibiting signs of confusion, overstrain and panic. Much of the firing seemed haphazard, a barrage for its own sake, and the searchlights were having difficulty in picking out and concentrating on single aircraft. When they did, however, they were as effective as ever, and the flak co-operated well, flinging a barrage into the apex of the cone. Every few minutes a bomber went down, watched in awe by the more fortunate crews who escaped.

At first, when the sirens had started in Cologne, people had stood about at the doors of their homes, waiting to see if it was a false alarm. For half an hour the sky was dark, no planes, no searchlights, no guns. It seemed that the bombers might be by-passing Cologne, flying on to some more distant target. Then, in the light of the rising moon, it was seen that the sky over Cologne was portentously clear. There followed the first thin rumble of aircraft engines, growing in volume minute by minute to a steady roar. The searchlights described their angular patterns, the guns barked and thundered. Hundreds of searchlights quartered the sky, hundreds of guns fired almost simultaneously. It made no difference to that steady oncoming roar.

The bombers were seen to be coming in on a broad front. Several of the first bombs fell some distance away. The defence lines to the west of the city seemed at first to be the object of the attack as bombs fell amongst the AA gun positions. The scream of aircraft engines rose above the barrage as bomber after bomber dived on the searchlights, their shrill falsetto machine-guns punctuating the stentorian bass of the flak. Still the mass of bombers came on. Soon, as though shaken and ignited by some natural phenomenon erupting within its boundaries, the limited area of the old city began to catch fire.

As the people of Cologne hurried into the vast underground shelters that had been constructed for them, many of them picked up scraps of paper that were falling from the sky. On them, in heavily printed capitals, they read of their destiny. 'The offensive of the RAF in its new form has begun.'

*

One of the first Stirlings on the target, after Macdonald and Gilmour, was the one piloted by Sergeant Wilf Davis, of 218 Squadron at Marham, the man who had vowed never again to dive out of searchlights. As usual Smithy – Albert Smith, the individualist gunner – had opted out of the radio job and was sitting in one of the turrets, this time the mid-upper. With second pilot Harry Guntrip they were an eight-man crew, the remaining members being Joe Borrowdale, the navigator from Cumberland, Chalky White, flight engineer, Harry Allen, wireless operator, Ken England in the rear turret and the American Tex Tate in the front. They were approaching Cologne from the north-west before settling down on their bombing run when suddenly the nightmare of Essen six weeks earlier was repeated; they were coned in thirty to forty searchlights and almost at once the apex of the cone was filled with flak. Wilf Davis weaved and jinked violently, but this time he did not send the Stirling into a dive. They could not escape that blinding cone, and soon they could hear the bursts of the flak.

Several times they heard the metallic thud of shell fragments on the fuselage. Then the port inner engine was hit. There were several other hits and they began to lose height.

'We'll get rid of the bombs and get out of here,' called Davis. 'Jettison the bombs, Joe.'

Down in the nose, Borrowdale dropped the bombs on the outskirts of Cologne. Then Davis turned away from the target, heading for Belgium. The searchlights lost them for a moment, then caught up with them. They were still boxed in by flak.

The next hit was on the mid-upper turret, where a tremendous hammer-blow struck Smith in the chest. He fell back for a moment, then slumped forward, blood spurting from his mouth. A jagged piece of metal had penetrated just above the heart and gone straight through, coming out at the left shoulder-blade. The whole of that side of his body was paralysed, but with his right hand he tore off his oxygen mask to save himself from choking. He knew he had been badly hit and that this was probably it, but his mind as always was clear.

He flipped on his microphone switch and called the crew. He could not hear his voice at all, and he realized that his intercom had broken and that he could not communicate with anyone. Movement seemed impossible and he thought he would probably never get out of the turret. He felt no fear of death, just a cold acceptance that this had been bound to happen to him sooner or later. It was a situation that he felt oddly familiar with. He was thinking not of himself but of the small terraced house in the narrow street outside Manchester, the place where he had lived all his life; he was imagining the shock that his parents would feel when they got the telegram. We regret to inform you. Killed in action.

He was coughing up blood now, but somehow he managed to crawl out of the turret. The Stirling had been at 18,000 feet when they were hit, and he was finding great difficulty in breathing without oxygen, but he found sufficient strength to get clear of the turret and begin the long crawl forward to the navigation compartment. He faltered several times, fighting to get his breath, and he was still some fifteen feet from the compartment when the blackness that had been surging round him suddenly enveloped him completely and he passed out.

When he regained consciousness about a minute later he could make out the shadowy figure of White, the flight engineer, ahead of him. He tried to shout to attract attention, but in his feeble state it was impossible to make himself heard above the noise of the engines. He remembered the torch that he always carried for emergencies. It was in the pocket of his flying jacket. He reached down and his fingers closed round it. Soon the flight engineer saw the light flashing and came back to help.

Between them White and Allen carried him back to the rest-bed. They plugged him into the inter-com so that he should know what was happening, and then White began to unzip his flying suit to give him first aid. But all the time they were losing height, and now the angle of glide suddenly steepened.

'The prop's flown off the port outer.'

That was two engines gone – both on one side. A Stirling just wouldn't stay up like that. They were down to 5,000 feet.

'Get ready to abandon aircraft,' called Davis. 'Smithy's injured so we'll get him out first. Have you got your chute on, Smithy?'

'No – it's back by the turret.'

'Harry – go back and get Smithy's chute.'

Harry Allen was working the radio and he didn't hear the order. Smithy rolled off the rest-bed and began to crawl back for it himself. He reached it and managed to unhook it, then crawled forward again. His left arm was useless and he couldn't clip the parachute on to his harness, but White helped him to his feet and fastened the parachute to the two breast clips. Then Smithy went forward, supporting himself as best he could, and squeezing past Davis and Guntrip, who were struggling to keep the nose up and the wings level. Behind them, in the narrow fuselage, waited White, Allen and England, the rear gunner.

Down at the nose hatch waiting for Smithy were Joe Borrowdale and Tex Tate. Another tragedy was threatened here. Borrowdale's parachute had been torn to shreds by flak and it was flapping uselessly in the draught from the open hatch. There seemed no hope for him. But Tex Tate offered to cling to him and jump with him, the two men coming down on the same parachute. It would be dangerous for both men, but for Joe Borrowdale it was the only chance.

Smithy scrambled down to the hatch and sat on the edge, hesitated for no more than a second or two, then gave the thumbs-up and dropped through the hole. His parachute opened and he landed safely, but the fall took him by surprise and he blacked out again. When he came to the Stirling had gone. Wilf Davis and Harry Guntrip must have got one of the port engines to pick up again. Perhaps they would all get back home. He thought wistfully of what now seemed the comparative security of the inside of the plane. He had forgotten the terror of that steep glide, and all he knew was that he was stranded alone in the middle of a field, weak from shock and loss of blood.

When the Germans found him they took him to a camp near Aachen, and there he met Tex Tate. There had been no time for Tate and Borrowdale to interlock their harnesses. Five men had been waiting behind them and they had had to get out immediately. Tate had dangled his legs through the hatch and Borrowdale had sat astride his shoulders; it was the only way to get through the hatch together. Between them they had improvised what had seemed an effective lock, and then they had jumped. When they hit the slipstream they had somehow held on. The next crisis had come when the parachute opened. The tug had been violent and it had jerked Borrowdale off. He had fallen to his death.

Tex Tate had watched the Stirling turn over on its back above him and then plunge straight in. All the rest of the crew had perished inside.

Smithy would not have been the first to jump had he not been wounded. The shell fragment that had so nearly ended his life had saved it.

*

So far the losses were frequent and the defences apparently unsaturated. In spite of the almost pathological fear of collision, many crews still had the danger from flak and fighters uppermost in their minds. Most pilots adopted their normal weaving technique over Holland and approaching Cologne. These pilots were flying on instruments, although the air was now crystal clear, having found from experience that the false horizon effect given by the various angles of the searchlights made it all too easy to get into an uncontrolled spiral. Weaving, too, was best done on instruments if a correct heading was to be maintained.

Thus the bulk of the force was either en route or approaching the target, rocking in the slipstream of other aircraft, altering course to avoid collision, and weaving continually to upset the flak predictors and to give the gunners a view of the blind spots underneath. Every crew-member kept an alert watch, partly for fighters, partly to warn the pilot when other bombers were weaving nearby or seemed likely to settle down on a converging course. Over the target itself it was also advisable to shoot a glance upwards at regular intervals, in the hope of avoiding any bombs that might be dropped from above.

To add to the obvious collision dangers, many of the crews, ignoring the briefing, and unable perhaps to break with long-formed habits of independence, were making their bombing runs direct, according to their direction of approach to the target. If they found themselves south of the target, they looked for a pinpoint on the Rhine and then flew northwards to drop their bombs, against the stream. Even some of the leading and most experienced crews did this. Others made their attacks across the stream, from west to east, or from east to west. Many crews after dropping their bombs were so fascinated by the sight of the burning city, with extensive areas of fire on both sides of the river, and cathedral and bridges illuminated, that they circled the area to take it all in. Thus one of the principal factors on which the estimate of the collision risk had been based – that all aircraft would be flying in approximately the same direction – proved to be illusory. Aircraft were converging from all directions in a criss-cross Clapham Junction of the air.

It was of course an achievement, in May 1942, to find the target at all, let alone the aiming-point. Many crews felt that it might be more dangerous to change course in order to attack from the north-west as briefed than to carry straight on. Any manoeuvring meant spending longer over the target and might mean as much flying across the stream as going straight in. And the light over Cologne was so brilliant that crews believed they could avoid collision if a good look-out was kept. Thus many of them chose the more direct course.

The first collision, however, was not due to this confusion of routes. Flight Lieutenant Brian Frow, an Englishman of No 408 (Canadian) Squadron based at Balderton, near Newark, was approaching Cologne in his Hampden from the north-west, at about twenty miles distance, on a straight and level course. Because of the wild and haphazard nature of much of the flak he had decided that there was nothing to be gained by weaving; he might fly into the flak just as easily as out of it, and at the same time he would be increasing the risk of collision. He believed, indeed, that orders for straight and level flight over the target – except for aircraft caught in searchlights – should have been given at briefing. Clearly, from the behaviour of many of the bombers around him, very few pilots agreed with him.

Half a mile ahead of him, soon after passing over Munchen Gladbach, Frow saw a burst of tracer dart across the sky, travelling it seemed no more than a hundred feet. Seconds later there was a bright glow in the sky, and then a ball of incandescent light fell slowly and gently out of the stream. Some poor devils had had it up front. It was a signal for a furious increase in the weaving and corkscrewing of the bombers ahead of Frow, the crews of which had seen the incident and were determined not to be caught in the same way. But Frow, shaken by the number of aircraft around him, was more frightened of collision than of fighters. He warned his crew on the intercom, but he kept the Hampden in straight and level flight.

Then he noticed that two aircraft not more than 400 yards ahead of him and slightly to starboard were settling down into the most dangerous position of all – one above the other. Unless someone in the lower aircraft was looking straight up from the astro-dome, neither crew would be likely to spot the other. The top aircraft was a Stirling. The one underneath was a Wellington.

It all happened incredibly quickly, in the space of perhaps ten seconds. As it weaved the Wellington rose slightly, while the Stirling sagged and then levelled out. Then the Wellington came up again under the Stirling, soaring this time just a few feet too far. As the two bombers touched, the fans of the Wellington cut the tail of the Stirling clean off. Both aircraft lifted together in a kind of mutual shock before dropping forward and then hurtling downward. Then the Wellington blew up. Frow watched the Stirling falling for several thousand feet, then lost it. A few seconds later a vivid explosion on the ground marked the spot where it had gone in. Frow and his crew had seen no parachutes from either plane.

*

The experience of the other squadrons in the van of the incendiary force was generally good. 9 Squadron had lost another crew in addition to Langton's, shot down by fighters near Eindhoven. The leading crews of 57 and 75 from Feltwell had got through without loss. Several crews had been put off their aim by flak and searchlights but most had dropped their bombs on or near the aiming-point and looked back at growing fires as they flew home. The first two Stirling squadrons, 15 and 149, had come through unscathed, and a crew of 149 had shot down an Me 110 over Munchen Gladbach on the way in. 214 Squadron had lost one Stirling in the collision witnessed by Brian Frow; the Wellington apparently came from 101 Squadron, making with Reece Read the squadron's second casualty. 218 had lost Wilf Davis. The target was well alight and the defences had seemed bewildered at first, but they were still active and by no means saturated. Across Holland and Belgium the fighter pilots were energetic and numerous and were just getting into their stride as the extent of their opportunity was realized. The first round had gone well, but the raid would succeed or fail on the performance of the main ruck of twin-engined aircraft, the Wellingtons, Hampdens, Whitleys and Manchesters, in the next hour. If they could spread the conflagration evenly in a concentrated area around the three aiming-points, the way would be open for the final shattering blow by the heavies.

2. *THE MAIN FORCE*

SOME OF THE first men to take off in No 1 Group were the crews of 103 Squadron at Elsham Wolds, timed to reach the target at the tail end of the incendiary force. One of the pilots was the tall New Zealander Clive Saxelby. Another was Hugh Constantine, the only group captain to fly that night as first pilot. One of the flight commanders was unwell and Constantine took over his crew. This was a shock for the crew, and it was grimly summed up by the navigator, Dizzy Spiller, the untidiest man on the station. 'Old Connie's bound to write us off,' groaned Spiller.

For Constantine, and indeed for all the crews, the flight across Lincolnshire and The Wash, then along the Norfolk coast to Cromer, in failing light, joining a swarm of black arrow-heads above and below them, all heading south-east, was a magnificent and thrilling sight, giving a comforting sense of security and power. Darkness came upon them as they crossed the North Sea, but still some of the crews kept their navigation lights on, anxious already about collision.

Constantine had not been unaware of the misgivings of his crew. Once he got airborne, the chief manifestation was the continual running commentary of advice that came to him over the inter-com. He realized that they were working off their nervousness and he did not silence them.

First man over the target from Elsham Wolds was Clive Saxelby. Another pilot, an NCO named Roberts, recently arrived on the station and unknown to Saxelby and his crew, had come along as second-pilot for the experience, and Saxelby had stationed him in the astro-dome. Their approach to the target was like a practice run, they were not picked out by the searchlights and the blaze below was already the biggest they had ever seen. It was becoming impossible to identify individual aiming-points, but they followed the Rhine in and dropped their bombs on the edge of the existing fires. Then they turned for home.

They had crossed the Dutch/German border and were approaching Eindhoven when the fighter picked them up. The first they knew of the attack was a succession of sharp cracks and a tearing, rending noise in the fuselage, followed by a strangled scream on the inter-com. The cockpit had escaped, but the middle section of the fuselage had been badly hit and was on fire. The fire quickly contaminated the oxygen system, half-suffocating the crew. Saxelby wrenched off his mask but he still couldn't breathe. He pushed back the cabin window and put his head into the slipstream, breathing deeply, and as he did so he stared straight into the silhouette of an Me 110, slanted into a 90-degree bank, turning in again towards him.

'Christ! He's coming in again!'

Saxelby put the nose forward and spiralled but the fighter followed him down, getting in another accurate burst. The fire in the mid-section had caught hold and the fabric was peeling and burning. Half of the tailplane, too, was denuded of fabric, and the trimmers had been shot away. The hydraulics were hit and the undercarriage and bomb-doors were drooping, greatly adding to the load on the control column as the Wellington spiralled. But the worst danger was the fire.

Pipkin, the navigator, was nearest to the flames. He had no gloves on, but he attacked them immediately with his bare hands.

McClean, the wireless operator, clipped on his parachute and went forward to open the hatch under the cockpit, expecting an order to bale out. He saw Saxelby struggling with the controls.

'Are you coming, Sax?'

'Not yet – I think I can hold it.'

McClean went back to help Pipkin, and between them they extinguished the fire, ripping off the affected fabric and pushing it out through the holes. The Wellington began to look bare and skeletal amidships, but it still flew. Pipkin went forward and shouted in Saxelby's ear.

'Everything's fine, we're doing well. I know exactly where we are. For God's sake keep her flying.'

But Saxelby was finding the weight of the controls too much for him. The plane was still locked in the spiral and the ground was coming up fast.

'It's no good – I can't hold her.'

Pipkin disappeared, then came back with a rope which he

tied round the control column. Saxelby noticed that the skin on Pipkin's hands was shrivelled and burnt. Pipkin lashed the stick back and the Wellington levelled out.

'Good work. But get ready to cut the rope in a hurry if I want to lose height.'

St Pierre, the French-Canadian in the rear turret, had been wounded in the leg. His inter-com was cut off, and he crawled forward to see what was happening. He thought he might have missed a bale-out order. Under the astro-dome, leaning against the side of the fuselage, was Roberts, the second pilot, apparently taking it easy. St Pierre gave him a prod to attract his attention, and like the body in the cupboard Roberts slid in slow-motion to the floor. This eager young pilot who had come along for the experience had been rewarded by the experience of death.

To the rest of the crew Sergeant Roberts was a stranger. He had bought it. The less said about it the better.

Although they were living with the daily expectation of sudden and violent death, and although they shrugged it off with jokes and euphemisms, the men of Bomber Command were not conditioned to the ugliness of the reality. St Pierre's reaction was typical. This was something he had to shut his mind to. He didn't want to see any more. He had to dissociate himself from it. There was a dead man in the fuselage – that was all it meant to him. As he didn't know the man, the incident would be that much easier to forget. Afterwards, over a few pints, he might tell the story of how he pushed the body and of how it slithered to the floor. He might even play it for laughs. Indeed, that was the only way. But right now he was scared, and he had to get away from it. After making sure that the plane was still under control, he turned on his heel and went back to the familiar isolation of his turret.

It wasn't until they were having a meal in the Mess after force-landing at Honington that they noticed St Pierre's leg. His left flying-boot was caked with blood. But St Pierre refused all demands that he go to the doctor. That would mean being left behind at Honington. Here was another typical reaction.

Stick to your crew, don't lose it. Hang on to the men you can trust. 'I'm coming widya,' said St Pierre.

There was no more poignant loss that night than that of Sergeant Roberts. A new man on a strange squadron, he was unknown and almost unmourned, even by his crew.

Back at Elsham Wolds, Dizzy Spiller was already telling the funniest story of the raid – 'How we got Connie to Cologne and back'. They really believed they had. Spiller would go through the whole operation, exaggerating the horror with which he had greeted the news that he was to fly with Constantine, repeating the full and slightly embellished dialogue that took place between 'me and the groupie'. 'What's our course for base, Mr Spiller?' Mr Spiller! He'd never been called that in his life. 'Flak's getting a bit close, Connie – better weave about a bit.' And then Spiller would caricature the group captain's evasive action, which he represented as smoother than the summer breeze. It was an act that went down well at parties in the Sergeants' Mess, but it was never quite so hilarious as when Hugh Constantine himself was there to hear it.

And so somehow the tragedies were forgotten, the tragedy of Roberts, and of two other NCO pilots and their crews, one lost over Germany, the other crashing on take-off next morning after being diverted. Both pilots were on their first trip as first pilot and captain. There were no survivors.

Only one crew was missing of the ten who came up to Elsham from Wellesbourne Mountford. The pilot was the most experienced man of the lot – Al Hamman, the South African. Hamman was shot down near the target, and only his wireless operator escaped.

*

At Marham, Paul Holder's time of take-off was about half-way down the list. Next to him in the second pilot's seat sat Jack Baldwin, a rotund figure now in Mae West, harness and flying kit, all borrowed from 'Square' McKee. One by one the Stirlings and Wellingtons rolled down the runway, disappeared over the ridge in the middle, then reappeared, navigation lights glowing, as they lifted their wheels. The sky of East Anglia was swarming with aircraft, those from Marham climbing steadily into the stream. One Stirling bounced badly on take-off, ripping off its port wheel, which bowled into the corner of the field. The sergeant pilot, warned from control that his undercarriage was damaged, decided to fly on. He would worry about it when he got back. He wasn't going to let a little thing like a damaged undercart keep him away from Cologne.

Holder and Baldwin watched all this from the cockpit. Then it was their turn to take off. As they climbed away they hit the slipstream of another Stirling, and the bump was something physical, rattling the plane and everyone in it. It was a timely reminder that there were many other bombers moving along stealthily with them.

'Captain to gunners. Keep your eyes skinned for other aircraft. Let me know at once if anything comes too close. State type when possible.'

The three gunners acknowledged the message, and Holder began a gentle but continuous weave. Soon they had crossed the North Sea. As they flew inland the searchlight concentrations grew more frequent and ahead of them they saw unmistakable signs of aerial combat. Tracer flitted prettily across the sky and a cargo of incendiaries was jettisoned, landing in a splash on the ground. Suddenly a huge flare glowed brightly, hanging in the sky like a lantern, then falling in idle slow-motion.

'What's that, skipper?' The question came from Baldwin, who had fallen naturally into the inter-com conventions.

'I'm afraid it's one of our aircraft, sir.'

They were still sixty miles from the target, but already they could see the fires. The searchlights and the flak intensified.

'Isn't it time we reached our bombing height, sir?' The plaintive request came from the navigator – in their continuous evasive action they had lost height. Holder pulled the Stirling back to 16,000 feet.

'Bomb-doors open.'

There was silence now except for the bomb-aimer's instructions. It was obvious that the defences were at full stretch. Searchlight beams groped sightlessly across the sky, giving no help to the ground gunners, who seemed content to put up a barrage over the target area to prevent the bombers from coming in low.

Another Stirling and a Wellington had settled down on the same bombing run. Both were clearly visible, one to starboard and slightly lower, the other to port and just above. Below them the city was becoming shapeless and obscured, hidden beneath vast areas of fire and smoke. Even the contours of the Rhine were dimmed under skeins of smoke. But the towers of the cathedral were still sharply outlined in the light of three immense conflagrations nearby. No one had expected to see such an area of fire.

'Enemy aircraft on our starboard quarter.'

This single interruption to the smooth flow of bombing instructions came from the rear gunner, a few seconds before the Stirling ended its bombing run. Holder held his course, relying on his gunners to keep the fighter at bay.

'Bombs gone.'

The fighter had selected another aircraft in the stream. Holder weaved and turned, while the bomb-aimer tried to get a photo. Then he turned west to clear the target area. Ahead of him, north-east of Cologne, the Ruhr defences were displaying their usual efficiency; several bombers that had wandered in that direction were coned by searchlights and boxed in by flak.

The increase in the burning area since their arrival over the target was most impressive; the fire was spreading like a plague. The major conflagrations were now roaring like blast furnaces, throwing up three enormous domes of flame.

The fires were clearly visible as they flew their corkscrew course home. Ninety miles from the target Holder turned and did a complete circuit, taking a final look at the glow that was Cologne. It seemed from this distance that the many thousands of individual fires had merged into a single inferno.

They landed at Marham just after half past three. Baldwin, somehow drawn into the crew comradeship, accompanied them to a breakfast of eggs and bacon. Even breakfast at Exning House after a ride on the Heath had never tasted better.

It was a wet, dismal morning, but one by one the Stirlings and Wellingtons returned in the grey light of dawn, until there was only one aircraft missing from each squadron. A third aircraft, the Stirling with the broken undercarriage, was circling the field, using up its fuel, its single wheel drooping in odd deformity, unretracted and unretractable. Two hours later its sergeant pilot made a successful belly-landing.

There wasn't much point in waiting any longer for the other two. Even if they hadn't been shot down they must have run out of fuel by now. First Jack Baldwin and then 'Square' McKee went to snatch a few hours' sleep before the day's work.

The fate of the two missing crews would not be known for some time – perhaps several weeks. Meanwhile they would be posted missing. In fact, the crew of the Wellington were all dead, shot down over the target. The missing Stirling was the one flown by Wilf Davis.

When Pamela Baldwin got up next morning she got an affirmative to her carefully casual inquiry as to whether her father was back. But while she was at breakfast the phone started buzzing, and it buzzed for the rest of the day as the news of Jack Baldwin's part in the raid got around.

For a subsequent attempted 1,000-bomber raid, on Essen, a postscript was added to Harris's executive signal. This is what it said:

'*No AOCs to fly without my permission, and none tonight.*'

It seemed that Bert Harris was not amused. But in fact, although Harris felt that he couldn't possibly have his knowledgeable group commanders straying about over enemy territory, exposing themselves to destruction and worse still capture, he privately wrote down Baldwin's effort as a good show.

When the New Year's honours list in January 1943 included a knighthood for the commander of No 3 Group, and was followed by promotion to the rank of air marshal, contemporaries muttered all over again that Jack Baldwin could get away with anything.

*

Jim Wilkie, the 19-year-old Manchester pilot from Skellingthorpe, was approaching the target at 9,000 feet. He had tried using extra boost but he could not get any more height. On reaching the Dutch coast he had wondered whether he ought to turn back, but with the very large number of bombers around him – mostly above him – he had decided that the risk of being picked out was still less than usual. He had stayed on course.

Presently a fleeting burst of tracer and a plunging bomber decided him to steer more to the north. Almost at once he hit a different sort of trouble – the Manchester was coned in a tripod of searchlights. He began to throw the aircraft about, trying to get away from that frightful glare. Soon he began to lose height. There was a loud thud, and then the port engine started running roughly and spitting fire. Wilkie cut the engine to prevent the fire from spreading, but the loss of height on one engine was alarming.

Wilkie had had plenty of experience on Manchesters and he did not subscribe to the general view that they wouldn't stay up on one engine. Yet this one clearly wouldn't. He jettisoned the bomb-load, still hoping to get the aircraft home. The searchlights were blinding him and he didn't know his heading, but he turned away from the target area. Light flak was beating on the wing and fuselage surfaces like hail, and he had to get away from those hideous lights.

Every manoeuvre seemed to cost him a hundred feet or more. Suddenly he was clear of the searchlights, but only at the expense of a further loss of height. He knew he must be very near the ground. There was no chance whatever of getting back, or even of reaching the coast, and he ordered the crew to bale out. A moment later Eddie Finch, the Cockney front gunner, strode past him from the nose turret. He did not even glance at Wilkie. Why hadn't he baled out from the front hatch? Was it jammed? Surely if it was Finch would have said so. Wilkie was mystified.

If he had had time to think about it, he might have found a perfectly reasonable explanation of Finch's conduct. Very probably there was nothing wrong with the front hatch. Finch had simply remembered his self-appointed responsibility for the young gunner Doug Baird. He was going back to make sure that Baird was clear of the rear turret and ready to bale out.

By applying opposite rudder Wilkie was able to keep the Manchester on a straight course for the balc-out, but he could not prevent it sinking. There was no chance of getting out himself – the moment he left the controls the aircraft would flip over on its back. In any case he knew he had left it too late. Very soon the plane would hit the ground. He wanted very much to see what was underneath him, and he switched on the landing lights. He was shocked to find that they were already almost scraping the trees. He didn't know how many of his crew had got out.

The tops of the fir trees would surely cushion the impact. He tried to level out, then felt a jolt underneath him and realized he had hit the ground. The trees had opened out on to a field and quite involuntarily he had made a perfect belly-landing.

Ahead of him, illuminated by the landing lights that still pierced the darkness, he could see a wire fence, and beyond it a row of gardens and houses. Both engines were on fire, the flames were spreading to the fuselage and Wilkie hurried back to see if anyone was left behind before climbing through the top hatch. He jumped down to the grass and was almost immediately surrounded.

'*Hände hoch!*'

There were Luftwaffe uniforms everywhere. He had landed on the airfield at Dusseldorf.

It was some time before Wilkie was able to piece together what had happened to all the crew. He met Tobias, the second pilot, and Jock Campbell, the gunner, in the German guard-room at Dusseldorf that night, and within a few days he saw the Australian Benn. He learned that Campbell and Benn, the nearest men to the escape hatch, had been the first to jump. Both had got down safely. Tobias, as second pilot, had chosen to go last and had been about to jump when the plane hit the ground. There was no news of Bee, Baird and Finch, except that Tobias had seen them jump and had realized afterwards that they must have been dangerously low. Wilkie was so worried about them that he disclosed the full crew list to the Germans, fearing that one or more of them might be lying injured amongst the fir trees.

Eventually he learned that Finch's unselfish action in going back through the fuselage had cost him his life. There had just been time for the first parachutes to open, but Eddie Finch, his friend Doug Baird and the cheerful Alan Bee, so animated as a rule and yet so subdued before this flight, had all jumped too low and had all been killed.

There were no medals to be won by the sort of deed enacted by Eddie Finch. The reconstruction of motive could be little more than conjecture – yet who can doubt what was in his mind as he hurried past Jim Wilkie? It was his sort of comradeship that enriched the tragic routine.

*

In the hotel near the station at Lincoln, Bette Baveystock sat in the lounge for half an hour reading the magazines before going to bed.

'Not many of the boys about tonight,' she heard someone say. 'There must be something on.'

At ten o'clock she went contentedly to bed. When she woke up Bave would be there. She read for a further half-hour, then put out the light. Almost at once she heard the drone of aircraft engines. One by one the planes seemed to circle the town before climbing away. The noise reverberated round the hotel for nearly an hour. There was something eerie about it all, lying there in a strange room in the dark, listening – listening and wondering. It was at one minute past eleven, had she but known it, that the plane carrying her husband on a one-way trip to Germany flew directly over her hotel.

Leslie Manser, the pilot, was having trouble with the aircraft. The Manchester wouldn't climb. It had behaved all right on air-test, but fully loaded its ceiling was no more than 7,000 feet. All attempts to get above that height overheated the engines. He was facing exactly the same hazards as Jim Wilkie.

Manser made a virtue of necessity. 'We may be better off at 7,000 anyway,' he told his crew. 'The Jerries will be plastering the main force above us and we might get by unnoticed.' But an hour later, as they approached Cologne on their bombing run, they were picked out by the searchlights, and there was no chance to escape at that height. Manser held the plane straight and level and they carried on to the aiming-point. 'Bang-on' Barnes went forward to drop the bombs.

They had watched the flak rising at other, invisible aircraft. Now it rose at them. Manser carried on coolly, never wavering from his course. They could see the Rhine on their left, and below them lay the burning city. Manser saw a dark area adjacent to the main conflagration and steered for that.

'Drop the bombs in the dark patch next to the fires.'

It meant a slightly longer bombing run, but it was in accordance with the briefing. The flak was insistent now, boxing them in. Two minutes later the dark patch disappeared under the nose.

'Bombs gone.'

Now, perhaps, to get more height. But the explosion of the flak was almost simultaneous and the plane rocked from a direct hit. Manser thrust the stick forward, diving to evade the searchlights, twisting and turning to confound the gunners. Baveystock, in a small folding seat next to Manser, hung on grimly. They were running into a hail of light 20-millimetre ack-ack, and the searchlights were shining through the cockpit roof. They were down to 800 feet before they finally escaped into the darkness. By that time they were sweating in a stench of fire and smoke.

The rear gunner shouted that he had been hit. Manser yelled back at him to hang on. 'We've got to find out what's on fire.' Their fear was that one of the bombs had hung up. Baveystock wrenched off the cover at the forward end of the bomb-bay but everything inside looked dark and normal; Horsley looked into the rear end and found he could see straight through to the ground. The rear part of the bomb-doors had been blown off by the flak-burst – but the bombs had gone.

Manser was climbing now on extra boost, striving for more height in case they had to bale out. He had tugged the Manchester back to 2,000 feet when there was a throaty growl from the port side as the engine burst into flames. This, thought the crew, is where we get out. But Manser made a different move.

'Feather the prop and try the extinguisher.'

Baveystock did so, but the fire in the engine did not lessen. The flames were streaking out to the rear and enveloping the whole width of the wing. Somewhere in the middle of that fire was a main petrol tank, holding nearly 600 gallons of high-octane fuel. It could be only seconds before the petrol boiled out through the main breather pipe. The explosion then would blow them all to kingdom come.

'Let's wait and see if the fire goes out,' said Manser. His composure astonished the crew. To them the situation was paralysing in its terror, and their instinct was to get out immediately. But Manser, having successfully bombed the target under direct fire, had his mind fixed on a new priority – getting the aircraft home.

Incredibly enough, Manser's refusal to panic proved right. In the next few minutes they watched the metal panels round the engine burn slowly away, then the flames flickered and went out. Manser was steering for Manston, on the Kent coast. 'Go aft and jettison everything you can,' he told Baveystock. They were still losing height. 'I doubt if we'll get to Manston but we might make the Channel. Then we can ditch and perhaps avoid capture.'

Baveystock found Naylor, the injured rear gunner, lying on the rest-bed. Horsley was bandaging his arm. Baveystock stuffed everything movable down the flare-chute – spare guns, ammunition pans, flares, oxygen bottles. But he knew he wasn't doing much to lighten the load. Manser was still struggling to maintain height. Barnes was still at the navigation table. Mills, the front gunner, was still in his turret. Thanks to the inspiration of Manser, every man was usefully employed. But Manser was finding it impossible now to keep the plane on course. The starboard engine was overheating under the strain – it might catch fire at any moment. In spite of all their efforts their only remaining chance lay in baling out.

'Put on parachutes. Prepare to abandon aircraft.'

Baveystock went forward to help his skipper. Horsley helped Naylor to the fuselage door (the rear hatch was permanently locked). The rest of the crew would exit through the front hatch, which Mills had already opened; he was standing by the hatch with parachute clipped on, ready to jump.

'Bale out, bale out!'

As Baveystock reappeared in the cockpit, Barnes was following Mills down to the hatch. Baveystock plugged in to the inter-com.

'Can I do anything, skipper?'

'No – get out! quick!'

Baveystock shot a glance at the flying instruments. Their speed was down to 110 knots – the critical speed for one-engine flying in a Manchester. The plane was almost on the point of the stall. Baveystock grabbed his parachute pack, clipped it on his chest, then unfastened the pack behind the pilot's seat and bent across Manser to clip it on.

Baveystock had not yet realized it, but for Manser all hope had already gone. He was in the same position as Wilkie had been. He could hold the plane more or less level for perhaps another half-minute – time enough for the others to get out. But he could not get out himself. The plane would dive into the ground as soon as he left the controls.

As Baveystock bent over him to fasten the chute, Manser thrust him roughly away.

'For God's sake get out – we're going down.'

The Manchester was juddering and shaking, about to stall.

Baveystock crawled down to the front hatch, doubled himself up and dropped through. He did not know that they were almost scraping the hedgerows. It was only a second or two later when he hit the dyke. There was no time for his parachute to open.

Almost simultaneously, less than a hundred yards beyond the dyke, the Manchester ploughed in.

For Leslie Manser, the succeeding priorities had been clearly defined. First, to reach and bomb the target. Second, to get the aircraft home. Third, when this proved impossible, to avoid capture. Fouth, to save the lives of his crew.

The men in the fuselage had got out just in time. Barnes and Mills, too, were safe. Only Baveystock, in a loyal attempt to help his doomed skipper, had stayed too long.

*

The vibrant roar of engines as the returning bombers turned over Lincoln shook the ornaments on the mantelpiece in the hotel bedroom where Bette Baveystock slept. She woke up, understood what the noise was and felt better. Now it was all over, and she could breathe freely again. She got up at seven o'clock, full of excitement, made up carefully to be at her best for her date and took extra trouble with her hair. At half past eight she went down to breakfast. There was no sign of Bave.

The resonant tones of Big Ben prefaced the nine o'clock news. 'Our bombers were out over Germany last night,' said the announcer. (It was Frank Phillips.) There was no mention of any losses. Bave must have been delayed at the airfield, or perhaps diverted. There were so many perfectly logical reasons why he should be late. He would show up soon. She finished her breakfast and wandered upstairs to her room. To fill in time she retouched her make-up. Perhaps he was waiting for her in the lounge. She went down to see, but there was still no Bave. Something must be keeping him. Why couldn't he phone?

At 9.30 she began to get really restless. Bave had said not to ring the camp, and she wandered about the public rooms, unable to settle. Her eyes ran over the print of the Sunday papers but her mind absorbed nothing. By eleven o'clock she could no longer keep away from the phone. She was still quite sure that Bave must be all right, that he would come in soon, but she had to know. She spoke to the squadron adjutant.

'Can you please tell me where Sergeant Baveystock is? It's his wife speaking.'

'Just a minute – I'll inquire.'

She waited in an uneasy dread, almost wishing she hadn't phoned. Then the same voice spoke to her again. This time the tone was quite different, the pitch controlled and even, the whole speech measured and tailored to fit the occasion.

'There's no news for you yet, Mrs Baveystock.'

'You mean he hasn't come back?'

'We can't say anything for certain yet. Quite a lot of planes were diverted. Where are you speaking from, Mrs Baveystock?'

'Lincoln.'

'Are you staying there?'

'Yes.' She gave him the name of the hotel.

'I'll get in touch with you as soon as we have anything to tell you.'

'Thank you.'

He hadn't got back to Skellingthorpe, but he must have got down somewhere else. In a moment he would come striding in. No other explanation was possible.

At twelve o'clock she went into the dining-room for lunch. She didn't feel like eating, but it gave her something to do. Hardly realizing what she was doing, she fumbled her way through the soup and the main course. A waitress brought the sweet. She looked up, and as she did so she saw the manageress peeping through the door, looking across towards her table. As the waitress retreated the manageress whispered something to her. Could it be her phone call? No one came to tell her so. Yet she felt sure she was being talked about. Then a spruce little man in a lounge suit appeared in the doorway and peered at her. For some reason she was being pointed out to everyone. What could they possibly know about her? Still no one came across to speak to her.

She finished her sweet and walked out of the dining-room, intending to sit in the lounge and await the call, but in the hall the manageress intercepted her.

'There's a gentleman waiting to see you.'

It couldn't be Bave. He would have dashed straight in. She was shown into a small private room.

She had known in her heart for an hour or more that Bave wasn't coming back, but she had somehow managed to pretend otherwise. Now, as she entered the room and her eye was drawn to the gleaming white of the padre's collar, the fact that Bave was missing hit her with full and numbing force, a stunning blow that landed right between the eyes. Yet as she felt the impact of the tidings that had been brought to her, it was the padre she felt sorry for. What a rotten job it was to have to tell a complete stranger that the bottom has fallen out of their world.

The padre did not try to soften the blow, but he talked about the possibility that Bave might be a prisoner, and told her something about the treatment of POWs, encouraging her to hope. He asked her about her family, and talked about his own. It was all so strange to be sitting there, oddly composed, talking about her life, knowing all the time that it was over.

When the padre had gone she enquired about the trains back to London. There wasn't one until six o'clock.

What a week-end.

In the next few weeks Bette Baveystock analysed almost every word of sympathy that was spoken to her, trying to assess just how much hope there really was. After about a fortnight the pension forms arrived. There was no further news. People began to annoy her by talking about what a fine fellow Bave had been.

It was five weeks after her week-end in Lincoln that she had a mysterious phone call. 'I can't tell you who I am,' said a voice that was heavily charged with a foreign accent, difficult to understand, 'but I have a message for you. You must keep it entirely to yourself. Do you promise to do that?'

'Of course.'

A Whitley V

A Stirling I of 149 Squadron

A Manchester of 83 Squadron

Above: Tea before the air test. Below: Crews of 106 Squadron at Coningsby with Guy Gibson in the middle, the morning after the raid

A section of Cologne, taken a week after the raid

The railway workshops at Cologne-Nippes – the biggest in Cologne – as seen by reconnaissance aircraft *above:* before and *below:* after the raid

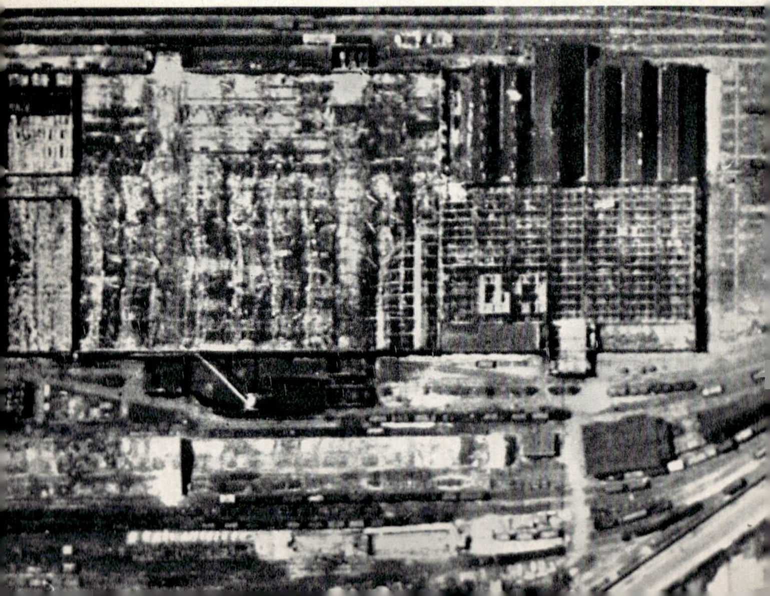

'The message is – the name and number you are interested in is alive and well, and is coming home.'

Before she could reply there was a click and the voice was gone.

For the next few days she endured the most excruciating mental torture she had ever known, alternating between radiant joy and the bleakest despair. How could anyone know anything about Bave if it wasn't official? Why should it be such a secret? And how could he be coming home? At times she was convinced that the whole thing was a hoax. But who could perpetrate anything so diabolically cruel?

The truth was that Baveystock, when he tumbled through the forward escape hatch less than 200 feet from the ground, had had his fall broken by the dyke into which he fell. His parachute hadn't opened fully, but it may have put a slight brake on his descent, and the four or five feet of water in the dyke had saved him.

He half-swam, half-waded to the bank, up to his neck in green slimy water. With the tension of the previous half-hour, the shock of the fall and the dowsing in cold water, he had an uncontrollable urge to urinate. He began to struggle with the zipper of his flying suit, then realized how ridiculous this was. His water could hardly be more unpleasant than the water he was already immersed in. Leaving his zipper alone, he let his muscles relax, luxuriating in the sense of release and in the warmth of the water that flowed round his loins. If I live to be a hundred, he thought, I'll never have a better one than that.

Peeling off his Mae West and harness, he crawled out of the dyke and ran across to the wreck of the plane. It was impossible to get near it, so fierce were the flames. A clump of trees around the wreck had caught fire, and ammunition was exploding with frightening rapidity. It was clear that Manser, holding on for those extra few seconds to give his crew time to escape, had been killed instantly as the Manchester ploughed in. He had given his life for his crew.

The plane had crashed three miles east of a small Belgian village called Bree, near the Dutch border. The villagers helped them to evade the Germans, and within forty-eight hours the whole crew, apart from Manser and Barnes – the latter having been injured in the fall and unable to avoid capture – were in hiding in Liège. In the next few weeks they were passed along the Comet escape line, through Brussels, Paris and St Jean de Luz, then over the Pyrenees to San Sebastian. They were in San Sebastian when the sympathetic intelligence officer put through the anonymous call. By a coincidence he had met an aunt of Bette's who had told him about her niece's loss. He had traced the crew through escape-route messages, but had not dared to pass any information until they were safely across the Pyrenees. It then became only a matter of days before they were in Gibraltar. A week later they were home.

When Baveystock and the rest of the crew told their story, Leslie Manser was posthumously awarded the Victoria Cross.

*

Ten, twelve and fifteen thousand feet above the target, the experience of individual crews was differing widely, even those at the same height and in the same wave. Some were hotly engaged by searchlights and flak and were forced down to low level, others flew through almost without interference. There was a period quite soon after the start of the raid – within about twenty minutes – when the ground defences seemed to give up altogether. The fantastic tracery of the searchlights was extinguished and the flak ceased. Then the searchlights were lit again, and while the flak remained silent the stage was set for the night-fighters based in the Cologne area to come in and pick off the bombers one by one. But the order to the flak batteries to cease fire was not followed by the arrival of the fighters. Through some administrative muddle or disagreement, permission for them to take off was apparently withheld. The result was that the bombers had a brief period without opposition of any kind, while very little fighter opposition was encountered at any time over the target.

Beneath the flames that covered the city like an impenetrable foliage, the people of Cologne were suffering a typical succession of miraculous escapes and tragic misfortunes, the predictable experience of any great city under aerial bombardment. Thousands of people had already been bombed out. Hundreds more were trapped in air raid shelters where all the exits were blocked by debris. Rescue work was hampered by blocked roads, burst water and gas mains, and the hail of incendiaries and high-explosive that continued to fall. In one cellar where 150 people were trapped, a high-explosive bomb fell through the half-destroyed building and penetrated the cellar ceiling, coming to rest in front of a wall. Miraculously it did not explode, but it was a delayed-action type and might go off at any moment. Efforts to reach the cellar from an adjacent building were intensified and a hole was finally cut through. Women, children and old men, together with a crowd of industrial workers, had just been evacuated when the bomb went off. Not all incidents had such a merciful ending.

*

The other Manchester crews at Skellingthorpe, like Wilkie and Manser, were also confined to a height of about 9,000 feet through the sheer inability of their machines to climb higher. But all the others – fifteen of them – got through safely, locating the target by following the river in bright moonlight and picking out the cathedral on their run-up, a floodlit oasis surrounded by a desert of fire. Just behind them were twelve Manchesters from 49 Squadron at Scampton. There should have been thirteen, but the CO – Wing Commander G. D. Slee – found his machine unserviceable at the last minute and went on the raid as second pilot with one of his flight commanders.

For Philip Floyd and his crew, this was their first operation over Germany in a Manchester. They had done seven trips on Hampdens, all to major targets in Germany, gone on leave and come back to find the squadron converting to Manchesters. They had done two minor trips on the new type – a leaflet raid and a mining sortie – and this would therefore be their tenth trip. This was a significant number for Floyd's 27-year-old navigator, accountant John Valentine, who had been told that his application for a commission would be forwarded when he had done ten trips.

Floyd soon experienced the same problem that had bothered all the Manchester crews so far – inability to reach a moderately safe height. In his case he could not climb above 7,000 feet, where they were an easy target for the searchlights. Thus, approaching Cologne, Floyd was faced with the classic dilemma – whether or not to dive out of a searchlight cone. He had so little height to spare that he was reluctant to try it, and he did everything he could to throw the cone off. But the concentration was too powerful – the flak centred on the apex of the cone and the Manchester was hit several times. The whole target seemed to be firing at them point blank. The engines escaped damage, but the hydraulics were punctured, rendering the turrets inoperable, and a pool of oil slopped about in the fuselage.

'We've had this,' said Floyd. 'I'm going to dive.'

The nose went forward, the speed built up and the searchlight cone was left behind. Floyd pulled out at 3,000 feet, but now he was within range of the light ack-ack batteries on the fringe of Cologne. The Manchester was hose-piped with tracer, but Floyd still headed for the target. Then he noticed that the oil temperature in the starboard engine was rising rapidly, and a shout from one of the gunners told him that oil coolant was streaming down the wing. He feathered the engine, realizing as he did so that he was too near the ground to have any hope of recovery on the remaining engine, and he gave the order to bale out.

Three men went at once to the rear hatch – two gunners and the wireless operator. Valentine went forward, and while the second pilot was jettisoning the front hatch, Valentine had a moment to talk to Floyd. He put a hand encouragingly on Floyd's knee.

'You've done bloody well, Philip. I'm going out in a second – I hope you'll follow me.'

Floyd took Valentine's hand and shook it, but he said nothing. They were still losing height, but he seemed to have the Manchester under control.

When Valentine got down to the front compartment he found the front gunner hesitating about the jump. There was no time to argue. The second pilot was waiting behind Valentine, and they had to leave time for Floyd himself. Valentine decided not to wait for the gunner. But in his excitement he pulled the ripcord of his parachute while he was still inside the plane, and it billowed out alarmingly in the draught from the hatch. He flung his arms round it like a pile of washing and jumped. He got through the hatch safely, the parachute didn't foul anything and almost immediately he found he was drifting gently down. The second pilot followed him, but in the next second the plane rolled over on its back, plunged forwards and blew up as it hit the ground. Floyd and the front gunner were still inside.

Floyd had been faced with the final dilemma that had killed Leslie Manser – he had managed to keep some sort of control while he stayed in the pilot's seat, but he must have known all along that directly he left it the plane would spin in. At their low altitude, there had never been any chance for him from the start.

In life the former pacifist Philip Floyd had made few friends. In death he won no honours. Perhaps he might have done if the five men whose lives he saved by his sacrifice had got back to England quickly, as Manser's crew did, to tell the story.

More frustrating still is the story of a second Manchester that was lost from Scampton. One by one the bodies of the crew were picked up next day out of the North Sea. The name of the pilot was Flight Sergeant Carter. There was no sign of the aircraft, no hint of what could have happened, no desperate radio call. It is probable that they got to the target, bombed it, suffered heavy damage themselves and struggled hard to get back. But the story of their heroism or ill-fortune lies beyond the power of re-creation.

*

The restrictions that had so irked Geoff 'Kid' Gane – the Australian gunner with the Eddie Cantor eyes – at Binbrook may have been less pointless than they seemed. No 12 Squadron was able to put up twenty-eight Wellington II's – the highest number of planes from any single squadron. And flying as second pilot with one of the crews was the station commander, Group Captain C. D. C. Boyce. But Gane's conviction of impending tragedy was borne out. As well as putting up the most planes, 12 Squadron suffered the heaviest casualties. They also had a high percentage of 'boomerangs', no less than six of their Wellingtons being forced to turn back.

One of the first planes to take off from Binbrook, piloted by 22-year-old Tony Payne, a flight lieutenant on his second tour, crashed on the outskirts of Amsterdam with the loss of the entire crew, probably shot down by fighters. The plane to leave immediately before Bruce Shearer's (Kid Gane's pilot), and flown by Sergeant G. H. Everatt (already mentioned), crashed at West Raynham thirty-seven minutes after take-off and again all the crew were killed. The plane to leave immediately after Shearer's, flown by a Pilot Officer A. Waddell, was shot down over Dusseldorf, and again there were no survivors.

In Bruce Shearer's case the take-off itself was nearly disastrous. The Wellington, loaded with high-explosive and incendiaries, refused to lift. Shearer rammed open the throttles, the engines screamed in warning, the plane bumped and lifted, then bumped and lifted again, and Kid Gane in the tail turret saw a hedge and then an anti-aircraft gun position flash past his face. They had been perilously near to staying behind in the UK for good.

'I'm going to get as high as I can,' Bruce Shearer told his crew. The intention was good but the execution disappointing – the Wellington would climb no higher than 10,000 feet. When they reached the coastal flak belt Shearer began to weave, but even before they were properly aware of enemy action against them, they noticed a trail of smoke from the starboard engine. 'It may be overheating,' said Shearer. 'Perhaps the engine's starved of oil.' There was no indication from his gauges, but he told Bruce Brown, the Sydney taxi-driver, to start pumping oil manually to the suspect engine. Brown operated the pump for more than a minute and the trail of smoke thinned to no more than a wisp. Shearer decided to go on.

They were approaching the Kammhuber Line now, and the searchlights began to spring up at them. The trail of smoke was persisting. Another Wellington close to them, caught in a cone of light, nosed forward gently and then plunged in flames. Shearer redoubled his efforts to evade the lights, but he still would not turn back. One extra-powerful blue searchlight was holding on to them tenaciously. In the distance they could see the burning target, with the Rhine snaking through it, bathed in moonlight. Another few minutes and they could drop their bombs and turn away.

The starboard engine was really hot now, the whole cowling emitting a dull red glow. Brown had left the manual pump and gone forward to aim the bombs. Eddie Ansford was trying to concentrate on the navigation. 'Mac' McKenna was listening out on the radio, oblivious to their danger. Gane, in the tail turret, took time out from his continual watch for fighters to shoot a glance at the sparks that flashed like tracer down the starboard side. Get your chute, he told himself. His fingers felt for it. Get ready. Get ready. He found it and clamped it on his chest. Then, as they came out of a violent stall turn, the engine caught fire.

'Pull the fire extinguishers, Eddie.'

As Ansford did so there was a sudden coruscation of sparks and embers and a huge chunk of cowling flew away behind them. Then the engine flowered into a mass of flame.

'We're getting out of this.' Giving up all hope of reaching the target, Shearer told Brown to jettison the bombs and then turned for home. He fought to maintain control, but the flames were spreading rapidly along the wing. There was only one more order to give.

McKenna, blissfully ignorant of everything that had happened so far, switched to inter-com just in time to hear the order to go. By the time he had tugged off his helmet, clipped on his parachute and made his way up front, Ansford had removed the main hatch just aft of the cockpit and jumped. McKenna followed. Shearer was still holding the plane steady. Brown kicked out the emergency hatch in the belly of the plane and jumped from there. That left Shearer and Gane.

In the restricted space of the turret, Gane was having difficulty in unfastening his safety-belt. He had turned the turret into position so that he could drop out backwards and he had ripped his gloves off, but his fingers tore clumsily at the harness and he could not free it. His biggest enemy now was panic. He knew his weakness, and with a great effort he calmed himself and started again, working at the harness slowly and methodically. At last it slipped away.

In the same moment the Wellington plunged into a violent spiral to port. Gane was thrown forward over the guns, pinned by gravity, feeble and helpless. He could not move. A second later the turret was flooded with light as the blue searchlight picked them up again. Blinded and enfeebled, trapped in a plane that was clearly in its final plunge, he controlled an insane desire to depress his guns and shoot it out with that piercing light.

Suddenly he was able to move again. The Wellington must have rolled out of its spin. He dragged off his helmet, reached backwards to open the emergency door behind him and depressed the lock. He heard the door click open in the wind, and then he dropped out backwards, cushioned by the rush of air. He pulled the ripcord of his parachute but nothing happened, and his heart froze with the certainty of death. He had known it was coming. For a moment he lay back and shouted with a kind of crazed laughter. He was still laughing ironically as he dived through the sky when there was a sharp crack above him, his dive was arrested and next moment he landed in a heap on a cart-track in the middle of a forest a few yards from the burning Wellington.

He had no idea what had happened to the others. He hoped they had got out safely. But for the moment he was obsessed with his own problems. He had no idea which way to go, and for a time he hid near the plane. Then he set off along the cart-track in a westerly direction. He had a terrible pain in his ears, and all the time he could hear those last few sentences from Bruce Shearer on the inter-com echoing in his brain. He had gone about half a mile when he nearly walked into a man on a bicycle. He jumped into a ditch and thought he had escaped being seen, but when daylight came he was easily caught. Reaction set in now and he slept in the local prison for many hours.

At three o'clock next afternoon a truck came to collect him from the gaol – he had landed near Duren, about twenty-five miles south-west of Cologne. There were three coffins in the back of the truck, and Gane and the two German guards sat on them – there were no seats. Soon they stopped at a cemetery. For a moment Gane wondered whether he was about to be shot, whether perhaps one of the coffins was for him. Then the caretaker opened the gates of the cemetery and led the Germans to another coffin. After some discussion they signalled to Gane, apparently asking him to come and look at the coffin. Uncertain what was required of him and still fearing treachery, Gane stepped slowly forward. The lid of the coffin was lifted, and there, pale but otherwise unmarked, was the face of his skipper, Bruce Shearer.

The shock brought a half-stifled cry from Gane, and while the German guards stood silently by, apparently in sympathy and reverence, Gane bit fiercely into his lip and fought back the tears. Shearer, like so many pilots that night, trying to make sure that his crew got out safely, had held on too long. He had got out all right, and the Wellington had crashed without him, but he had left it too late.

*

Some of the last of the squadron Wellingtons to take off were those of the three Polish squadrons, Nos 300, 301 and 305, all based in Lincolnshire. Their late appearance was governed by their load – many of them carried 4,000-pounders, calculated to harass and hamper the fire-fighting after the incendiarists had done their work. They found visibility still good except for the pall of smoke that lay over the city, and several large bursts were seen where the 4,000-pounders fell. One flight sergeant named Kubacki had his petrol tanks holed and his starboard engine put out of action, but he got back to Ingham, where the ground crews counted twenty holes in his aircraft. Kubacki himself described it as 'a very nice trip'.

All the Polish crews returned safely, including Flight Lieutenant Hirszbandt, the 43-year-old pre-war major in the Polish Air Force. With Hirszbandt went the station commander at Lindholme, Group Captain A. H. Garland. It was Hirszbandt's twentieth trip.

Alone among the squadrons and units taking part, Lindholme defied superstition by sending thirteen aircraft. Two nights later, in the big raid on Essen, they sent thirteen again, but this time they were not so lucky. Veteran flier Hirszbandt and all but one of his crew were killed when they crashed at Swanton Morley on the return flight and the aircraft burnt out. That night the station commander had stayed on the ground.

3. *THE TRAINING UNITS*

AT THE FARMHOUSE at Cottesmore, Tom Ramsay had gone back for a cup of tea at five o'clock, reminded his wife Muriel that he would be night-flying and might not be home till daylight, and had then walked across the airfield to the briefing room. Still she suspected nothing – night flying at an OTU was no more than routine. After briefing Ramsay crossed the airfield again to work on his Hampden aircraft, which was dispersed only 250 yards away from the farmhouse. He and the upper gunner, Sergeant Falk, worked for the rest of the evening on swinging the compass, which had given trouble on air-test, and both men missed their pre-flight supper. They didn't even have time to call in at the farmhouse for coffee and biscuits before take-off.

At half past ten Muriel Ramsay went to bed. Soon she heard the Hampdens, thirty of them, taking off one by one. Unknown to her, practically the whole station had turned out to see them off. Tom Ramsay taxied right past her bedroom window to the bottom of the runway before taking off, but she didn't even look out. Some hours later she awoke in sudden panic to the certainty that someone – she was sure it was Tom – was calling her name. 'Mu!' called the voice. 'Mu!' It was Tom all right. But now that she was properly awake, listening intently, she could detect no further sound. The moon shone brightly through the curtains, deceiving her for a moment into thinking that dawn was breaking and that Tom might be back, but after a glance at her watch she sank back and relaxed. It was two o'clock. She must have been dreaming. Within a minute she was asleep again.

At six o'clock she was dimly aware that 'Rickie' Richman, the other trainee pilot living at the farmhouse, had come home and gone to bed. She awoke at eight o'clock to find that there was still no sign of Tom. She remembered now the words of the NAAFI man. She recalled the odd manner in which Tom had stood in the doorway before he said good-bye, as though he had wanted to tell her something. She remembered the vivid dream she had had in the night. She went along to her landlady's bedroom.

'I don't know what's happened to Tom. He's not home.'

'I'll ring up the station.'

They came out to see her, first the flight commander, then the padre. She shouldn't worry too much just yet. There were three planes missing from the station, but rescue boats were out looking for them. Later in the day they confirmed that Tom was missing. On Monday morning she went by train to her parents' home in London.

For Tom Ramsay, the flight to the target had been uneventful. Although it was his first operation, and it wasn't easy for him to judge, he got the impression that something was seriously wrong with the defences. He arrived over the target soon after one o'clock, one of the first of the OTU crews, but already much of the work of the searchlights seemed aimless and undisciplined, and there was no great concentration of flak.

His briefed height was 10,000 feet, which he gained without difficulty, and his target was the railway station near the cathedral. He had a full load of incendiaries in the bomb-bay, with a 250-lb high-explosive bomb slung under either wing.

At the end of his bombing run he banked round to try to see the effect of his bombs, but he couldn't pick out his own from the many others. Strings of incendiaries were burning in numerous lanes round the railway station and the whole area was a mass of fire. Ahead of him the defences seemed more active, so he continued his turn until he was heading north-west, away from the target. At this point the compass started playing tricks again. After a time he discovered that instead of heading back for the Dutch coast south of Rotterdam, as he had intended, he must have been flying almost due north. Forty-five minutes after bombing he found himself deep in northern Holland, almost as far north as Amsterdam and fifty miles farther inland. A lone Hampden, in danger of becoming lost, they had lost the protection of the bomber stream.

'There's an aircraft below us.'

The German ground control system, disorganized though it was, had no difficulty in directing a fighter on to the straggling Hampden. Immediately after the warning there came a fierce, spitting noise, as of a high voltage jumping across a gap, and the cockpit was lit up like day. Swords of lightning stabbed and pricked convulsively at the starboard engine and the next moment it burst into flames.

At once the Hampden started an involuntary turn to port, while a shower of sparks and flashes danced before Ramsay's eyes and filled the cockpit. He throttled back the burning engine and turned off the petrol, but the whole fuselage was still being raked with cannon. Within two or three seconds the port engine, too, had burst into flames. He throttled that back too, turning off the petrol, and the Hampden settled into a gentle glide.

Ramsay called his crew on the inter-com but could get no reply. Several times he gave the order to bale out. The pilot's position in a Hampden in this sort of circumstances was hopelessly confined; Ramsay was sitting in a tiny enclosed space from which he could neither see nor reach any of his crew. The observer was down in the nose, while the gunners were in the upper and lower turrets respectively, half-way down the fuselage, with no communicating passages to the cockpit. All Ramsay could do was hope that they had baled out already and prepare to get out himself.

The lonely, isolated, claustrophobic feeling of being inside the Hampden cockpit was intensified by the fire in the engines, a wall of flame on either side hemming him in. His entire horizon was restricted to this tiny area between the engines; he could see nothing beyond them, so fierce were the flames. Thus, as he pulled off his mask and unlocked the cockpit hood, he had no sensation of being about to jump off into space. He was merely about to step out of a tiny cell in which he was incarcerated by fire.

He pulled back the hood and stood up, released his straps and took off his helmet. The Hampden held steady in a gentle dive. About eight feet from him on either side were the burning engines. He began to clamber out of the cockpit, letting himself down on to the wing on the starboard side. The slipstream was not violent, but it would be enough to sweep him off the trailing edge of the wing, so there was no danger of his falling forward and being hit by the propeller. The greatest danger was of hitting one of the booms of the twin tailplane, but in the aircraft's present diving attitude he ought to fall clear. He was letting himself out backwards, head first, feet last, on to the wing, and he was almost clear of the cockpit when the Hampden nosed forward rather more steeply. As it did so the cockpit hood slid forward on its runners, jamming against and firmly pinning his right leg.

He kicked hard with his leg and tugged desperately at the hood but he could free neither. He would have to twist and worm his way back into the cockpit, get the weight of his body off his leg, push the hood back from inside and lock it securely, and then try again. All this took some time. He was working in a sort of vacuum, the only need he was conscious of being to step out of a burning cubicle. That was how it seemed to him. He was only half-aware of his real predicament, of the rapid loss of height and increasing proximity to the ground. He had very little sense of urgency, and therefore none of panic. Thus he was able to worm his way back into the cockpit without undue strain or tension and free himself quite easily. He locked the hood back firmly this time, climbed out again and dropped clear.

He was conscious that he had fallen on to the wing, and then, in spite of the nose-down attitude of the Hampden as it dived with engines burning to destruction, he slid backwards under the force of the airstream, over the trailing edge of the wing and down into space. Then he pulled the ripcord.

Now that he had escaped from his cell he was struck by the beauty that surrounded him. The countryside beneath him was bathed in moonlight and he was coming down on the edge of a village. He had had about a thousand feet to spare. He landed in a tree in someone's back garden, and the Hampden crashed no more than a field away, burning fiercely, discharging bullets in unrhythmic profusion. After unsuccessfully trying to attract the attention of someone in the house, he freed himself from the tree, lay down in the garden, covered himself with his parachute and went to sleep. He was captured next day.

Ramsay's crew – the tall, serious-minded navigator Bill Gorton and the two gunners, Vic Woolnough and Fred Falk – must have been killed in the fighter attack. It is inconceivable otherwise that they could have failed to get out. All three were found in the burnt-out wreck of the Hampden.

It had been exactly two o'clock when Tom Ramsay had first tried to bale out. It was as he lay half in and half out of the Hampden, pinned by the leg, that Muriel Ramsay awoke from her nightmare after hearing him call. Five weeks later, after controlling a recurring impulse to destroy the china jug, Muriel Ramsay heard that her husband was safe.

*

At Feltwell the despatching of aircraft from two runways

simultaneously was going on apace. Inevitably the four Wellington Ia's of Flying Training Command – three of them from Sutton Bridge – had to wait till last. Among the pilots at the back of the queue was the tall young pilot officer David Johnson.

Every evening since her husband had left Sutton Bridge on Tuesday 26th May, Dinny Johnson had telephoned through to Feltwell and talked to him for a few minutes. Throughout that week the gang at Sutton Bridge had given her no real chance to brood, to feel lonely or neglected. They had visited her every night. Tonight, Saturday, they called for her and took her to a dance on the station.

At ten o'clock a private call was booked to Feltwell on her behalf. Half an hour later the operator announced that Feltwell were not accepting calls. This could have only one meaning. The operation was on and Feltwell were in it.

Dinny tried to keep the party going but it was no use. At half past eleven she asked to be taken home. In fact, her husband was still on the ground at Feltwell, waiting to take off.

*

John Russell, the young, artistic squadron-leader commanding the blind-approach training flight at Driffield, took off in his Whitley at 23.10 and set course for the target. Four other Whitleys in his flight took off soon after, but for one reason or another – mostly due to the heavy icing which had driven back the 158 Squadron Wellingtons from the same airfield – all were forced to turn back. Russell, who also had to contend with severe icing, did not blame them. As CO he had chosen the best available Whitley – he regarded that as his prerogative – and he was able to climb more quickly than the others through the worst of the cloud.

As a bomber the Whitley was obsolescent. There were, in fact, no Whitley squadrons left in Bomber Command, though this was partly due to the enforced transfer of the last three Whitley squadrons to Coastal Command. When plans for the return of these squadrons for the raid fell through, the only

Whitleys remaining to take part were those of No 10 OTU at Abingdon plus the handful from Driffield and from a target-towing and gunnery flight at Grimsby, thirty-one Whitleys in all.

Although able to cruise at little more than 120 miles an hour, John Russell was able to climb to 12,000 feet, and his flight to the target was uneventful. His crew was a scratch one. Only the wireless operator, the short, dark-haired, placid Dennis Foster, DFM, was a member of Russell's flight. Foster, too, was on rest from operations. The crew was made up by a New Zealand second pilot named Box, from Auckland, a Canadian navigator named Godbehere, from Montreal, and an English gunner. All were straight from training units and without operational experience.

The long, rectangular, box-like fuselage of the Whitley, with its in-line Rolls-Royce Merlin engines, carried them in its typical nose-down flying attitude safely to the target and a good deal of the way back. They were somewhere between Brussels and Antwerp on the return flight when the cannon shells from a German fighter suddenly hummed past Foster's ears at the radio and clattered against the armour-plating up front. Foster's first thought, translated at once into action, was to reach down, grab his parachute and clip it on. It was a reaction born of experience. His next thought was for the rear gunner, isolated some fifty feet behind him in the tail turret. Foster plugged into the inter-com and was not surprised to hear the gunner shouting.

'We've been hit. I've taken a bashing myself. I can't see the fighter.'

From his position at the radio, directly behind the pilot, Foster could see that the port engine was on fire. He was glad he had kept his parachute handy. In the cockpit, another look at the port engine convinced John Russell that there was no time to waste. The fire had spread to the fuselage. He gave the order to jump, easing back the throttles and reducing speed to make the exit easier. The other crew-members were not so well prepared as Foster, but Box, the second pilot, scrambled quickly down into the bomb-well to get his own and Russell's chute. He went forward again and stood next to Russell, ready to clip on his chute for him, but in that moment the fighter attacked again. This time the entire port mainplane ripped out of its housing and dropped away, pirouetting down like a leaf. At once the broken Whitley turned over on its back and started a vicious, jerking, irrecoverable spin.

Russell did all he could to check the spin but the centrifugal force pinned him to his seat. His feet reached vainly for the rudders, the stick flapped uselessly in his stomach, the heat was becoming insufferable and the smoke asphyxiating. Behind him, Foster had been thrown helplessly forward when the wing flew off and now he was crouched on his knees on the radio table behind Russell's seat, head down and forced backwards between his knees, so that the nape of his neck was pressing hard against the armour-plating. When we hit the deck, he thought, it'll knock my head clean off. There was nothing he could do about it – he couldn't move so much as a finger. Just as he was thinking what a bloody pity it was, he passed out.

Russell had his hand on the carrying strap of his chute, but he could get no farther. The spin prevented it. The Whitley was inverted, spinning upside down, and Russell was dragged from his seat and precipitated against the perspex roof, to which he stuck like a fly, still clutching the chute. The Whitley was still revolving, and as it rotated he caught glimpses of the ground. It wouldn't be long before they crashed.

From somewhere underneath him there was an explosion, and in the next instant he felt himself falling through space. The strap of the chute was still held tightly in his clenched hand. Only a few seconds, a firm grip and a lot of luck stood between him and a violent death. He brought his hand up towards the two parachute clips on his chest, but he could only fasten the pack on one side. The other side refused to click into position, and the pack dangled in front of him. The ground was very close now, and all he could do was pull the ripcord and hope that the single clip would hold.

He felt the tug as the parachute opened, at what seemed little more than tree-top height. He landed heavily and his leg crumpled underneath him. Bits of his aeroplane rained down around him, but he was safe.

Box and Godbehere had been thrown out similarly, but they had not been holding their parachutes. Both men fell to their death. Box had helped to save his captain by getting his chute. Foster, who had clipped on his chute at the beginning, was the only other man to survive. He, too, was thrown out when the Whitley blew up, still unconscious, and when he came to he was gently swaying to earth. He had no recollection of pulling the ripcord and his parachute must have jerked open as he fell out. The only man left in the Whitley was the tail gunner, Orman, who was killed in his turret.

Russell's leg was broken in two places, giving him no chance to attempt to escape. Foster, too, was taken prisoner.

This was the only Whitley lost on the raid. Of the twenty-one Whitleys which went on the raid from Abingdon, all attacked the target and all returned safely, and although one crash-landed at Manston there were no casualties. Only one of these obsolescent Whitleys met fighter opposition (apart from Russell's) and only three were damaged by flak. It was an astonishing record for an OTU, one that was not approached by any of the squadrons.

*

The first aircraft to leave the unfinished satellite airfield of Graveley was piloted by a wisp of a man named Fred Hillyer. The time was 23.05. By opening the throttles unevenly Hillyer was able to counteract the unequal boost that the Wellington still suffered from; the aircraft climbed well and they crossed the North Sea at 13,000 feet. 'Fly down the Rhine,' they had been told at briefing, 'and you'll see the target long before you get there.' They were between sixty and seventy miles away when they first saw the glow of Cologne.

Above the Rhine to the north of Cologne the long fingers of the searchlights pointed skywards. Ahead of him Hillyer saw two searchlight beams meeting to form an arch, right on track.

He decided to duck through the centre, but knew he had done the wrong thing when the cockpit was suddenly flooded with light. At once the flak was right on target, buffeting the Wellington so that it juddered and jumped at each burst. Then the port engine started racing. Hillyer throttled back immediately and pushed the nose forward, and as he struggled to keep control he realized that his sudden loss of height had shaken off the searchlights. He carried on for the target, still some 10,000 feet above the Rhine.

The darkness was soothing but it did not last long. Soon they were caught in another glaring searchlight beam. Hillyer remembered the advice of Flight Sergeant Ford, the instructor he had met at Wing. 'Fly straight down the beam,' Ford had said, 'then pull out, and you'll lose it.' Hillyer tried it, diving as steeply as he dared, and it worked. Once again they knew the blessed relief of darkness. But the port engine was running roughly now, ebbing and surging like a gasping lung. They were on the northern outskirts of Cologne.

Straight ahead Hillyer could see the two central bridges across the Rhine. His target, the railway station near the cathedral, was just to the right of the first bridge. He eased the throttles gently forward and pressed the control column towards him, trying to regain some of the lost height. Soon he was back at 10,000 feet, settling down on his bombing run.

Cyril White, the bomb-aimer, went down into the nose, preparing to drop the bombs. Hillyer could see the fires raging ahead of him; it was difficult to believe that anyone could be alive down there. All around him he could see other bombers converging on the target. He stared at one of them incredulously – it was a Heinkel 111, probably a training aircraft, well off course on a night cross-country from some Luftwaffe OTU.

'Steady. Steady.'

The crews had been warned to avoid the cathedral, and White was keeping his run well to starboard. (Some of the crews of the training units, though, had been briefed to aim at the cathedral direct, on the principle that if they did this they would never hit it.)

'Bombs gone.'

Hillyer felt the nose come up and the whole aircraft rise buoyantly as the load fell away. He did not intend to carry on to the turning point south-west of Cologne. The port engine was failing badly now, the airspeed was falling and was soon down to barely 90 miles per hour, and his one concern was to clear the target area.

'Steer 310,' called Vincent, the navigator.

Hillyer turned to starboard, still above the burning city, and soon the sky was empty of other aircraft. But the Wellington was labouring at little above stalling speed. He glanced at his fuel gauges and they seemed surprisingly low. Then he remembered the 120 gallons that had been taken out before take-off. The trouble with the port engine had upset their economical cruising and they would be hard pressed to get across the Channel, even if the plane held up.

'Check up on the dinghy drill,' he called to the crew, 'we may have to ditch.'

Straight ahead of him he saw a tiny green light which seemed to be approaching at great speed. Suddenly he realized what it was. It was the cockpit light of a German fighter.

'Fighter ahead and below.'

White, now back in the front turret, had already seen the fighter, and he fired a burst as Hillyer finished his warning shout. Then there was a tremendous racket of firing from behind. Some of it, Hillyer knew, was from his own turrets, but not all of it. The fighter dead ahead must have been a decoy. Another fighter had turned in to attack from astern.

The nose of the Wellington started to drop. Hillyer dragged back on the stick with all his wiry strength, but there was no response. The port engine had stopped, the cockpit was full of smoke, the rear of the plane was on fire.

'Bale out!'

There was no reply on the inter-com. That might be because connections had been severed, or it might be that everyone else in the aircraft was dead, shot to pieces by that lethal burst from the second fighter.

Most pilots were aware of the touching faith and confidence that their crews resposed in them. None was more keenly conscious of this than Fred Hillyer. It was this awareness that stimulated so much self-sacrifice amongst pilots. But in this instance Hillyer was uncertain what to do. If his crew were already dead, there was no point in staying at the controls.

He chopped the throttle back on the starboard engine to prevent the aircraft spinning, and felt it settle into a steepening dive. He began to clamber out of his seat. He could see no sign of movement behind him. Just before he left the cockpit he glanced down through the windscreen and saw that the guns of the front turret were pointing sideways. The power for the hydraulics came from the dead port engine. That meant that Cyril White was trapped in the turret.

In an involuntary movement of haste and near-panic Hillyer jumped down from his seat, catching the cord of his parachute pack on the swivel-stop of his seat as he did so. Now, as he crawled forward to operate the 'dead man's handle', the handle external to the front turret that operated the turret manually, every movement was hampered by the billowing canopy.

No nightmare could have been more madly conceived. The burning aircraft plunging to destruction, the trapped front gunner, and the would-be rescuer hardly able to move, chained and fettered as in a dream.

Somehow Hillyer fought his way through to the turret. He grabbed the dead man's handle and wrenched at it. It was jammed. He banged his fist on the side of the turret itself, but there was no answering tap. Cyril White must be dead, or unconscious. Silk and shroud lines still enveloped Hillyer, there was nothing he could do for White, and a single phrase hammered at his brain. 'Get out, for God's sake get out.'

Abandoning what he was now quite certain was a dead crew, he swung himself down through the escape hatch in the floor, bunching the parachute in his arms as best he could. It was no use. The lower half of his body dropped clear of the fuselage and was buffeted by the slipstream, but he was trapped at the waist by the billowing chute. He could feel his legs being dragged backwards by the speed of the dive, hitting the underside of the fuselage, and one of his flying-boots was torn off.

He couldn't get out of the plane and he couldn't get back in. He was in the most wretched situation imaginable. The means of escape had lain in his hands and in a moment's carelessness and panic he had deprived himself of it.

It was in this moment, which should have been one of extreme mental torture and anguish, that Fred Hillyer underwent one of the most uplifting experiences ever recorded in the heat of war. He thought back on his life, his home, his family, even his schooldays, and he thought of Lillian, the girl he had met at Lichfield, and all the terror and the tension evaporated and he relaxed into a calm, spiritual serenity. This was the moment that all but the most unimaginative aircrew looked forward to with fear and apprehension and yet with a morbid curiosity at what it must be like. This was it, and he feared it no longer, the snuffing out of the spark that had been Fred Hillyer. For the last few seconds of life he had attained the cool elation of the martyr.

It may be that the more Hillyer struggled the more tangled his parachute lines became, and that when he relaxed they untwisted the more readily. It seemed to Hillyer, though, that in that moment of supreme oneness with creation there was a flashing green light, as though the aircraft above him had exploded. He felt himself drop away, and saw the tail wheel of the Wellington pass directly over his head. Below him the trees were upside down, and he struggled to right himself. A large dark shape raced across the ground just beneath him, and his eye followed it uncomprehendingly until he saw that it was the shadow of his own parachute, projected by the brilliant moonlight. Then he hit the ground heavily and passed out.

He was taken prisoner next day and driven to nearby Utrecht. His strange mood of elation stayed with him until his German guards drove him to the scene of the crash. All his crew were dead. His only consolation was that what he saw confirmed his conviction that they had been killed in the fighter attack.

Of the other crews from Graveley, Edwin Ford, the man who had advised and befriended Hillyer, was shot down by a fighter and crashed in flames near Leeveroi, all but one of his crew being killed. The exception was the wireless operator, Denis Caswell. The only other crew lost from Wing was the second Lichfield crew, piloted by Flying Officer W. R. H. Whiting. They too were shot down by a fighter over Holland. Strangely enough all the aircraft and crews operating from Lichfield got back safely.

For Fred Hillyer, the reaction from such an experience could only be one of the most heartrending depression and despair. It caught up with him that night in Amsterdam gaol. Yet the basic serenity that had so appealed to the WAAF in the fabric section at Lichfield helped him in the years of captivity. And she waited for him.

*

John Bulford, the dark-haired young man with the bushy eyebrows and the penetrating, deep-set eyes, reached Cologne towards the end of the OTU wave, flying one of the Bassingbourn Wellingtons. He had only recently come off operations, but he could see that nothing to compare with the destruction below had ever been achieved before. One or two searchlights picked him out and he had to fly through some desultory flak, but he thought the aircraft had escaped. They had left the city well behind and were settling down to their post-target coffee when the starboard engine started running jerkily and the rev. counter oscillated violently. Flames streaked back from the nacelle and soon the engine packed up altogether. Then the dead propeller fell forward and dropped clean away.

Already they had lost a lot of height, and now the searchlights picked them up. Bulford took evasive action, and he finally got the Wellington within sight of the coastline. If only he could get well out to sea and make a ditching they might avoid capture. But suddenly he found he was down to ground level, too low to bale out, faced with an immediate emergency landing. There was no time to strap himself in. Fortunately he put the Wellington down in the middle of a swamp and the crew escaped injury.

In these circumstances, some men liked to keep together, others preferred to take their chance alone. Bulford, always something of a lone wolf, favoured splitting up. The others compromised, pairing off in twos while Bulford went off on his own. None of them got very far before they were captured.

For John Bulford, as for many of his kind, being taken prisoner was to feel an overwhelming if unreasonable sense of personal failure. It was the end of a freedom that young men straight from school had never previously known, and would perhaps never know again. It was the beginning of frustration and disillusion, the end of ambition. All this, coupled with continual hunger and sickness, was mentally and physically debilitating. It was one's duty to escape – but once in the well-guarded prison camps, surrounded by searchlights, machine-guns and barbed wire, what a forlorn hope for most men this was. For a time, thoughts of escape smouldered. Then, after three months or so, all but the most naturally rebellious knuckled down, made the best of things. For John Bulford, what rankled most was his failure before capture to obtain a commission. He would never get one now.

There was no snobbery amongst air crews about rank. A pilot was a pilot. But like the ripples from the stone in the pond, the difference made by commissioned rank was felt most at the perimeter. There were a thousand little ways in which rank affected you, especially if you didn't have it. It even extended into captivity, where officers and NCOs from the same crews were segregated.

Being taken prisoner, an obvious last hope for the men of Bomber Command, was somehow rarely considered by them in this light. You got back, or you got the chop. You rarely heard of anyone who had been taken prisoner. A number of crews were missing from a raid, and that was that. By the time news of capture came through, if it ever did, the squadron personnel had changed and the names of prisoners were often unfamiliar and therefore unreal.

Escape and evasion – yes, this was taken seriously by many crews, some of whom carried elaborate escape aids in addition to those issued to them. But men just could not see themselves as prisoners. When it happened to them, the shock and frustration reduced their morale to a low ebb. Most of them had so much unfinished business. It seemed that the war might last for ever, certainly for five or ten years, a lifetime to a young man. The prisoner knew he was lucky to be alive, knew that his tragedy was insignificant compared with the death of comrades and the destruction of cities; but his was a tragedy just the same. The experience of being a prisoner left its mark on most men.

There was of course a second stage, the stage of resignation and acceptance, which most men needed for their sanity. In this period men knew an attenuated happiness. They read and studied, developed a sense of purpose to replace the vacuum of waste. John Bulford, for instance, studied for and passed his inter-B.Sc. (Economics). Then came the final, tantalizing stage, of hopes raised by the noise of Russian guns, or of the airborne operation at Arnhem – no group of men felt the tragedy of Arnhem more keenly than the prisoners of war. This period was accompanied by a disruption and chaos difficult to accept after the ordered life of earlier years. Why couldn't the Germans realize they were hopelessly beaten? The whole world was against them, they were surrounded, their cities were crumbling in ruins, why couldn't they give in? This bewilderment and exasperation at German obstinacy and myopia was tempered by a puzzled admiration for the astonishing tenacity of the race.

Most prisoners found their German guards human and likeable. There were few cases of brutality, and these were mostly incited by Nazi fanatics. However the Germans treated other races, they did not set out to treat British prisoners badly, the outstanding exception being the shooting by the SS of the fifty officers following the mass escape from Stalag Luft III. Only 1·5 per cent of RAF prisoners died in captivity.

*

Among the last of the OTU aircraft to reach the target were the two Wellingtons from Harwell piloted by the two Jacks – Jack Paul and Jack Hatton. The target was to Jack Paul a fantastic sight. Whereas in his days in the Middle East he had seen no more than occasional splashes in a pool of darkness, the whole area below was a sea of fire and explosions and the darker patches had to be looked for. He could distinguish individual buildings and see the flames flickering even at 10,000 feet, but recognizing definite target areas or aiming-points – except near the river – looked impossible.

He made his bombing run from the south-east, turning over Bonn and following the left bank of the river. As he approached the two central bridges he saw the cathedral, nestling close to the river, floodlit by the surrounding fires. There was a dark patch north of the cathedral and the navigator aimed his bombs at that.

'There's an aircraft coming up behind us.'

Almost simultaneously, the first shells from the German fighter tore into the fuselage. Cannon shells the size of tennis balls whipped past Paul's ear and shot off through the starboard fabric with a tearing, metallic roar, leaving a choking smell of cordite. There seemed to be no fire and the controls all answered well, but when Paul called the crew he got no reply.

The direction of attack had been from the port quarter, and instinctively Paul turned towards that side, pulling back the stick to make the fighter overshoot. As he turned he looked down and stared straight at the perfect silhouette of an Me 110. The front gunner, a pupil named McCormick, saw it too and opened fire. Then the fighter disappeared into the dark side, obviously manoeuvring to get them silhouetted against the moon.

Paul continued to turn to port, looking for the refuge of cloud, but the sky was appallingly bare. The best thing to do seemed to be to stick around and shoot it out. He had done this twice in the Middle East and got away with it. There was one serious drawback – the breakdown in the inter-com. No one could give him a running commentary on which way to turn as the fighter came in. Equally serious, but unknown to Paul, was the fact that the tail turret had been hit and put out of action. In that turret the tall, fair-haired Bunny Evans, one of the really aggressive gunners and a veteran of fifty operational sorties, sat helpless and completely cut off.

In spite of all Paul's turning and weaving, the Me 110 pilot attacked again from the dark part of the sky and the Wellington was hit a second time. A third time the fighter came in, firing at point-blank range. This time there were direct hits in the port engine, port wing and fuselage and the wireless operator, Tommy Lyons, was killed. A long flag of flame trailed back from the port engine, and Paul knew that this time there would be no escape. Here was one Wimpey that wouldn't get home.

He banged with his fist on the door behind him to attract the attention of Green, the navigator. 'Get the front gunner out of the turret, then bale out,' he shouted. But already it was too late. The crew of the Me 110 had had no difficulty in keeping the burning bomber in view, and already the pilot was diving in for his fourth and last attack. At the end of it the Wellington was spiralling slowly downwards in a shallow dive, burning freely, and the only man still conscious was the tail gunner, Bunny Evans.

Evans began to crawl out of the turret and into the fuselage. He could see no sign of life at all up front – the rest of the crew had either baled out already or they were dead. The Wellington was still floating down, rocking from side to side. There wasn't much time. He grabbed his parachute, clipped it on and dropped through the diamond-shaped escape hatch in the rear of the plane, kicking it out as he went. He landed in a tree in the back garden of a miner's cottage in the village of Marcinelle, near Charleroi, and the Belgians soon found him a hide-out.

Meanwhile the burning Wellington had continued in its faltering dive until it hit a house in a nearby village, knocking down one side of the building completely, depositing one crew-member in the ruins, and then carrying on into an orchard on the far side of the road, where it steadily burnt itself out. The three men still inside it were already dead.

At her parents' home in Coventry, Joyce Paul listened to the one o'clock news on the radio (read by Alvar Lidell) and heard the report that over a thousand bombers had raided Cologne. Forty-four of our aircraft, said the report, were missing. She thought at once of the relatives of those men. With so many planes missing, there would be many unhappy homes by the end of the day. She could not resist a warm feeling of gratitude that her husband of a fortnight was not at the moment exposed to these dangers. The telegram she was expecting would be so different, telling her what train to catch to Didcot, where Jack would be waiting for her. It was no good feeling guilty about it. One had to take one's happiness when one could.

As that Sunday afternoon wore on and there was no telegram, Joyce Paul began to wonder whether she would be able to get to Didcot that night. All her bags were packed and she was ready to leave, but Jack was leaving it late. Then, at half past four, she saw her father-in-law, who lived nearby, coming through the gate, carrying what looked like a telegram. For some reason the message must have gone to him. The expression on his face startled her, and when she opened the door to him she knew that something was wrong.

He handed her the telegram. 'It came to me,' he said, 'they can't have changed the next-of-kin address. It's happened, what I always said might happen. He's missing. He must have been on that raid to Cologne.'

Joyce Paul read the telegram in disbelief and bewilderment, her basic calm untouched by the news. 'There must be some mistake. He's not flying on the raids. He's instructing. He's meeting me this evening in Didcot. This telegram is a mistake.'

Jack Paul's last recollection had been of bending down to release his oxygen and inter-com plugs. In that moment the fighter had attacked again and he had passed out. His next awareness was of being in the centre of a holocaust of fire, smoke, dust and exploding ammunition. He tried to move but found he was trapped.

When Bunny Evans had taken that last terrified stare at what had seemed an empty fuselage, Paul had been slumped over the control column, unconscious. He remained that way until the plunging Wellington hit the house in the village of Montigny-le-Telleul. It was Jack Paul's body, limp but relaxed, which was deposited in the ruins of the house as the plane careered on. Now, half-buried in smouldering rubble, completely baffled by his surroundings and still barely conscious, he roused himself instinctively for some sort of effort. 'You've got to get out of here,' he told himself firmly, 'you've got to get out.' In front of him was a kind of doorway, and he began to drag himself towards it, somehow freeing himself from the pile of rubble under which he lay. Next moment an apparition appeared in the doorway, an old man with white hair and a white beard and moustache, dressed in a white robe. In his confused, concussed state he was quite certain that he must be dead. The apparition said nothing, then left as suddenly as it came. It was in fact, the owner of the house, dressed in his night-clothes. Paul crawled through the open doorway, realized with relief that he was in a garden and passed out again.

When he came to he was being cradled in the arms of a Belgian woman who was speaking to him in perfect English. Again he was baffled – how could he possibly be back in England? The dream was short-lived. 'Be careful,' the woman was saying, 'the Germans will be here any minute.' Her name was Ruby Dondeyne, and she explained that escape was out of the question – far too many people knew about the crashed plane, and with his injuries it would be impossible to move him. He gave the woman his wallet and escape papers, passed out again and came to as the Germans were lifting him into an ambulance.

He was taken to the Belgian hospital in Charleroi, and next day, when he was admitted to the operating theatre, the German guards were somehow excluded and a Belgian woman consultant named Dr Louise Biernans told him about his crew – that three of them were dead and one was missing. She asked if he wanted to send a message home. He scribbled a few words to Joyce on a slip of prescription paper and signed it with a drawing of the Leslie Charteris 'Saint', which he had always used when writing to her, but he could not see how she could possibly get it. He began to hope that she might two days later, when the nurse accompanying one of the Belgian doctors on his rounds turned out to be a disguised Ruby Dondeyne. She slipped a scrap of cigarette paper in his hand, and on it was written a message from Bunny Evans. 'Baled out,' it read, 'am in good hands, yours, Bunny.' Clearly the Belgian underground was well organized. Joyce Paul did in fact get her husband's message, the first intimation she had that he was alive. Twelve weeks after the raid, Bunny Evans was safely in Gibraltar after a tense crossing of the Pyrenees, helped along the escape route by many brave but anonymous hands. The tree into which he fell in the village of Marcinelle is still known locally as 'the Tommy tree'.

After a few days Jack Paul was moved to a hospital in Brussels. In the next ward he was astonished to recognize a voice he knew – it was the second of the two Jacks from Harwell, Jack Hatton, the ex-Cranwell apprentice. Hatton too had been shot down over Belgium and had been too badly hurt to escape, although the Belgians had offered to hide him. That he had recognized would be too dangerous for them, and he had asked to be given up. Hatton's wireless operator, Bob Collins, an Australian from Brisbane, also reached Gibraltar safely; the rest of the crew were captured. The two Jacks, finding themselves by an odd coincidence in adjacent wards, were the only pilots to be lost from Harwell.

The money in Jack Paul's wallet – totalling £8 – was passed to Louise Biernans, who buried it in her garden. After the war she had the satisfaction of handing it personally to Jack Paul. The money was used to open a bank account for the Pauls' first child, for whom Louise Biernans acted as godmother.

*

In the streets of Cologne, thousands of fires had taken hold and the whole city shook continually with the blast from the growing weight of high-explosive. Tens of thousands of people were crowding the aid centres, many of them evacuated from the blitzed and burning areas, others completely bombed out. All over the city the tale was the same. From the suburb of Niehl in the north, through Bickendorf, Ehrenfeld and Lindenthal to the west, and worst of all in the old city, the skeletons of buildings shook off their attire of rubble, brightly illuminated by surrounding fires. Water mains in all areas were breached, power and telephone cables torn up, gas mains punctured. Civil defence and fire-fighting forces were swamped by the weight of the attack. Emergency detachments and mobile squads were cut off by disrupted communications and hampered by blocked roads and the shortage of water. Railway stations, platforms, goods depots, locomotives, trucks and rails were wrecked. Seventeen major railways centres were reporting severe damage. Bombs fell with grim impartiality on industrial buildings, empty city offices, crowded hospitals, empty churches, hastily abandoned homes and crammed air raid shelters. Even so, prompt action by individual and group self-protection forces and industrial civil defence units prevented many incipient fires from developing. Incendiaries were quickly collected and doused and energetic efforts made to control and extinguish roof-top fires. The top floors of many buildings were gutted while lower floors escaped.

Areas of severe damage were not confined to the west bank. Mulheim, Deutz and Kalk on the east bank were all heavily bombed. The docks, too, were ablaze. Customs sheds were showered with incendiaries and completely destroyed, together with the goods they held. A huge eight-storey warehouse had its roof gutted, silos were destroyed, dock buildings wrecked, ships and barges sunk, all traffic halted. At Cologne-Rheinau an electric semi-gantry crane shifted and crashed into the river, damaging the passenger ship *Amicitia*, which was already on fire, and severing its moorings. The blazing ship drifted helplessly down-river, finally beaching itself near Mulheim Bridge, where it burnt itself out.

And all the time the tale of human tragedy and of dramatic rescue went on. Hundreds of people had been trapped in air raid shelters where buildings had collapsed on top of them.

Scores had already been killed or suffocated in this way. Yet amongst those who had not gone to ground the casualties were heavier still.

At the top of Rheingasse a man was trapped on the third floor of a block that was burning fiercely. He climbed out of the window. Two feet below the sill of the fourth-floor window immediately above him, a cable was suspended across the street to the block on the opposite side, carrying the current for the street-lamp which dangled from the cable half-way across. The man stood on the third-floor sill, reached up and grabbed the cable. Then he stepped off the sill and began to work his way hand over hand out across the street. The cable sagged perilously, but it held his weight. Swinging round the lamp in the middle, the man carried on to the block on the far side, let himself down on the window sill and climbed in.

Cologne was a city under siege, beleaguered by an unprecedented aerial bombardment. Only daylight could bring relief.

4. THE HEAVIES

FOR THE TWELVE squadrons of heavies, together with their conversion flights and the conversion unit at Marston Moor, a total of over 200 new four-engined bombers – about 130 Halifaxes and 75 Lancasters – the moment to strike the final pulverizing blow had come.

One of the first Halifaxes to take off was piloted by a young squadron leader commanding the conversion unit at Marston Moor. His name was Leonard Cheshire. It was exactly 23.20 as the port engine of his plane, 'E' for Edward, roared into life. It had done so countless times for conversion training of squadron pilots in the previous seven months, but this was something different.

The sky was still light enough for Cheshire to see the host of bombers floating irresistibly above him towards Cologne. Then someone flashed a green at him from the control tower, and at

23.44 his Halifax moved forward down the flare-path and took off. There was a call from the tail gunner.

' "N" for Nuts is taking off just behind us. She's airborne now.' Then the night closed in.

To Cheshire the faces beside him were unfamiliar, but the spirit seemed the same as he remembered from earlier tours. 'I had wondered', he wrote afterwards,[1] 'if it would feel different, starting again: I wondered too if the sight of gunfire would frighten me, or if the absence of the old, trusted faces would take away the confidence I once had known. All this, and more, I had asked myself during the hours of preparation, and then, when the night closed in and the flare-path disappeared behind the port wing, I knew that the answer was no.

'As we flew on across England, in the sky and on the ground there were signs of inexhaustible activity: flare-paths, aeroplanes and lights pointing out the way . . . And then as we turned over the Dutch islands on to the last lap, the most monstrous sight in all the history of bombing. The sky, helped by the moon, was very light, so that the stars showed only dimly and infrequently. The ground too was light, but in a curious manner mauve, so that the contrast was very beautiful. Against this pale, duck-egg blue and the greyish-mauve were silhouetted a number of small black shapes: all of them bombers, and all of them moving the same way. One hundred and thirty-four miles ahead, and directly in their path, stretched a crimson glow: Cologne was on fire . . . ablaze from end to end, and the main force of the attack was still to come. I looked at the other bombers, I looked at the row of selector switches in the bomb compartments, and I felt, perhaps, a slight chill in my heart. But the chill did not stay long: I saw other visions, visions of rape and murder and torture. . . . No, the chill did not last long.

'I glued my eyes on the fire and watched it grow slowly larger. Of ack-ack there was not much, but the sky was filled with fighters. Every now and then we saw air-to-air tracer, and usually something would fall burning from the heavens. . . . In the tail and down the fuselage the gunners kept an even

1. In *Bomber Pilot* (Hutchinson).

stricter watch; and all the time the fire grew larger and larger. . . . When Cologne came in view beneath the port wing there was a sudden silence in the aeroplane. If what we saw below was true, Cologne was destroyed. We looked hastily at the Rhine, but there was no mistake; what we saw below was true.'

Stanley Wright, the tall, fair-haired pilot who had 'buzzed' the King and Queen by mistake, took off from Marston Moor fifteen minutes after Cheshire, at the bewitching Service hour of 23.59. Wright was flying a Mark I Halifax with a scratch crew – he had left his regular crew behind at the time of his precipitate posting from Leeming. The Mark I Halifax was faster than the Mark II and had a better range, but its ceiling – the crucial factor when it came to enemy defences – was lower. This wouldn't matter so much if, as was hoped, the defences were saturated by the time the new four-engined bombers went in.

The Halifax responded well up to 15,000 feet but above that it wallowed badly, and Wright eased it down to that height. He passed directly over Eindhoven and approached the Maas to the south of the night-fighter airfield at Venlo on the Dutch/German border. Ahead of him the target was a bright orange glare. Then, as he was crossing the Maas, he saw what looked like the glow of a hundred cigarette ends streaming away from the nose of the Halifax. It took him a moment to realize that it was tracer, fired not from one of his own turrets, or he would have heard the burst, but from a fighter sitting on their tail.

He was puzzled that he had heard nothing from the tail gunner, but he soon guessed the reason. The elevators and rudder were virtually useless, suggesting serious damage to the whole tail section. In fact the tail unit was shattered and the gunner, taken by surprise as the fighter crept up underneath out of the darkness, was unconscious or dead, knocked out before he could fire a single shot.

Wright turned away as best he could to escape further attack, but the starboard aileron, too, was damaged, and he had very little control. He called Cookson, the navigator.

'Jettison the bomb-load. Prepare to abandon aircraft.'

Cookson jettisoned the bombs, then climbed up into the cockpit to give Wright his parachute, laying it on the floor beside him. As he did so the fighter attacked again. Wright could sense at once that what little control he had managed to retain had gone. Fire, too, was streaming from one of the petrol tanks, and he gave the order to bale out.

He was vaguely aware, as he struggled with the control column, that the three surviving crew-men, Cookson, Tavener and Lowman, had gone forward to the front escape hatch. Then he was staring down at a blotch of fire which he guessed must be the burst of his own bombs. As he stared at the blaze it rotated like a roulette wheel, round and round, in a clockwise direction, spinning like a top. But he knew it couldn't be the ground that was spinning. It must be the plane.

Down at the front escape hatch the rest of the crew lay in statuesque terror as the centrifugal force of the spin pinned them to one side of the fuselage. Although within three feet of the hatch they couldn't get to it.

Consumed by panic, dizzy with the whirligig of fire that filled his windscreen, Wright struggled with useless controls to correct a spin that became more vicious every minute. Above the roar of the motors, still turning at near full power, he shouted at himself to pull himself together. The only hope seemed to be to throttle back the engines. He had tried all the usual spin corrections without effect. Now, fighting against the centrifugal force that dragged his right hand into his lap as he took it from the control column, he forced his hand towards the throttles, gripped them, shut the two port engines and opened up to full power on the starboard side.

At once the Halifax came out of the spin. But it was still diving straight for the ground. The spin had lasted from 15,000 feet down to 6,000 and the airspeed had built up to just under 400 miles per hour. The maximum safe diving speed of a Halifax was 340. The airframe must be in immediate danger of breaking up.

As soon as the Halifax stopped spinning, Wright evened up the throttle settings to get equal power from port and starboard sides. The centrifugal force which had pinioned the rest of the crew to the side of the fuselage was at once removed, and the three men at the open hatch baled out. Then, without any pressure being exerted on the control column, the Halifax began to pull out.

But the plane now performed like a runaway horse. The reins were slack and useless but the power was undiminished. In spite of Wright's efforts to level off, the Halifax came out of the dive as though catapulted from the base of a switchback, soaring straight up. As it soared Wright could sense what was going to happen next. The Halifax, unbridled and headstrong, was about to perform a loop.

The terrific speed built up in that 10,000-foot dive had given the plane the impetus for the most far-fetched aerobatics, and Wright felt the nose come up and over. As the Halifax lay on its back at the top of the loop the engines faltered momentarily, then picked up again as the loop was completed.

For a moment the aircraft dived for the ground, engines racing. Then of its own accord it began to pull out a second time, climbing into another uncontrolled loop. This time the speed was insufficient. As it got to the top of the climb it stood on its tail, slipped back and stalled. In that plunging moment of stall Wright's parachute, which Cookson had put ready on the floor beside him, hit the perspex dome with such force that Wright thought it must go through. Then, as though tiring of its gyrations, the plane dipped forward at a steep angle, diving headlong for the ground.

Wright hurriedly unstrapped himself, grabbed his parachute, which had fallen back to the floor beside him, and made for the hatch. He sat on the trailing edge of the hole, dangling his feet through, took a grip on the ripcord and pushed off. As the tail of the plane passed over his head he pulled the cord. Very soon afterwards he hit the ground. His knees buckled and hit him in the chest, winding him completely, and he lay writhing on the ground like an injured footballer, struggling for breath.

Wright had landed near the village of Tegelen, four miles south-west of Venlo and just inside the Dutch border. Most of the population of Tegelen had gone to the shelters, but one man, Anton Rijvers, had stayed in his garden to watch the raid and had seen the spectacular gyrations of the Halifax, traced for him through the sky by the burning petrol tank. The writhing descent had seemed to last for several minutes. All the time the plane was getting lower and lower – and nearer and nearer to Tegelen. Rijvers, too interested in the plane's fate to run for shelter, stood transfixed as the plane seemed to right itself and then glide towards his own house. It missed the roof by no more than a few feet, spilling burning petrol over it as it went. Fifty yards away it struck a line of trees before ploughing in. In the same moment the roof of the house caught fire.

Rijvers did not stay to put out the fire. The house was empty, and he was more concerned to do what he could for the crew of the crashed bomber. He ran across to the wreck and found that wings and engines had been torn off by the trees but that the tail was intact. He peered into the turret and saw the gunner sitting upright at his guns. Rijvers pulled him out but he was dead. He looked at the gunner's papers and found that his name was Sergeant K. J. A. Manley and that he had a wife and two children.

The fire had taken hold in his house and by morning it was gutted. During the day the German fighter pilots from Venlo came to have a look at their kill. The man who claimed it was Oberleutnant Reinhold Knacke, a prominent German ace who was credited that night with his twentieth kill.

Wright made a good attempt at escape and was going well when he entered a forest and, crossing from one fire-break to another, had the misfortune to clash with two German guards. It was the end of his freedom for three years.

In common with most of the men taken prisoner on this raid, Wright passed through Cologne a few days later on the way to prison camp. Most men found that Cologne was still almost impassable – road traffic was still taking wide detours and rail communications were almost non-existent. A woman conductress on the bus which took Wright and three other prisoners from one blitzed railway station to another pointed out some of the damage. Repeating the propaganda line, she insisted that all they had hit was hospitals and schools, all they had killed was women and children. A large and sullenly hostile crowd gathered round them at the railway station, and Wright was not the only one to feel more frightened at this stage than at any other. He had little doubt that if one person acted violently and defied the guards the rest would follow, that only the guards and an instinctive German respect for them saved the prisoners from a rough handling or worse. This was the impression of more than forty prisoners taken after the raid who subsequently passed through Cologne. It was their worst moment. Yet there were no actual incidents and not one of them was harmed.

All Wright's crew except Manley were taken prisoner, and all but Manley survived the war except Lowman, the flight engineer, the only man known to Wright prior to the raid. Lowman was killed in April 1945 by strafing from a low-flying British plane while on a forced march.

*

At Croft, high on the Yorkshire moors, Bob Plutte, Paddy Todd's pilot, took off at exactly midnight. Twenty minutes earlier, the tall instructor Peter James had taken off in a Halifax of the conversion flight. It had been an uncomfortable experience. In the middle of his take-off run, when he was trundling along the runway at 90 miles an hour, the blackout curtains above him had started to flutter and the hatch over the cockpit had begun to lift. James shouted at his second pilot to grab it but it was too late. Before anyone could do anything the hatch had blown open and locked itself fully back in the upright position. The draught, and the noise of the engines and airstream, was terrific. But for the moment James had to concentrate on somehow completing the take-off. He was committed to it and it was too late to throttle back now.

Once airborne he urged the crew to try to close the hatch, but they couldn't get up into the airstream to do it. They tried to lasso it, and the flight engineer got a rope round it, but it refused to budge. Eventually James decided to leave it; if they pulled at it any more it might snap at the hinges and blow back against the tail. That could do enough damage to end their ambitions of going to Cologne or anywhere else.

To the surprise of his scratch crew, Peter James made no attempt to turn back. They were briefed to fly at 15,000 feet, and the cold was so intense when they climbed up through the icing that James had to hold the control column with his elbows, his hands were so numb. It was colder than it had been in the early Whitleys, when they had had no heaters at all and hoar frost had formed inside the plane. But this was one party James didn't intend to miss.

In common with many other pilots in the last wave, he mistook the burning city 150 miles ahead for the rising moon and altered course accordingly, unable to believe it could be Cologne. And shortly afterwards he met further misfortune; the port outer header tank blew up and he had to feather the engine. He continued to steer for Cologne for a time, but the odds were now too much against him and he was reluctantly forced to turn back.

Meanwhile Bob Plutte was getting the usual greeting from the Dutch islands as he crossed the enemy coast. Paddy Todd, in the rear turret, was pleased enough to see the flak – the part he dreaded was the North Sea crossing. They were hitting the slipstream of other bombers frequently now, but their run to the target was otherwise smooth. Nearing Cologne Todd brought out his own unofficial and entirely unauthorized camera, but there was too much smoke to get any good pictures. They dropped their bombs, Todd pushed out the parachute that had embarrassed him for so long, and they turned for home.

They were still inside Germany when Todd spotted a Ju 88 crossing above them in the opposite direction. He disappeared into the dark side, and Todd lost him.

'There's a Ju 88 just gone over the top. He's somewhere to starboard.'

The other gunners peered into the darkness but saw nothing. Then, a minute later, the Ju 88 pilot suddenly opened up at them, 500 yards astern and slightly below.

'Pluto! Corkscrew!'

The German pilot was a cautious man. As the Halifax swung to and fro he sat out at 500 yards and lobbed his cannon and machine-gun fire into it from long range. His fire at that distance was surprisingly accurate; he hit the port outer engine, riddled the port flaps and damaged the starboard outer as well. Cannon shells thudded into the plating and tore through the fuselage to the front, where Tubby Porter, the flight engineer, promptly closed the armour-plated door. Todd and the mid-upper gunner, Jack Winterbotham, now had the fighter all to themselves.

'What's happening?' called Winterbotham. He had suffered a flesh wound in the first attack, but he still could not see the fighter.

'He's on our tail.'

Todd was not only thoroughly scared; he was thoroughly enjoying himself. Sooner or later the German pilot would come in for the kill – he would hold his fire until then. He had developed a trick at these times of somehow shrinking his body to present the smallest possible target to enemy bullets, taking advantage of every available piece of metal in the turret as a shield, and he was doing this now. In many ways it was little more than a self-deception, a pretence that his body had contracted very much more than it had; but it made him feel safer. And when, a moment later, his reflector sight was shot clean away in front of his eyes and he suffered no injury, it seemed that the contraction was not entirely imaginary.

In spite of the explosion in front of his face, Todd did not take his eyes off the fighter for more than a moment. He blinked, he swore with all the melody and resource of the Ulsterman, though with underlying good humour, and when he looked again the fighter was closing in.

'The cheeky bastard!'

Todd still held his fire. It was a dangerous game, but he meant to get that fighter. He gave him one short burst at 300 yards, just to warn the German not to come in too close, and then he waited for the breakaway. At 200 yards, just as the

German pulled up and away, Todd gave him a five-second burst. It was a perfectly-timed riposte, and the Ju 88 turned straight over on its back and plunged downwards. As it went, Winterbotham followed it with a long burst of fire. There was no recovery. Nearly all the crew, including Todd himself, had the satisfaction of seeing it explode as it hit the ground.

Bob Plutte got the Halifax back on two engines and they force-landed at Honington. The plane was riddled and they landed on the rims, the tyres having been punctured in the scrap. They reported for de-briefing behind an OTU crew who were in the middle of describing an air combat they had seen. The position, time and height accorded exactly: it was their own scrap.

For several days afterwards, Paddy Todd had a slight squint, but it disappeared after a week. He was glad to have got rid of the parachute. He guessed that the Germans must have had a long and unsuccessful search for his body. That was the best laugh of all.

Last off at Croft was Sam Lucas, the new commanding officer of 78 squadron; and because he had also given himself the task of photographic reconnaissance, which he decided to undertake first, prior to his bombing run, his was the last Croft aircraft to bomb. It was his first operational flight as first pilot.

As Lucas circled the target area and his navigator took the pictures, it seemed that the defences had now been completely drenched. Cologne, or what they could see of it through the smoke and fire, seemed an empty honeycomb, thousands of walls with hardly a roof between them. It was an awesome sight – it didn't seem possible that anyone could survive in that holocaust. The feelings of the crew were similar; they were appalled by what they saw, and none of them spoke.

While Sam Lucas was taking his pictures, the main weight of the final wave was concentrating over the target. Fighter opposition along the route was still intense. Another risk that was undiminished was collision. Indeed, as this was the most concentrated part of the raid the risk was bigger now than at any time.

Squadron Leader Evan Griffiths, senior flight commander of No 102 Squadron at Dalton, a satellite of Topcliffe, climbed into cloud after setting course and did not emerge from it until he had reached 11,000 feet. He was maintaining course on Gee, and as he emerged from the cloud it was plain that other crews were doing the same. Griffiths found himself uncomfortably close to two other Halifaxes, one on each side, and he had to alter course to avoid them. Several times his Halifax rocked as it hit the slipstream of unseen aircraft, and once or twice he picked out the exhausts of other bombers directly ahead. But Griffiths believed that the danger from fighters still remained greater than the danger of collision, and he adopted his usual gentle weaving technique over Holland.

'Unidentified twin-engined aircraft high on the port quarter. Looks like a Ju 88.'

They were about fifteen minutes short of the target when the call came from 'Mac' McIlquham, the tail gunner, on the inter-com. Griffiths stared back over his shoulder but he could see nothing. 'Let me know if he turns towards us.'

'He's turning now.'

Griffiths executed a sharp turn to port in the hope of throwing the German pilot off, and the enemy aircraft passed safely underneath them. Griffiths turned back on course and resumed his gentle weave. Two minutes later McIlquham called him again.

'He's dead astern now. I've got him in my sights but he's a long way back.' Half a minute later there was an excited shout. 'He's closing in. Here he comes!'

Griffiths turned quickly to port but he still couldn't see his attacker. He was shocked next moment by the racket of machine-gun fire and a prolonged shouting on the inter-com. 'I've got him! I've got him! He's on fire! I've got him, Skip!'

Griffiths turned left and right but was unable to see the plunging fighter. The sky was latticed with the bright tilted avenues of the searchlight beams. He set course again for Cologne, bombed the target successfully and then started orbiting to watch the fireworks. After seeing several other four-engined bombers pass close underneath and over the top, he gave this up as too dangerous and set course for home. His conclusion was that had it somehow been possible to switch daylight on during that last hectic fifteen minutes over the target, or during the multiple criss-crossing of routes as the bombers returned over the North Sea, no one would have wanted to repeat the experience.

In fact there was probably only one collision over the target in this latter part of the raid. It was seen by a sergeant pilot of 78 Squadron and probably involved a Lancaster of 61 Squadron from Syerston and a Halifax of 405 Squadron from Pocklington. Both crews were lost over the target and there were no survivors.

The Lancaster crews of No 207 Squadron from Bottesford looked down on what seemed a single immense fire raging in the town with hundreds of smaller ones scattered round the perimeter. The whole of Hohenzollernring, in the north-west part of the old town, was a mass of flames. It was impossible to identify individual bomb bursts, but they were so frequent that they resembled the incessant gun-flashes of an ordinary raid.

Crews of No 44 Squadron, flying Lancasters from Waddington, found a solid area of fire three miles long and two miles wide covering the whole town, surpassing anything in their previous experience. They had been the first squadron to get Lancasters. Even from a distance of a hundred miles they had detected what appeared to be large explosions. Most crews decided that bombing the centre of the target area was a waste of time and looked for areas that had so far escaped the main concentration. Dummy fires on the edge of the city were easily recognized by their comparatively dim obscurity.

This is what it looked like to a second pilot/navigator of No 97 (Lancaster) Squadron, tall 17-stone Rhodesian Flying Officer 'Bull' Friend: 'As we crossed the town there were burning blocks to the right of us while to the left the fires were immense. Buildings were skeletons in the midst of fires; sometimes you could see the frameworks of white-hot joists. The blast of the bombs was hurling walls themselves across the flames. I remembered what had been said at briefing: Don't drop your bombs on the buildings that are burning best, go in and find another target for yourself. At last I found one, in a heavily built-up area, and I let the bombs go. As we came away we saw more and more of our aircraft below us, silhouetted against the flames. Above us there were still more bombers, lit by the light of the moon. We set course for home.'

Harold Batchelder, another pilot on 102 Squadron from Dalton, experienced a depressing sense of futility as he gazed down at the awful destruction of the city that was Cologne. He began to shrink from adding to it. Then, quite unbidden, came a vision of a scene he had witnessed when going on leave for Christmas 1940. Passing through London, he had caught a brief glimpse of the troglodytic life of Londoners in the Underground, seen the tall skeletons of buildings, the shells that had once been churches, the sudden wide open spaces where the rubble had been cleared. It cured him of his squeamishness, and he began to look for a spot where the fires weren't going too well.

Overwhelmed as the ground defences were, they were still capable of concentrating on single aircraft and giving them an unpleasant passage over the target. The accuracy of the bombing then depended a good deal on the calibre of the crew. An astonishingly high percentage of bomber pilots – perhaps at this stage in the war as many as one in three – were utterly dedicated men. The others were mostly brave men who did their duty, but where there was a reasonable let-out they would probably accept it. One of the dedicated kind was 25-year-old Squadron Leader Tony Ennis, dark, lean and merry, a flight commander on No 10 Squadron at Leeming, the squadron timed to be last over the target. Ennis's Halifax was picked up by searchlights at 14,000 feet approaching Cologne and held in them for twenty-five minutes. His tail gunner, the tall, pensive, reticent Sergeant Bertram Groves, was wounded by flak. In the end Ennis was forced to jettison his bombs, but he dropped them no more than a mile north of his aiming-point before diving to fifty feet to evade the searchlights. The whole way down the wounded Groves was firing down the searchlight beams and at enemy gun positions. He was hit again, blinded in one eye and severely wounded in the leg, but he went on firing. In any case the doors of his turret were jammed and he couldn't get out. The port outer motor was hit and stopped, but Ennis finally evaded the defences, pulled up to 400 feet and set course for the Dutch coast. Only when they were clear of the target area did Groves mention his wounds or the fact that he was trapped in the turret. Likes attracted each other when it came to forming crews. Ennis managed to get the damaged Halifax back to Manston, where Groves was rushed to hospital. He was later awarded the DFM.

Tony Ennis was one of the coolest and most aggressive of all bomber pilots. Awarded the DSO and the DFC, he was killed in action in 1943.

The only aircraft lost from Leeming was a Halifax piloted by a Sergeant A. R. Moore, shot down by a night-fighter near Eindhoven. Four crew-members escaped but Moore and his two gunners were killed.

The aircraft scheduled to be last over the target was the Halifax piloted by Willie Tait. Tait's timing was good, but the concentration was thinning out now and his aircraft was picked out by the ground gunners. He lost an engine over the target, and this delayed his attack, but he finally dropped his bombs in the 100th minute of the raid, at 02.34.

Willie Tait was not, as he should have been, the last pilot to bomb. There were several late-comers. Sam Lucas, for instance, having taken his time over the photographs, was only just settling down on his bombing run. His navigator had found a tiny semi-circle of black near some railway marshalling yards and they motored towards it and aimed their bombs. The time was 02.38.

The greatest raid of all time was virtually over, but there were still a few stragglers to come. There were some stragglers, too, amongst the many hundreds of bombers now on their way home. Not all of them would make it.

5. *THE STRAGGLERS*

LAST AIRCRAFT OF all on target, hopelessly late, was the Lancaster of the conversion flight at Syerston piloted by Yorkshireman George Gilpin. At eleven o'clock that Saturday night, all trussed up in their Mae Wests and parachute harnesses, Gilpin and his crew had arrived at the flight dispersal to find their aircraft deserted. There wasn't a single bomb on board, and hardly a gallon of fuel. Gilpin could not understand it – until he saw that the ground crews were still working flat out on the squadron aircraft. It was inevitable that the single Lancaster of the conversion flight should be left till last.

Gilpin looked a hundred times at his watch. Half-past eleven came, and midnight, and still his pleading calls to the armourers and refuellers brought no response. Soon the first aircraft would be on target. Even the squadron Lancasters at Syerston, part of the last wave, were beginning to line up now. Soon after midnight they took off, all sixteen of them. Then at last, reinforced by a squad of eager young Air Training Corps cadets, came the ground crews. Gilpin doubted very much if it was worth bombing up now, but he let them carry on, he and his crew stripping out of their flying gear to lend a hand. It was after one o'clock when they finished.

All crews were supposed to be off target by 02.25. The orders were that no one was to bomb after that time. Anything up to fifteen minutes late one might get away with. But even if he pushed the throttles through the gate, Gilpin knew he couldn't be on target within half an hour of the deadline. The controller would never let him go.

Gilpin taxied out stealthily to the bottom of the runway, but there he had to wait for the controller's signal. On duty tonight, he knew, was a WAAF known as the 'Duchess', a girl named Alice Adlard whose blonde, regal, slightly forbidding beauty had earned her this soubriquet. Gilpin had waited no more than a few seconds when the lamp at the control tower flashed green.

'Hurray for the Duchess!'

Before she could change her mind, Gilpin pushed the throttles open and the Lancaster sped down the runway. He did not glance again at the control tower. In fact, no orders to discontinue take-offs had come through, though Gilpin was still bound by the instructions he had received at briefing. The time was 01.15.

Ahead of Gilpin lay the city of Nottingham, wholly blacked out. Gilpin had a sister living on the northern outskirts, and often on daylight or dusk take-offs she came out into the garden to wave to him. The moon was glinting on the white marble tombstones in the churchyard next to her house, but if his sister had waved tonight it would have been to the others, an hour or more ago. She would have gone to bed by now.

Suddenly, as he turned over the middle of Nottingham, there was a shattering clatter of machine-gun fire and Gilpin almost froze on the stick. Then came the realization that the racket could only have come from the front turret. Brewer!

'What the hell are you up to, Brewer?'

Brewer had wisely decided to familiarize himself with the turret controls and with the feel of turret rotation in the air at the earliest opportunity. In doing so he had inadvertently fired the guns – a burst which must have fallen like summer hail on the roof-tops of the city. But he had the presence of mind to find a casual answer for Gilpin.

'Just firing off a trial burst, Skipper.'

Gilpin's nerves were calmed a little by the nonchalance of the reply, but they were still frayed. 'For Pete's sake leave things alone.' They set course for the target, climbing to 17,000 feet as they crossed the North Sea, and before they reached the Dutch coast they began to run into a stream of returning Stirlings and Wellingtons, most of them several thousand feet below. There was absolutely nothing going their way.

Gilpin called his navigator, his old school contemporary John Beach. The two men had known each other for fifteen years and had done their first tour together. 'Now then, John,' called Gilpin in his bluff Yorkshire manner, 'what time are we going to get to Cologne?'

Beach, tall and thin, with an unusually small head that nevertheless carried a brilliant brain, had been a schoolmaster before call-up. Physically awkward and ungainly, he was mentally the most graceful man Gilpin knew. A fortifying streak of obstinacy ran through the brilliance.

'We shall reach the target,' announced Beach, 'at five past three.'

'What was the last time we were supposed to attack?'

'All aircraft are supposed to turn for home,' quoted Beach with infuriating accuracy, 'at 02.25, whether they have bombed or not.'

'Forty minutes late, eh?'

Gilpin was no rebel. He flew to orders. It was the only way to run an organization like Bomber Command. A sound planner himself, he respected the plans of others.

'It's no good, John, we can't go. We can't go to Cologne. It's all against orders.' But Gilpin was determined not to take his bombs back. 'Give me a course for Gelsenkirchen.'

But now, straight ahead of them, throwing the oncoming bombers into crimson silhouette, lay the great glow in the sky above Cologne, drawing them towards it like a moth to a candle. No word came from Beach about a change of course for Gelsenkirchen. Gilpin did not repeat his request. There was tacit agreement throughout the crew that this plane went to Cologne.

There was scarcely any need for navigation. They merely pointed the plane at the glow. Soon the stream of returning bombers began to thin out. Then they were down to the stragglers, and finally a quarter of an hour from the target, they were completely alone. The defences, too, seemed to be dead; there wasn't even a lone searchlight over Cologne, not a single flak burst. The sky was an empty arena, the carnage and litter of battle burning itself out monstrously below.

The bomb-aimer's position was in the nose, but Brewer

could not drop the bombs so Beach went forward. The centre of the target was a mass of flames, surrounded by smaller fires, and smoke was pouring up to a height of 15,000 feet. Gilpin went in steadily, aiming for the middle of the main fire. There were no dark patches now.

Exhausted as the defences were, they would surely give a hostile reception to a lone bomber. One by one, as though controlled by some sleepy lamplighter, the searchlights flickered on. Soon a beam picked out the intruder and focused on it. More and more tentacles of light swept the sky, tactile as an octopus. It was an unforgettable sight – the burning city, the criss-cross tendrils of the searchlights, the black gleam of the trapped bomber. Gilpin, blinded by blue light, tried in vain to see a way out. A searchlight beam looked no more than a pencil of light from a distance, but when you were caught in it the area of light seemed infinite. It was like drowning in a vast lake of blue, swamping, all-embracing, entire. He didn't know if he was caught in one searchlight or twenty, and it hardly mattered – the effect was the same.

Beach, he knew, would lie there stubbornly in the nose, oblivious of the barrage, or pretending to be, concentrating on his bomb-sight. Somehow he would have to keep the Lancaster straight and level until Beach had dropped the bombs. He lowered his seat to the floor and began flying on instruments – he daren't expose his eyes any further to that appalling glare. When the flak-bursts started he weaved gently, waiting for the signal from Beach. Why didn't the fellow drop the bombs? They were right on top of the target, and on a night like this one place was as good as another. But that he knew wasn't John Beach's way. To him, aiming-points were sacrosanct.

'Steady. Steady.'

In the next instant Gilpin felt and heard a terrific clout directly behind him. A huge shell fragment had torn through the roof and down through the navigator's seat. Had Beach been sitting there, as he certainly would have been if they had been able to find a bomb-aimer, he would have been obliterated.

'Bombs gone.'

Now Gilpin tried everything to get out of the searchlights, turning steeply to port and diving at more than 300 miles an hour before pulling up almost into the stall. All the time they were flying through puffs of flak. They could hear it and smell it, even when they weren't hit. Several times Brewer came up on the inter-com with facetious comments about their situation, infuriating Gilpin. At these times, if there was nothing important to be said, it was axiomatic to keep quiet. Even for experienced aircrew it was a terrifying experience, and Gilpin found that he was sweating profusely. Brewer was almost playful, yet he ought to be paralysed with fright. Perhaps he just didn't understand the danger, or perhaps he was talking to keep up his spirits. But he sounded as though he was being thoroughly entertained.

'They're not very pleased to see us, are they?' intoned Brewer, as though expecting an answer. 'And they're not such bad shots after all, are they?'

'For Pete's sake,' said Gilpin, 'shut up and let's get out of here.'

They lost an engine on the way out, but Gilpin was quite happy on three. And the fighters which had harried the returning bombers over Holland and Belgium had packed up for the night. The last of the thousand had somehow got safely away. When they reached the Dutch coast it was daylight.

*

David Johnson's crew was a scratch one that included four men from the Central Gunnery School at Sutton Bridge plus a second pilot and a navigator picked up at Feltwell, six men in all. The second pilot was a Czech. The last of the forty-seven crews that took off from Feltwell, they bombed the target successfully; but like Tom Ramsay before them they must have turned almost due north away from the target area, presumably due to some navigational or compass error. At some stage, though, they were almost certainly chased by a fighter. Their Wellington eventually crashed in flames in the Hessen Allee in Klarenbeek, fifteen miles north-east of Arnhem, at 02.30 that

Sunday morning. In the burnt-out wreckage were found the bodies of five of the crew-men. Among them was David Johnson. Only one man, the rear gunner, Sergeant Waddington-Allright, escaped. He was taken prisoner.

News that her husband was missing reached Dinny Johnson next day. The gang wangled her some petrol, and one of them insisted on driving her that evening with her 6-months-old baby to her parents' home in the north. For Dinny Johnson it was the end of an idyll.

*

Even when the last bomber had left the Dutch coast on the homeward flight the danger of losses was not yet over. Many crews were struggling across the grey spume of the North Sea with faltering engines and damaged controls. Another hazard was that of dangerous cumulo-nimbus cloud in the latter stages of the crossing and over the east coast. Those who got across safely faced deteriorating visibility and lowering cloud over the bases. With a large number of bombers returning in a short space of time, many of them crippled and facing crash-landings, runways and circuits were congested.

Pilot Officer Bob Ferrer, of Stetchford, Birmingham, was one of the pilots who was struggling to get home in a crippled plane – the old drogue-towing Wellington Ic from No 12 OTU at Chipping Warden. Home for Bob Ferrer, as for his wireless operator for the night, Ronald Grundy, meant furnished rooms in a row of cottages in a village outside Banbury. Both men were hoping to get back to their wives that night.

They had bombed the target about half-way through the raid, when the huge column of smoke belching up into the moonlight was flattened out at about 8,000 feet and spewing away to the south-east. Up to that time the danger to the Wellington had seemed general and impersonal. But soon after leaving the target they had been shadowed and then attacked by an Me 110. The fighter's first burst had been right on target. Grundy, sitting at the radio behind the pilot, had seen blue tracer darting from behind along the fuselage and ricocheting off the electrical panel on the starboard side. As he ducked there had come a stifled groan from Mackenzie, the Canadian rear gunner, over the inter-com. To Grundy, unused to these extrovert Canadians, it had sounded like something out of an American film.

'They got me, Bob.'

Ferrer put the Wellington into a steep dive, determined to shake off the fighter, and they had lost nearly 10,000 feet and were well clear of the target before he levelled off and set course for home. Then Grundy and the flaxen-haired Lucki went back to help Mackenzie. They made their way along the catwalk, negotiated the drogue winch, opened the turret doors and pulled Mackenzie clear. But as they lifted him forward they stumbled over the winch and fell in a heap around it. Mackenzie was in great pain and the fall was a disaster, but at last they got him on the rest-bed in mid-fuselage. Ferrer was calling for radio bearings, so Buck went back from the front turret to help Lucki while Grundy returned to his set. They gave Mackenzie morphine, then returned to their crew positions.

One of the engines was running roughly but they made steady progress across Holland to the North Sea, losing only a little height. They were at 4,000 feet as they crossed the Dutch coast. Grundy began to use his loop aerial, tuning in to the Ely radio beacon to take a bearing, but when he switched in the fixed aerial to try to sense the bearing the needles wouldn't respond. He looked out of the astro-dome and saw that the fixed aerial had been shot away. As he reported this to Ferrer, the starboard engine failed.

At once they began to lose height more rapidly, though Ferrer still hoped to complete the sea crossing on the remaining engine. 'Get me a fix,' he called to Grundy. 'Make it priority.' Grundy reeled out the trailing aerial and called the D/F station at Hull. He passed the fix to Lucki who plotted it on his chart. It put them forty miles from the English coast, heading straight for the bulge of East Anglia. 'There's a chance we may have to ditch,' called Ferrer. The port engine was complaining now as Ferrer struggled to maintain height. Below him the sea was like glass, bathed in moonlight. The altimeter showed 1,500 feet. 'Send an SOS,' he told Grundy, 'and get another position.'

Grundy sent the distress message and got an immediate acknowledgement. The fix put them less than thirty miles from the coast. Fifteen minutes flying. If only Ferrer could coax the plane along just a little longer they would be safe.

Back in the row of cottages at Wardington, the wives of Bob Ferrer and Ronald Grundy were asleep, unaware that their husbands were flying at less than a thousand feet over the North Sea, fighting for their lives.

'Ditching stations.'

The port engine was faltering. Buck came out of the front turret and took up his ditching position next to the bed, under the astro-dome. Lucki sat on the floor of the cabin, to the right of the radio, his legs splayed out into a V to make room for Grundy. As the port engine finally cut, Grundy clamped down the key, shut the ply-wood door leading to the cockpit and slotted his body into the opening made by Lucki, bracing his legs against the main cross-member of the wing a few feet in front of him. Alone in the cockpit, Ferrer was facing the almost impossible task of judging his height above the still mirror of the sea.

Within another thirty seconds the plane hit the water, before Bob Ferrer was ready for it, slightly nose-down. The force of the impact sprang the trap-door under the nose and precipitated a tidal-wave of water through the fuselage, smashing the ply-wood door and flooding the cabin with a wall of green. As the waters rushed in so Grundy and Lucki were catapulted forward, doubling the impact. Grundy was hurled through this wall of water into the cockpit and then sucked out through the trap-door as the Wellington floated to the surface, suffering multiple injuries as he went. By this time he was unconscious.

Somehow the Wellington passed over Grundy's body and allowed it to float away freely. As he came to the surface his first awareness was of opening his eyes and feeling like a blinkered horse, unable to see anything except in a narrow aperture dead ahead. He was staring straight into the guns of the rear turret, which constituted his entire horizon. On either side of the turret was complete darkness.

He was so confused and concussed that he didn't have the presence of mind to pull the gas bottle on his Mae West. Somehow he started swimming, and then he saw the dinghy and struck out towards it. He wondered why it was that he couldn't swim properly, but even when he reached the dinghy and lifted his arm round the outer tube to hold on he was too bemused to take stock of his injuries. In fact he was suffering from compound fractures of both legs and one arm, several ribs were broken, his lip had been cut open and was flapping like a letter-box and he had lost all his front teeth. Unaware of why he was doing so, and with no hope of being heard, he found himself shouting weakly for help.

The Wellington was rising and falling gently on the swell. All the others must still be inside. Then Buck appeared as if from nowhere, swimming powerfully across to the dinghy, pulling Mackenzie behind him. Somehow Buck had got Mackenzie off the bed and pushed him through the astro-dome before climbing out himself. Even Buck didn't have the strength to get into the dinghy, still less to hoist up Mackenzie, and the three men huddled together at the rim, with Buck holding on to Mackenzie to keep his face clear of the water. There was still no sign of Ferrer and Lucki when, a minute later, the Wellington settled deeper into the water and sank slowly down.

It was still dark when they were picked up by a naval launch and taken to Harwich – Grundy's SOS had been quickly acted upon. They had been very near the coast when the aircraft came down, they had so nearly made it. There was even a report, which found its way later that morning to Bob Ferrer's wife, that they had all got down safely. She even called on Ronald Grundy's wife to tell her the good news.

Mackenzie died from his wounds later that morning; Buck's great effort to save him had been in vain. The bodies of Ferrer and Lucki were never recovered. Telegrams were sent later in the day to the two cottages in Wardington. One brought Ronald Grundy's wife to see him in the naval hospital at Shotley that evening. The other, to Bob Ferrer's widow, doubly cruel after the false report that he was safe, seemed to signal the end of all meaning to life.

Kenneth Buck, his crew gone, joined another one and was posted to a squadron a few weeks later. He was reported missing almost exactly a year afterwards and was subsequently presumed dead. Ronald Grundy made a partial recovery and was transferred to the technical signals branch with a commission, but he developed tuberculosis of the spine as a result of his injuries and spent two years in bed before being invalided out of the Service in 1947. His most ironic moment, however, came about a month after the raid, when he lay completely immobilized in the RAF hospital at Ely, one leg in plaster, the other leg in a splint, one arm in plaster, his face and ribs still only partly healed. It was fairly obvious that he would never fly again. It was at this moment that he had a visit from a clerk in the hospital orderly room.

'Flight,' said the clerk, 'I've got some good news for you. Your pilot's course has come through.'

*

Rumours that Ansons and even Tiger Moths took part in the raid on Cologne have no substance, although the Ansons of No 13 OTU at Bicester did make a contribution by taking part next morning in air/sea rescue sweeps. Another rumour without substance was that the North Sea was littered with dinghies. The elaborate preparations for search and rescue proved to be an unnecessary insurance. Apart from Bob Ferrer and his Wellington, the only planes to come down in the sea were the Manchester of 49 Squadron flown by Flight Sergeant Carter, and a Wellington from 142 Squadron, from both of which the bodies were recovered next day.

The cumulo-nimbus, too, claimed its victims. Sam Lucas, one of the last to leave the target, came safely through the night-fighter belt and crossed the North Sea at 12,000 feet. The advice at briefing had been to lose height and come in under the cu-nim, but when Lucas saw the build-up directly ahead he had just crossed the Lincolnshire coast and he hesitated to go down into the rain and murk beneath it. While he was debating what to do he found himself in the cloud-tops. He climbed as steeply as he dared, but he could not get clear.

Once or twice he saw the moon, revealed suddenly and encouragingly before the cloud once again enveloped them. Violent turbulence threw the Halifax about like driftwood, and Lucas could hear the ice from the airscrews hitting the fuselage. So far from gaining height to get out of the cloud, he was finding it impossible to maintain it. The only thing to do was to turn back out to sea, let down and come in again underneath the cloud.

He had just started his turn when the Halifax fell right out of his hands. The instruments collapsed and the plane began a tight spiral through the cloud. He put the stick hard forward to regain flying speed, then tried to stop the rotation, concentrating on getting the bottom of the turn-and-bank indicator to stay in the middle. The spin became sloppy, but the Halifax showed no sign of coming out.

The one instrument that was still registering correctly was the altimeter. When they got down to 3,000 feet, Lucas gave the order to his crew to bale out. At least he knew they must be over land. Nothing had been said in the aircraft up to that point, but the crew were all ready to go and they left in about five seconds. Lucas stayed where he was. In that long spiral it had been impossible for the others to get his parachute, and his only chance lay in regaining control.

The spin continued. All the hatches were open and the screech of the wind was deafening. It was a solitary feeling, plunging alone in a four-engine bomber to one's death. But he still tried every trick he knew to get out of the spin. The thought that he could still have been sitting behind an Air Ministry desk but for his own impatience did not occur to him. Small inconsequential details imprinted themselves on his mind: lying on the cockpit floor was a sandwich which someone had trodden on; a lighted torch was rolling to and fro with the spin. The darkness and the cloud seemed to insulate him from fear.

He had never known what it was to panic. He thought he could detect a faint response from the controls, and he kept working them, determined to get the aircraft out. He was below a thousand feet when with the help of the throttles he finally made it, the spiral flattened out and the instruments clicked back into focus. He was feeling strangely breathless, but his hands were steady and he wasn't even sweating.

Underneath the cloud the night was pitch black and it was raining heavily. He didn't know his fuel state and he couldn't remember the engineer's settings; there was no automatic pilot and he couldn't leave his seat to look at the gauges. The undercarriage was up and locked, so were the flaps, and he could alter neither from the cockpit. He was considering his next move when he saw the searchlights of a 'Sandra' guiding system to the south and he headed for these.

He didn't know what airfield it was, but that didn't matter. He flew round to get a mental picture of it, then did a low dummy run alongside the runway, switching on his landing lights to see what the ground surface was like. As he did so there was a bright flash behind him – the trailing aerial was still out and it had fouled a line of high-tension cables. The aircraft was undamaged, and he turned back, made another approach and set the Halifax down neatly on its belly parallel to the runway. He found he had landed at Wittering. The rest of his crew had come down near Spalding in Lincolnshire. All were unhurt except one. Sergeant E. Webb, the tail gunner, had fallen heavily and awkwardly in the high gusting wind and broken his neck. He died on the way to hospital.

One other pilot had an almost identical experience. Warrant Officer Ernest Smith, flying a Wellington from No 16 OTU at Upper Heyford, got into a spin in cumulo-nimbus cloud ten miles east of Southwold; at 2,000 feet he ordered his crew to bale out. They were still over the sea, but three of them went. One man, Sergeant Cuddington, the tail gunner, didn't have time to get out. Smith pulled out of the spin at 200 feet, almost scraping the water as he brought the Wellington under control and climbed away. The three men who baled out had been within sight of the coast as they parachuted down, but the most intensive search failed to find them and they were presumed lost at sea.

*

Above the Cambridgeshire fens the first traces of light, clearly visible from the air, were obscured on the ground by a curtain of cloud at 2,000 feet. Donald Falconer, 'Uncle' Falconer, of No 14 OTU at Cottesmore, returning with his Hampden after successfully bombing the target, began his let-down through cloud soon after crossing the Norfolk coast. He broke cloud safely in almost complete darkness over the small north Cambridgeshire town of March. The time was just after four o'clock. Letting down immediately above him, on a similar course, was the 78 Squadron Halifax piloted by Geoffrey Foers.

Sitting in the engineer's position in the Halifax, back-to-back with the pilot, immediately beneath the astro-dome, was Sergeant Harold Curtis, an artisan from Melton Mowbray whose long fair hair that normally flopped over his left eyebrow was at present held in position by his flying helmet. Curtis was a former engine fitter who had volunteered for training as a pilot only to find himself posted to the newly created role of flight engineer. He was making up his engineer's log, and he called Foers.

'What height are we, Skipper?'

'Two thousand feet.'

He was about to make the entry in his log when there was a thump to his left – the starboard side, since he was facing aft – and the Halifax started to quiver and vibrate with staccato violence. He turned instinctively to look at the pilot, hoping for reassurance, and there was Foers fighting to hold the control column, which was jerking back and forth under some irresistible outside pressure. None of the men in the Halifax had the slightest idea what had happened, but it was instantly clear that they would have to get out.

'Bale out!'

Foers went on wrenching at the controls, knowing that there

was no chance whatever at this height of getting out himself. The Halifax was bucking and swerving downwards and would hit the ground in seconds. What the hell could be the matter? Meanwhile Curtis, ignoring for the moment the order to bale out, stood up, still facing aft, and peered through the astrodome. Everything looked normal towards the tail, but looking forward over his left shoulder he could see the starboard wing. The starboard outer engine had disappeared altogether – it must have fallen out – and the inboard engine was on fire. This was enough for Curtis. He grabbed his parachute and ran down the fuselage to the side door, clipping on his chute as he went. In an emergency bale-out like this it was every man for himself. He could do nothing for anyone else. He got the side door open and went straight out, and even in the semi-darkness he could see the grass slipping by not very far beneath him as he did so. He pulled the ripcord, and the tug of the opening canopy almost coincided with the bump as he hit the ground. He picked himself up quickly, shaken but unhurt. Two hundred yards ahead of him, in the same field, he saw the Halifax crash.

In those last few moments Geoffrey Foers had somehow kept the Halifax on a fairly even keel, but the impact with the ground was heavy. Curtis ran over to the wreck to pull out his crewmates only to find that they had all been thrown out on impact. He located three of them at once, but they were so badly injured that he doubted if they would live. Two of them died almost immediately. He helped the third to light a cigarette. There was no sign of Foers.

He stared unbelievingly at the shattered cockpit. Foers could not possibly have baled out. He must be somewhere near. Curtis stared around him, still half-dazed by his own fall, and there on the edge of the field, staggering about in a severely concussed state in the near-darkness but amazingly still on his feet, he saw his pilot. Although sustaining critical head injuries which put him on the D I list for several days, Geoffrey Foers had escaped with his life.

Two fields away, Curtis saw another aircraft burning. He had seen so many fires on the ground that night that he did not connect this one with his own crash. It wasn't until nearly an hour later, when fire and ambulance parties had collected the injured and dead men and he himself had been taken to March policc station, that he met a short, thick-set RAF officer with a pipe in his mouth who was stripping off his flying kit.

'Where have you come from?' asked the officer.

'Out of that Halifax.'

'What Halifax?'

'In the field down the road. We'd just broken cloud when something went wrong. The starboard engine fell clean out.'

'Good God! So that was what I hit.'

Immediately after Donald Falconer had broken cloud, the slight seepage of light into the cockpit had been cut off from above. He thought it had been more cloud – but in fact the Halifax was right on top of him. That was what was shutting out the light.

The two starboard engines of the Halifax had churned through the cockpit hood of the Hampden, virtually cutting it in half, ripping off the hood. Falconer, thrown out before he had time to think about it, was the only man in the Hampden to escape. His seat-type parachute saved him. His crew of three, one of whom, Sergeant Knowling, had been with him throughout his operational tour, were killed instantly when the plane hit the ground.

In spite of his injuries, Geoffrey Foers was back on operations with 78 Squadron at Croft that August. He was shot down by a fighter near Duisberg in October 1942 and killed with all but two of his crew. Donald Falconer, too, returned later to operations, completing a second tour with the Pathfinder Force. On New Year's Eve 1943 he volunteered to do an extra sortie, from which he did not return.

PART V

ASSESSMENT

AT 04.00 HOURS on 31st May, long before the last of the bombers had landed back at their bases, the first Mosquito ever to operate against Germany took off from Horsham St Faith in Norfolk on a bombing and photographic sortie against Cologne. The pilot dropped his bombs in the target area, but although it was daylight by then it was impossible to see the results owing to cloud and smoke. Numerous fires were burning in the centre of the city and in the adjoining industrial and residential areas on both sides of the Rhine, and a huge pall of smoke covered the city and rose to a height of 15,000 feet. Conditions for photographic reconnaissance were impossible.

Two men at least had no doubt by this time of the success of the raid. Both Harris and Saundby, still unable to sleep, had rung the operations room at High Wycombe a few minutes after 4 am from their bedside telephones, quite independently of each other, to reassure themselves about the raid. Both asked the same question.

'What was the weather like over Cologne?'

The answer, that there had been a full moon and no cloud, was all that either man wanted. Both were confident now that the raid must have been a success.

A second Mosquito took off at 06.30 that morning, but it failed to return. Three more PRU Mosquitos went to Cologne during the day, but not one was able to get pictures because of the smoke. 'When at last that Sunday morning dawned,' wrote a German eye-witness later, 'a tremendous fire-cloud hung over the city. The sun was dimmed and all we could see of it was a purple disc behind the writhing smoke, a circle which at its edges broke up into the colours of the rainbow, then into deepest black. Suffering and death, fire and destruction raged in the streets in the ghostly twilight of a total eclipse. For many hours the glare of the flames was brighter than daylight.'

A full evaluation of the raid would have to wait until the fire-cloud dispersed. Meanwhile, Bomber Command counted its losses. Of the total force of 1,046 bombers, forty-one were missing, of which three were known to have come down in the North Sea. (Another seven bombers had crashed in the UK with the loss of most or all the crew.) Of the eighty-eight aircraft of the intruder force, three were missing. So of a combined force of 1,134 aircraft, forty-four had failed to return. The percentage bomber loss was 3·9, which was slightly higher than the previous average for attacks on Cologne but lower than the previous average for attacks on similar targets in conditions of moonlight and no cloud. Taking into account the large number of OTU and fresher crews employed it was clear that the concentration had greatly reduced casualties. Even more striking were the comparative figures for the three successive waves; the first wave suffered 4·8 per cent casualties, the second wave 4·1 and the third, the most concentrated, only 1·9. This very low figure also reflected the general superiority of the Lancaster and Halifax.

The estimated rate of one collision per hour over the target had proved exactly accurate: in just under two hours there had been two collisions. The third collision, over Cambridgeshire, was of a kind that was always a potential danger when low cloud covered the bases. There was only one report of an aircraft being hit by falling bombs – it was an OTU Wellington – and although the tail gunner had been killed outright the damaged aircraft had got back safely. Dr Dickins and his research team had been right.

The other major prophetic advice given by the research scientists – to go to Cologne – was depressingly vindicated two nights later, and again before the end of June, in the thousand-bomber raids on Essen and Bremen, both of which were failures.

One surprising feature of the casualty figures, often remarked on before, was the lighter percentage of losses suffered by the

OTU groups as compared with the front-line squadrons. There is in fact a simple explanation of this. The OTUs were not the only units that night to put up inexperienced crews. As has been noted earlier, in order to make use of all the available aircraft the squadrons were forced to employ crews who would not normally have been sent against a major German target without further training. An analysis of the casualty lists reveals again and again the tragic loss of some new crew on their first major operational flight.

Of the forty-one missing crews of the bomber force, twenty-four were from squadrons and seventeen from training units. Among the twenty-four squadron pilots as many as ten were on their first operation over Germany as first pilot and captain, accompanied by inexperienced crews. Two more were on their first trip as Manchester captains, another two had completed only three operations. Thus the bulk of the squadron losses were raw crews. Only ten could be described as fully fledged, and half of these had done less than ten trips.

Again, of three squadron pilots involved in fatal crashes on take-off or landing during the operation, all were on their first trip as first pilot and captain. There were no survivors from these three crews.

Here then was the reason for the apparently incongruous fact that the squadrons had suffered heavier percentage losses than the training units. It was one of the most poignant and significant lessons of the operation, yet the human factor behind the figures was not apparently made available to the operational research scientists at High Wycombe – or not asked for – and the inference was therefore not drawn in their raid report, illustrating the dependence of such analysis on the quality of the information fed into it.

It is not suggested that commanders did not appreciate the much greater vulnerability of raw crews; they most certainly did. New pilots were normally required to do five trips over Germany as second pilot, followed by two or three mining sorties and one or two trips to targets in occupied Europe as first pilot before captaining an aircraft to a major target in

Germany. This was regarded as about the best compromise in the circumstances – like a pilot's first solo flight, it was a plunge that sooner or later had to be taken. But deeper analysis of the figures for the Thousand Plan might have brought an order from Command for an even stricter qualifying programme, to the ultimate good of the bomber offensive.

The heavy losses of these raw crews would have been a particularly severe blow to Harris had he known of them. The responsibility was one he would have accepted personally: the whole tempo of the operational planning after the last-minute defection of Coastal Command had demanded the employment of every available crew. But despite these many human tragedies, and in a very real sense because of them – because of the determination to reach and pass the figure of a thousand even without outside help, and because of the enthusiasm and readiness for sacrifice of the rawest crews – the raid had demonstrated in a necessarily spectacular manner the possibility of delivering vast blows against Germany's industrial cities without incurring crippling losses. Other inferences awaited thorough photographic reconnaissance of the target area. It was a week before the dust had settled sufficiently for successful photography and interpretation, but long before then the impact made by the raid had become clear from other sources.

First, on 31st May, came a communiqué from the Fuehrer's headquarters that was remarkable for its subdued tone. 'During last night,' it read, 'British bombers carried out a terror raid on the inner city of Cologne. Great damage was done as a result of explosions and fires, particularly in residential quarters, to several public buildings, among them three churches and two hospitals. In this attack, directed exclusively against the civil population, the British air force suffered severe losses. Night fighters and AA artillery shot down 36 of the attacking bombers. In addition, one bomber was shot down in the coastal area by naval artillery.' In the circumstances it was a remarkably accurate communiqué, and the admission of 'great damage' was unprecedented, as was the implied admission of the accuracy of our bombing in the phrase 'the inner city of Cologne'.

Another event without precedent was the tone of the newspaper *Kölnische Zeitung* when it resumed publication three days later. 'Those who survived,' it said, 'were fully aware that they had bade farewell to their Cologne, because the damage is enormous and because the integral part of the character, and even the traditions, of the city is gone for ever.'

German propaganda sources, however, after dwelling at length on the heavy RAF losses and the great success of the German air defences, ridiculed the British claim that more than a thousand bombers had attacked the city, dismissing this figure as pure fantasy and putting the actual number at about seventy. (In fact it was not less than 910.) Later, after the raid had attracted world-wide publicity, some German reports admitted that several hundred aircraft had probably taken part but that only about seventy had reached the target area. 'More than half the planes which attacked Cologne,' said the German radio, 'were shot down.' The British had put out this imaginary figure in an attempt to explain their losses.

For world consumption, German commentators were at pains to claim that the 'barbarous British terror raids' were a new departure in air warfare, which would be returned with interest, but that up to that point the German conduct of the war had been exemplary throughout. Earlier bombing – and atrocities – apart, the notion that the conduct of an aggressive war against neighbour states could be carried out in an exemplary fashion was an odd one.

The raid stung the Germans into several reprisal raids, including one on Canterbury on the following night, mostly as a sop to morale at home. Numerous reports said that the attack on Cologne was of no military consequence, and one report added cryptically that the force would have been 'far better employed elsewhere'. This was to be a recurrent German theme. For our part we were convinced from our own experience at the receiving end that bombing on a heavy enough scale must have military consequences in time. With the advantage of hindsight the arguments on how the bomber force might have been more profitably employed continue, but it is noteworthy that when the Germans turned from the attack on our airfields and radar stations in the Battle of Britain to attacks on ports and towns, which suited us well enough in that particular battle, we were careful not to hint that their planes might have been better employed elsewhere.

In evaluating the raid the Nazi leaders were hampered at first by the complete severance of telephone and teleprinter lines and later by the difficulty of getting accurate and disinterested reports. A week after the raid Goering was still insisting that the number of bombers penetrating to Cologne was no more than seventy, of which the Luftwaffe had shot down forty-four. Goebbels dismissed this as absurd and preferred the evidence of the Gauleiter of Cologne, from which he judged that the destruction surpassed that of all earlier raids. On the whole though he was inclined to shrug off the raid as an isolated one. 'I still cannot believe,' he wrote,[1] 'that the English have the power to continue such bombing attacks. . . . However it can't be overlooked that such night attacks can damage us considerably.' Goebbels was himself a disciple of area bombing. 'Once again I have been proved right in my view that there is no point in starting a bombing war with the English from the military standpoint: we can only hurt them by hitting their civil population and cultural centres.' Conversely, he clearly believed that this was our best way of hurting them.

Goebbels promised speedy retaliation in kind, and he wrote at first of the reprisal attack on Canterbury as though it were equal in scale with Cologne. When he realized that there was no comparison he wrote that his 'fingers itched' with frustration. 'It would be wonderful if we were able to get so far this summer in the East,' he wrote, 'that we could again concentrate our air power in the West.'

Perhaps the most convincing evidence of all is that provided by an entry in Goebbels's diary six months later, by which time the lesson of Cologne had had time to sink in. The entry showed

1. From an unpublished portion of Goebbels's diary (National Archives of the United States).

how Goebbels's public propaganda pronouncements on British bombing were the exact opposite of his private view. In our bombing offensive against German cities, he confided to his diary, we were striking at our enemy's weakest point.[1]

At last the thoughts of the Nazi leaders had been turned inwards. Directly after the raid Goering announced that first-category SHD units – the professional units already organized by the Reich authorities for fire-fighting, decontamination, demolition and rescue work in the more important areas – had been placed within the uniformed police under the sphere of command of Himmler. This was the first of many measures involving the expansion and reorganization of the German air defences and radical changes in plane production and overall strategy. These changes, while making Bomber Command's task progressively harder as the months went by, were ultimately to have serious military consequences for Germany. The war in the West took the first step towards a decisive phase with the raid on Cologne.

When at last photographic interpretation could give an accurate assessment of the results of the raid, the damage revealed was on a far greater scale than anything yet seen in any German city. Not only were large areas of the city itself devastated, but industrial and residential properties in all the main suburban areas had been seriously damaged. It is not intended to dwell on the sufferings of the people of Cologne; no doubt another, differently-angled book could be written around their human experience and individual courage. But the broad details must be given.

According to the report of the Police President in Cologne, the bombing was spread evenly over the entire city area and had no recognizable centre of impact. This is consistent with the plan for the attack, which was to spread outwards from the three main aiming-points. Nevertheless it was clear from photographs that the crescent of the old city, aiming-point for the incendiary force, suffered very severe damage indeed.

Biggest damage of all was to so-called 'accommodation

1. *The Goebbels Diaries*, 13th December 1942 (Hamish Hamilton).

units', complete homes accommodating whole families in blocks of flats and in houses. More than 13,000 such homes were completely destroyed and a further 6,000 badly damaged, over 45,000 people being homeless. Fifteen hundred commercial and industrial undertakings had their premises completely destroyed and a further 630 were badly damaged. Thirty-six major factories were completely destroyed with 100 per cent loss of production, seventy were badly damaged with 50–80 per cent loss of production, and more than 220 others sustained medium or slight damage. Movements of trains from stations within the city area had to be suspended for several days, main water, electric power and gas supplies were cut off over large areas, many roads were impassable and tramcar traffic was entirely suspended for a week. Large detachments of the German Army had to be brought in to assist in clearing the rubble.

Of the numbers bombed out, two-thirds were able to lodge temporarily with relatives or friends and a third were left without accommodation. Thousands of refugees still clogged the rail centres a week later when RAF prisoners were still passing through. For the Nazi authorities these refugees presented a serious problem of morale. The damage could not be hidden from the people of Cologne, but rumours of the disaster elsewhere in Germany had to be suppressed. All evacuees from Cologne were required to sign the following declaration:

'*I am aware that one individual alone can form no comprehensive idea of the events in Cologne. One usually exaggerates one's own experiences, and the judgement of those who have been bombed is impaired.*

'*I am, therefore, aware that reports of individual suffering can only do harm, and I will keep silence. I know what the consequences of breaking this undertaking would be.*'

In England, the bombed-out at least had the satisfaction of telling their story afterwards to those who would listen. Even this consolation was denied to the Germans. Perhaps the pledge of secrecy made the telling all the more piquant.

Past experience, good shelters and the energetic work of the civil defence forces combined to keep casualties down, but even so they were heavy, bigger than in any other raid on Germany up to that time. The total was just over 5,000, of whom 469 were killed. In 106 earlier attacks on Cologne, 139 people had been killed and 277 seriously injured. Most impressive were the material results of the raid as compared with the previous Cologne raids and those on German targets in general: the damage was vastly more than the aggregate of all previous air raid damage in Cologne, 600 acres – including about 300 acres in the centre of the city – being completely destroyed. This was not far short of the total estimated area of destruction to targets in Germany wrought by the entire bomber offensive up to that point.

When he learned of the success of the raid Churchill sent an immediate signal to Harris. 'I congratulate you and the whole of Bomber Command,' he said, 'upon the remarkable feat of organization which enabled you to despatch over a thousand bombers to the Cologne area in a single night and without confusion to concentrate their action over the target in so short a time as one hour and a half. This proof of the growing power of the British bomber force is also the herald of what Germany will receive, city by city, from now on.' It was this last sentence, with its clear indication of the Government's intention to support a bomber offensive against Germany's principal cities, which for Harris justified the gamble of Cologne.

It remains to evaluate the raid more fully in terms of short-term and long-term failure and success. Harris's overt and declared object had been the destruction of the city of Cologne. Clearly this was not achieved, nor even approached. The city had been paralysed for a week, crippled for a fortnight, disrupted for a month, seriously inconvenienced for from three to six months. But by the end of 1942, information on the reconstruction of Cologne, based on the latest aerial photographs, led us to the conclusion that almost every damaged industrial plant that had been re-photographed was either reconstructed already or in the process of repair, and that very few, perhaps only two or three, had been left derelict. This after a raid that still, seven

DIE SCHWERSTEN ANGRIFFE DER LUFTWAFFE VON DER R.A.F. WEIT ÜBERBOTEN

Mehr als 1000 Bomber auf einmal eingesetzt

IN der Nacht vom 30. Mai griff die Royal Air Force Köln mit weit über 1000 Flugzeugen an. Der Angriff wurde auf anderthalb Stunden zusammengedrängt. Der deutsche Sicherheits- und Abwehrdienst war der Wucht des Angriffs nicht gewachsen.

Premierminister Churchill sagte in seiner Botschaft an den Oberbefehlshaber des britischen Bomberkommandos am 31. Mai:

„Dieser Beweis der wachsenden Stärke der britischen Luftmacht ist auch das Sturmzeichen für die Dinge, die von nun an eine deutsche Stadt nach der andern zu erwarten hat."

Zwei Nächte darauf griff die Royal Air Force das Ruhrgebiet mit über 1000 Maschinen an.

Die Offensive der Royal Air Force in ihrer neuen Form hat begonnen

Translation

THE ATTACKS OF THE RAF FAR SURPASS THE HEAVIEST ATTACKS OF THE LUFTWAFFE · MORE THAN 1000 BOMBERS IN ONE ATTACK

On the night of May 30th/31st, the Royal Air Force attacked Cologne with well over 1,000 planes. The attack was concentrated into an hour and a half. The German civil and anti-aircraft defences were not equal to the weight of the attack.

In his message to the Commander-in-Chief Bomber Command on May 31st, Churchill said:

'This proof of the growing power of the British Bomber Force is also the herald of what Germany will receive city by city from now on.'

Two nights after this the Royal Air Force attacked the Ruhr with over 1,000 planes.

THE OFFENSIVE OF THE ROYAL AIR FORCE IN ITS NEW FORM HAS BEGUN

(*Thousands of these leaflets were dropped in the weeks following the raid on Cologne.*)

months later, was far outside the normal capacity of the Command.

The lesson of the raid was that the destruction of German industry, industrial life and industrial potential by bombing was not within our power, then or in the foreseeable future, and that to achieve conclusive results a massive expansion of the bomber force was necessary, together with improved aids to target-finding and bomb-aiming. With the weapons and means available, large industrial areas were virtually indestructible. Somehow life went on.

What of the effect on morale? It is apparent from the operation order that in May 1942 Harris shared the popular misconceptions on German morale and its susceptibility to shock attack; it is also apparent from his subsequent utterances that he revised his opinions radically some time after this raid and before the end of 1942. Later experience clearly demonstrated that four main factors stood between the bombing offensive and outright victory. First was the known inadequacy of effort; the Air Staff had always held that 4,000–6,000 bombers would be needed for the successful prosecution of a bomber offensive as a war-winner on its own, which was probably an accurate estimate, but it was a figure that was never approached, not even by the ultimate strength of the British and American bomber forces combined. Second was the enormous amount of slack available to be taken up in German industry; although the Germans had been ready for a short war, they had not mobilized their vast industrial resources for a long one. Third was the over-estimate of the powers of permanent destruction of the bomber. Fourth was the under-estimate of the resilience and powers of recovery of a totalitarian State, and especially of the German people.

But if it seemed that the raid had failed in some of its overt, immediate objects, on the whole it had been a success. Serious damage had been done in the short term to the industrial capacity of Germany's fourth largest city. The blow to morale had not been fatal, but it was the first of many scars that over a period would weaken the tissue. For the Allies themselves, still in desperate straits on all fronts, Cologne burned like a beacon of hope. The very fact that Britain alone was capable of dispatching more than a thousand bombers in one night to a great German city had an incalculable impact, inspiring and uplifting for the Allied fighting man, alarming and depressing for the Germans and humiliating for their leaders. What the German soldier thought about it is revealed in many captured letters; he was stunned and apprehensive. What was it going to be like when the Americans joined in? The effect on his fighting heart is less easy to assess, but it may not be altogether without significance that Cologne preceded El Alamein and Stalingrad, places where despondent letters about the bombing of Germany were captured. For the fighting man on both sides, Cologne was a turning point of the war.

But to judge the raid purely on its material and moral results would be to forget that its main purposes, undisclosed in the operation order, were strategic and political – the preservation and expansion of Bomber Command as a war-winning weapon. 'The exertions and the risks to which Air Marshal Harris had exposed his command had been justified by the event,' comments the official history.[1] 'Furthermore, a convincing and practical demonstration had been given of the argument for a great and speedy expansion in the front-line strength of Bomber Command.' This was what Harris had been after, and he followed up the raid with the strongest possible representations to the Prime Minister. 'The success of the Thousand Plan,' he wrote, 'has proved beyond doubt in the minds of all but wilful men that we can even today dispose of a weight of air attack which no country on which it can be brought to bear can survive.' He called for the immediate return of all bomber aircraft from Coastal Command, the ultimate return of all bombers from the Middle East, the return of all suitable aircraft and crews from Army Co-operation Command, the extraction of every possible bomber from America, an approach to Stalin to transfer his bomber force to Britain and the highest possible priority for the production of heavy bombers at home. With the

1. *The Strategic Air Offensive Against Germany* (HMSO).

force envisaged, Harris believed that bombing could win the war, as quickly and as surely as the devastating American area bombing, culminating in the dropping of the atom bomb, was later to precipitate the surrender of Japan.

Churchill's support of Harris, which was always considerable and always vital, fell short of endorsement of Harris's belief that bombing either could or should be relied upon to win the war by itself. Impressed as Churchill was by the achievement of the Thousand Plan, he saw the growth and development of the bomber offensive as the first essential to victory, but a victory by land armies for whom the way had been prepared. Thus it is possible to argue, since Bomber Command never reached the Air Staff estimate of its required strength, and was therefore never strong enough to win the war by bombing alone, even in conjunction with the Americans, that the raid failed politically and strategically. But Harris's minimum object was the preservation of Bomber Command as a formidable weapon, the first and main source of victory. In this the raid succeeded. Up to this time the existence of Bomber Command as a major strategic force had been in doubt. The arguments went on, but the outcome was never seriously in doubt after Cologne. 'My own opinion,' wrote Harris afterwards, 'is that we should never have had a real bomber offensive if it had not been for the 1,000-bomber attack on Cologne.'[1] It was in the forging of the weapon that Cologne was a turning point, and it was here that Harris's basic war conception was met – the avoidance of major land campaigns until the enemy was fatally weakened by bombing. This policy was finally endorsed at the Casablanca Conference in January 1943.

The immediate material and moral results, then, important though they were, were not catastrophic for Germany and the area offensive which followed had disappointing results for some time; but the raid had significant and decisive effects which stemmed naturally from its main purpose, notably in the assumption of an offensive air posture and the forcing of a defensive posture on the entire German air force. And by the

1. *Bomber Offensive* (Collins).

end of 1943, with the aid of developments in radar and target marking, a weapon had been forged for the more selective and precise bombing that was often demanded and often accomplished.

In view of the doubts that have since been cast on the value of the bomber offensive, would it have been better if there had been no Thousand Plan, better if the Commander-in-Chief of Bomber Command had been a lesser man than Harris, not prepared to take such a fearful risk with his forces? In answering this question one turns inevitably to the strategic bombing surveys that were compiled immediately after the war, and to the four volumes which comprise the official British history of the strategic air offensive. From these we learn that the bombing of Germany did little to reduce the production of war material prior to about July 1944. This was for two reasons. First, the main weight of the air offensive was not brought to bear until 1944; of the total tonnage dropped by the RAF and USAF in the European war, 83 per cent was dropped after 1st January 1944, and of all tonnage dropped on Germany herself, 72 per cent was dropped after 1st July 1944.[1] So it is not surprising that the effect was hardly felt in earlier years. The effort was too small. Secondly, as already stressed, Germany had such enormous idle resources on which to draw; to appreciate Germany's vast untapped industrial power it is enough to record that in aircraft, tanks, trucks, self-propelled guns and many other types of armaments, British production alone exceeded German from 1940 to 1942. When, under Speer, Germany began to mobilize her resources and put her economy on a war footing for the first time, an inadequate bomber offensive was quite unable to keep pace with the rapid industrial expansion inside Germany. Even so, as soon as the air war was launched on its full and final scale, the effect was immediate and widespread.

Most big cities took about three months to recover to 80 per cent production after a heavy raid and six months for a return to 100 per cent. These figures have often been cited to disparage the bombing offensive, to show how quickly German industry

1. United States Strategic Bombing Survey.

shook off the effects of our bombing; but in retrospect they seem impressive enough. Some cities indeed never returned to 100 per cent at all. The figures do not take into account the diversion of productive and military effort from other areas for repair work – which was certainly enormous – and they quite ignore the fact that but for our bombing the production of armaments in these cities must otherwise have reached 150, 200 and even 300 per cent of the original figures under Speer's expansion schemes.

An impression, exaggerated if not actually falsified, has been built up over the years of German resilience and increased productivity under bombardment. Certainly the ability to take punishment and to come back with renewed energy was astounding and admirable. There is no intention to belittle this. But the stamina was not inexhaustible. Every bomb that fell on German cities from 1942 on widened the crack in morale, drove in the wedge between the German people and their leaders. Perhaps one of the greatest achievements of Allied bombing lay in the way it discredited the Nazis and their propaganda, bringing home to millions the tangible proof of Nazi miscalculation and of Allied power. Herein lies the reason for the pathological hatred of our bombing by the Nazi régime and their desperate efforts to present it as pointless and of no military value. The violence of their reaction gives the vital clue to its insidious cumulative effects: they have protested too much. The bombing was a cancer that the Nazis could not isolate; no amount of propaganda could explain it away. 'If I could hermetically seal off the Ruhr,' wrote Goebbels in his diary, 'if there were no such things as letters or telephones, then I would not have allowed a word to be published about the air offensive. Not a word!' That was how much it hurt the Nazis. It was the one thing they had failed to take properly into account. The entry in Goebbels's diary referred to earlier, that we were striking at Germany's weakest point, survives and rings true.

By the beginning of 1944, even before the invasion of Europe, three-quarters of the German people regarded the war as lost, bombing having played a major part in producing a conviction of Allied superiority, even though up to that time it had had only a limited effect on production. It may be, after all that has been said to the contrary, that it is here, in the field of morale, that bombing scorcd its greatest victory. 'Bombing,' said the United States Strategic Bombing Survey, 'appreciably affected the German will to resist. Its main psychological effects were defeatism, fear, hopelessness, fatalism, and apathy. It did little to stiffen resistance through the arousing of aggressive emotions of hate and anger. War weariness, willingness to surrender, loss of hope in a German victory, distrust of leaders, feelings of disunity, and demoralizing fear were all more common among bombed than unbombed people.' Here was one of the great imponderables, whose effect on the disintegration of the German war effort, at home and at the front, defies scientific analysis and can never be accurately assessed.

*

In its early stages, up to the time of Cologne and well beyond, the British people identified themselves with the bomber offensive, recognizing as they did so that they were making a Hobson's choice. The air was the only element where we could get to grips with Germany; bombs were the only things we could hit back at the Germans with. The shrewdness and resolve of our air leaders, the strength and quality of our aircraft industry, the skill and courage of our aircrews – these were the answer to criticisms that we were leaving Russia to fight the Germans virtually alone. This perhaps explains the disappointment still felt at the allegedly modest results of that offensive compared with the extravagant hopes held out for it. It should be added that in espousing this weapon they fully expected powerful German retaliation in kind, and that they backed themselves to trade punch for punch and rely on their own stamina to last the longest, never perhaps suspecting that German resilience might equal or even surpass their own. Then, some time in 1943, with their free speech, critical attitude towards Government and sympathy for the under-dog, together with a natural human amnesia about pain and injury, moral and physical, they moved into a climate in which it was possible to feel sorry for the Germans. The blitz was forgotten, the V-weapons were as yet unknown and the whole question of the moral rectitude of a bombing campaign on industrial cities was raised again and again. It is true that the Government's most vociferous critics were often people of pacifist tendencies, but it is also unfortunately true that the questions asked were seldom answered honestly and fearlessly. Those, like Harris, who *did* answer them honestly and fearlessly embarrassed the Government, who, with one eye on world opinion and the other on minority opinion at home, and strangely unsure of themselves, preferred at this stage to hide behind euphemisms and evasions. Even Churchill, whose earlier statements and forecasts could have left the British people in no doubt where they stood on the bombing of Germany, was silent. This was a serious mistake, one that we are still paying for. As Harris said repeatedly at the time, it was the Government's responsibility to keep the case for the bombing of Germany and the Germans firmly and clearly in the public mind, and not smother it with specious jargon about military targets, thus letting it go by default.

Harris practiced what he preached by keeping his own Command well informed on this point. In an official publication called the *Bomber Command Review*, published quarterly, the following appeared in mid-1942:

> Our bombers now have two main tasks:
> (a) to destroy the enemy's ports, ships and the mainspring of his offensive against our ocean convoys.
> (b) to inflict maximum damage on German and German-controlled war industries.
>
> In the course of such operations it is now part of our policy to create havoc in those German towns and cities which house the workers on whose efforts the Nazi war machine is dependent.

The precedence of the two main tasks is worth noting. In this period, more operations and more bomb tonnage was still being directed against naval than industrial targets; the defeat of the U-Boat remained the first charge on all our resources.

But the crux of the policy statement lay in the qualifying sentence at the end.

*

War has its own evolution: an early operation cannot necessarily be compared with a late one. Yet a comparison with the atomic attack on Hiroshima must be faced. The raids have obvious similarities. The object of the Thousand Plan was frankly stated – to destroy the city of Cologne. That the expected scale of destruction was not achieved is beside the point. Undoubtedly Harris believed that in mounting the raid he was aiming what was fundamentally a military as well as a political blow. But there was the tangible hope, expressed by Harris himself and transmitted to the crews at briefing, that the raid might precipitate a German surrender. 'At best the result may bring the war to a more or less abrupt conclusion ...' wrote Harris in his personal message to his group and station commanders just before the raid. This can only be interpreted as an intention to terrorize and intimidate the enemy into giving in, an intention surely the same as Hiroshima. It is pointless to deny it, and a great deal of harm has been done in trying to evade the issue. Cologne was conceived in the heat and fear of a struggle for survival that was both national and individual and yet transcended the bounds of both, a world-wide struggle against an evil tyranny, with the fingers of our enemies at our throat. To justify it, and indeed the whole conception of area or so-called terror bombing, it is necessary to put the clock back to 1939, 1940 and 1941, as well as 1942, as has been attempted earlier in this book.

The Thousand Plan stands as the most portentous air raid in history before Hiroshima. Its exact relation to Hiroshima is harder to define. Cologne was demonstrably necessary for the easing of the German stranglehold on all fronts and the forging of a war-winning weapon; the same cannot be said of Hiroshima. With the atom bomb, too, there is the question of the genetic aftermath. But we believed initially that we had killed at least 20,000 people in Cologne, perhaps many, many more.

Five weeks afterwards the Ministry of Economic Warfare gave the figure as from 1,000 to 6,000. There was incredulity and even disappointment when neutral sources gave the figure as under 500. This seemed a perfectly natural reaction at the time. In such a raid it was of course accepted that there must be many thousands of maimed or injured. The truth, unpalatable though it may seem when quoted out of context, is that we would have been well content to stop the war that night by the complete destruction of Cologne and its people. Indeed we would have been jubilant. The end would have justified the means.

*

Area bombing on a vast enough scale could certainly have finished the war. But the lesson of Cologne was that to defeat Germany by this means alone was beyond our power, anyway up to the end of 1944. Long before that, political ends, for which wars are fought, had demanded the occupation of territory, and it might have been disastrous if land forces had been sacrificed earlier to provide a bigger bomber offensive. (The land situation was disastrous enough as it was.)

It was such an enormous task to win a war against a great industrial nation by area bombing with the weapons available up to mid-1945 that both the USAF and the RAF tried at various times to find a short cut by attacking selected industries. When they had a big enough bomb, the Americans also plumped for area bombing; belief in it had its final enunciation at Hiroshima.

What, then, did Cologne lead to? What did the bomber offensive really achieve?

After the blitz on Britain, the bulk of the Luftwaffe was transferred to the Russian front. By concentrating their forces in this way the Germans were for a long time able to achieve air superiority almost anywhere; they were able to assemble a force of 2,750 aircraft for their Eastern offensive in the summer of 1942. This force, substantially weakened later by transfers to the Mediterranean, was fatally restricted both in numbers and potential by the new major commitment which appeared with Cologne – the defence of Germany itself.

During 1942, German night-fighter defences in the West increased by almost exactly 100 per cent, while the first-line strength in the East fell below 2,000. Then, from early 1943 until D-Day, the combined Anglo-American bomber offensive became the dominating factor in the air war. It forced the reduction of the German air force in the Mediterranean to a point at which its influence on operations became negligible, it forced the transfer from Russia to Germany of single- and twin-engined fighter units at the very moment when the growing strength of the Soviet air force demanded a stiffening of German fighter opposition. Above all, it forced a changeover in aircraft production from bomber to fighter, from offensive equipment to defensive, which altered the whole character not only of the German air force but of the entire German prosecution of the war. Germany was forced to abandon her strategic plan in a vain attempt to meet our own.

This concentration by the Germans on the defensive in the air did not save the situation for them. On the contrary, it led to the complete defeat of the German air force, and it was German impotence in the air that made possible the Allied invasion of Europe in 1944.

The battles of Stalingrad and El Alamein have been rightly emphasized as two great turning points of the German war, the one on the Russian front, the other in the Middle East. But there was a third water-shed in the same period, this time in the West, equally emphatic if not so freely recognized. This was Cologne.

In spite of the valuable confirmation the raid gave of the theories propounded by Harris and Saundby, it did little to solve the problems of a bomber offensive. It was far more fundamental than that; it began them. The struggles for support, the clashes of opinion, the diversion to other tasks, continued, and with them all went an unceasing battle for tactical, technical and scientific supremacy over the German defence mechanism. But the combined air offensive was on.

'At the beginning of the war,' said a paper prepared by the German air historical branch dated 6th October 1944, 'the operations of the German Air Force determined the character of events. . . . The enemy, however, exploiting the experience gained in the first years of the war, built up a strong air force suited for both strategic warfare and for ground support operations and thereby achieved the supremacy which facilitated his great successes in the West.' The bomber offensive must be seen as the foundation of victory in the battle for air superiority, the decisive element of World War II.

Had the V-weapons not been largely stillborn through Allied bombing, a situation might have arisen in which the whole Allied effort in the West would have been directed towards checking these weapons. The result could have been the regaining of air superiority by the Germans, which would have meant the certain failure of the invasion.

'Allied air power,' concluded the United States Strategic Bombing Survey, 'was decisive in the war in Western Europe. Hindsight inevitably suggests that it might have been employed differently or better in some respects. Nevertheless, it was decisive. . . .'

The official British history of the strategic air offensive against Germany, after nearly a million words of closely reasoned argument and detailed appendices, reached the same conclusion. '. . . both cumulatively in largely indirect ways and eventually in a more immediate and direct manner, strategic bombing, and also in other roles strategic bombers, made a contribution to victory which was decisive. Those who claim that the Bomber Command contribution to the war was less than this are factually in error.'

This was the weapon, the decisive weapon, that was forged that night over Cologne.

Appendix A

THE GEE SYSTEM

Prior to the introduction of Gee, navigation in Bomber Command had been based largely on dead reckoning, assisted by drift-taking and by three methods of position finding – visual pinpointing, radio loop bearings and astro. All three methods were subject to very considerablc error, as indicated by scientific analysis and proved by the examination of photographs. The basis of the Gce system was a wireless pulse signal transmitted simultaneously by two stations, a 'master' and a 'slave' station, and displayed on a cathode ray tube in the aircraft. By measuring the difference in time between the reception of the two signals, and by keeping this difference constant, it was possible to keep the aircraft on a pre-determined line – the line of constant difference between the two stations. Further, by means of a second pair of transmissions from the same 'master' and a different 'slave' station, an exact point on the line could be determined, with the help of specially prepared charts. For blind bombing and homing, the operator could reverse the process and set up his equipment in advance, directing the pilot to steer the aircraft so that when the pulses intersected the plane would be over the pre-selected position.

Appendix B

EXTRACT FROM THE FILES OF POLICE PRESIDENT, COLOGNE

105th[1] Air Attack on Cologne during the Night of 30th/31st May 1942

During the night of 30th/31st May 1942 Warning Control Cologne issued the following alerts:

2353 hours: Yellow alert.
2359 hours: Red alert.
0017 hours: Air-raid sirens sounded.
0335 hours: All-clear sounded.

The air attack lasted from 0047 until 0225 hours. The number of enemy aircraft over the city could not be estimated.

During the attack the following bombs were dropped:

864 HE bombs (250–500 kg), among them 23 duds or delayed-action bombs.
20 aerial mines (1,800 kg).
about 110,000 stick incendiaries.
565 incendiary canisters and phosphorus incendiaries.

The following damage resulted:

12,840 residential buildings were affected, of which:
3,330 were completely destroyed,
2,090 were badly damaged, and
7,420 were slightly damaged.

Damage to these buildings was caused by some 12,000 fires, remaining damage being caused by HE bombs.

'Accommodation units' in the above-mentioned buildings were affected as follows:

13,010 completely destroyed,
6,360 slightly damaged,
22,270 slightly damaged.

1. According to British records it was the 107th.

APPENDIX B

The following losses to commercial and industrial undertakings were reported:

1,505 completely destroyed,
630 badly damaged and
425 slightly damaged.

Factories and industrial installations with Works Civil Defence organizations suffered the following losses:

36 completely destroyed with 100% loss of production,
70 badly damaged with 50–80% loss of production,
222 sustained medium or slight damage with less than 50% loss of production.

The following damage also occurred:

Water mains were breached at 17 places.
Main electric power cables were damaged at 32 places.
Main telephone cables were damaged at 12 places.
Major breaches of gas mains occurred at 5 places.

Casualties:

(a) Police
(1) Killed — 1 outside shelter
(2) Injured — 9 outside shelter
(b) Civil Defence Police:
(1) Killed — 18 outside shelter
(2) Injured — 16 outside shelter
(c) Civil Defence Unit No 27 (motorized):
(1) Killed — 8 outside shelter
(2) Injured — 4 outside shelter
(d) Armed Forces:
(1) Killed — 58
(2) Injured — Not known
(e) Civilian Population:
(1) Killed — 384
(2) Injured:
Hospital cases — 531
First aid treatment — 4,467

Total Killed: 469, of whom
181 were in shelters
248 were outside shelters
27 were performing Civil Defence duties and
13 were not classified.

Total Injured: 5,027, of whom
1,410 were in shelters
3,114 were outside shelters
149 were performing Civil Defence duties and
354 were not classified.

Bombed Out: 45,132, of whom some 14,825 are temporarily without accommodation.

Effect on Transport:
Tramcar traffic in the city area was practically at a complete standstill for a week after the attack. Movements of trains from stations within the city area also had to be suspended for a few days.

AA Barrage: Very intense at times.

Weather: Starlight night, with full moon.

Employment of Forces:
The Civil Defence Police of Civil Defence Area Cologne and appreciable forces from outside were employed with good results. In addition, flying squads were used effectively in dealing with damage, cordoning off areas etc.
Individual and group self-protection forces and Industrial Civil Defence played an energetic role in dealing with damage.
Furthermore, Armed Forces' emergency detachments in some strength were brought in to assist the local Civil Defence Control in dealing with and clearing away damage.

Type of Attack:
The attack was quite clearly carried out by strong forces operating in a large number of successive waves. HE bombs were dropped for about 1½ hours, incendiaries being dropped throughout this period. Bombing with HE commenced about

$\frac{1}{4}$ hour after the first incendiaries fell. Some of the enemy aircraft flew over the city at low-level. From the outset, bombing was spread almost evenly over the entire city area and was repeated to the same degree at brief intervals. The attack had no recognizable centre of main effort. Residential areas, including numerous public buildings, hospitals, churches etc., were primarily affected.

[The document continued by listing, by street and number, every building destroyed by incendiaries and high-explosive in two 'main areas of damage', Koln-Altstadt (the old city), and Koln-Nippes to the north. There followed a list of seventeen major railway installations in all parts of the city – passenger and goods stations and repair works – to suffer serious damage, and four main dock areas which had been severely disabled.]

Appendix C

Analysis of bombs dropped by type and weight

A/C known to have attacked		High explosive bombs dropped					Incendiaries dropped	
Type	No	4,000 lb	2,000 lb	1,000 lb	500 lb	250 lb	30 lb	4 lb
Wellington	496	20		44	575	38	488	213,251
Stirling	71		32	35	143		3,016	61,280
Whitley	23				42		32	7,940
Hampden	71				50	2		25,470
Manchester	35						1,364	25,470
Halifax	105			302			2,504	81,270
Lancaster	67	66					112	41,550
TOTAL	868*	86	32	381	810	40	7,516	456,231

* These were provisional figures, and the total number of bombers known to have attacked Cologne was later amended to 898. Subsequent research into the fate of missing aircraft shows that the actual figure was well over 900 – probably about 910.

INDEX

(Only place-names of direct significance to the story have been indexed)

[1] Nos 21 and 25 O T Us also took part.

[1] Also in the Bomber Force were Squadrons No 7, 35, 150, 156, 420 and 460

General War Series